DRINKING COFFEE
WITH A FORK

THE STORY OF STEVE CARLTON
AND THE '72 PHILLIES

Chic —
Nice to meet
Christine
and Adam
at Barnes
Noble —
Keep rooting for
the Phillies, and
hope you enjoy
the book!
David Brown

Steve Bucci and Dave Brown

Foreword by Jamie Moyer

Camino Books, Inc.
Philadelphia

Manufactured in the United States of America

1 2 3 4 5   14 13 12 11

Library of Congress Cataloging-in-Publication Data

Bucci, Steve.
   Drinking coffee with a fork: the story of Steve Carlton and the '72
Phillies / Steve Bucci and Dave Brown; foreword by Jamie Moyer.
          p. cm.
   Includes bibliographical references and index.
   ISBN 978-1-933822-25-9 (alk. paper)
   1. Carlton, Steve, 1944–. 2. Baseball players—United States—Biography.
3. Philadelphia Phillies (Baseball team)—History—20th century. I. Brown,
David W. (David Wesley), 1960–. II. Title.
   GV865.C317B84 2011
   796.357092—dc22   2010053592
   [B]

ISBN: 978-1-933822-25-9 (paperback)
ISBN: 978-1-933822-32-7 (hardcover)

Cover and interior design: Jerilyn Bockorick

This book is available at a special discount on bulk purchases for promotional,
business, and educational use.

Publisher
Camino Books, Inc.
P.O. Box 59026
Philadelphia, PA 19102

www.caminobooks.com

**"Hitting him [Carlton]
tonight was like
trying to drink coffee with a fork."**

Willie Stargell
Pittsburgh Pirates
August 9, 1972

Contents

Acknowledgments *vii*
Foreword by Jamie Moyer *ix*
Introduction *xi*

1 **The Trade** *1*

2 **The Strike** *14*

3 **Opening Day...at Last** *26*

4 **The Showdown with Gibson** *33*

5 **The One-Hitter** *43*

6 **He's Only Human** *55*

7 **The Losing Skid** *61*

8 **The Streak Begins** *75*

9 **The Brawl** *84*

10 **On a Roll** *93*

11 **Ten in a Row and Counting** *97*

12 **Return to St. Louis** *116*

13 Win Day *124*

14 Taking 20 Bows *134*

15 The Niekro Game *139*

16 Playing Out the String *147*

17 The Rest of the Squad *162*

18 The Case for Carlton *168*

19 Beyond '72 *180*

Sources *188*
Index *190*

To view box scores of Steve Carlton's victories in 1972, visit www.caminobooks.com.

Acknowledgments

There are numerous people that the authors wish to acknowledge for their generous help in this endeavor. First and foremost is Larry Shenk, the Philadelphia Phillies' Vice President of Alumni Relations, without whose assistance this book would not have been possible.

We extend special thanks to the following people for their gracious cooperation and insight: Gene Alley, Steve Arlin, Bob Bailey, Glenn Beckert, Frank Bilovsky, Steve Blass, Vida Blue, Bob Boone, Larry Bowa, Darrell Brandon, Ruly Carpenter, Skip Clayton, Gene Clines, Bob Costas, Billy DeMars, Denny Doyle, Bill Giles, Dave Giusti, Ross Grimsley, Terry Harmon, Ken Henderson, Stan Hochman, Tommy Hutton, Bill James, Fergie Jenkins, Dave Kaplan, Fred Kendall, Bruce Kison, Jerry Koosman, Tim Kurkjian, Davey Lopes, Frank Lucchesi, Greg Luzinski, Ernie McAnally, Joe McDonald, Don Money, Jamie Moyer, Brad Nau, Phil Niekro, Fred Norman, Al Oliver, Claude Osteen, Danny Ozark, Milt Pappas, Wes Parker, Ray Rippelmeyer, Ken Rosenthal, Bob Robertson, Manny Sanguillen, Dan Schlossberg, Larry Shenk, Ted Simmons, Jayson Stark, Joe Torre, Wayne Twitchell, Tom Verducci, Bob Watson, Rich Westcott, Chris Wheeler, Rick Wise, Jimmy Wynn, Betty Zeiser, and Don Zimmer.

A debt of gratitude is owed to Mary Russell Baucom and Colin Frey of the Major League Baseball Players Alumni Association. We also greatly appreciate the efforts of members of the media relations departments of several major league teams: Meagan Swingle (Atlanta Braves), Monica Barlow (Baltimore Orioles), Pam Ganley (Boston Red Sox), Kevin Gregg (Philadelphia Phillies), Danielle Holmes (Chicago Cubs), M.J. Trahan (Houston Astros), Amy Summers (Los Angeles Dodgers), Debbie Gallas (Oakland Athletics), Joe Billetdeaux and Monica Robinson (Pittsburgh Pirates), Karen Madden (San Diego Padres), and Carmen Molina (Tampa Bay Rays).

Our warm thanks go to Brenda Galloway-Wright of the Temple Urban Archives for her kind assistance.

Many thanks go to our publisher Edward Jutkowitz and our editor Brad Fisher for their belief in our book idea and their efforts to help us carry it out.

We're grateful to Hal Bodley for his many insights and for granting us permission to reprint excerpts from his 2009 interview with Steve Carlton.

Steve Bucci wishes to thank Larry Platt, Mike Sielski, and John Feinstein for their advice and encouragement. Many thanks to Sean Forman and his wonderful Web site, Baseball-Reference.com, as well as to "Video" Dan Stephenson for providing a copy of the Phillies' official highlight reel from Lefty's greatest season. Steve is also indebted to the good folks at the Philadelphia Free Library. And lastly, but most of all, his thanks to Gina, who makes it all worthwhile.

Dave Brown wishes to thank his wonderful wife Kim for her support, patience, and hard work in typing manuscript copy throughout this project, as well as Doug Brown, Mike Jones, and Jeff Rodimer for their helpful suggestions.

Foreword

It was in 1972 that Steve Carlton became my boyhood idol. I was nine years old that summer, going on 10, and baseball had already become my passion. My family and I were living in Souderton, Pennsylvania, a small, blue-collar town not far from Philadelphia, and naturally, the Phillies were my favorite team. Summertime is always full of fun and excitement when you're a kid, and that summer had the added excitement of the Phillies' new pitcher and the incredible run of success he was enjoying.

Even at that age, I understood the type of year Steve Carlton was having, and was well aware that you don't often see pitchers do what he was doing. That dominance is now chronicled by Steve Bucci and Dave Brown in *Drinking Coffee with a Fork: The Story of Steve Carlton and the '72 Phillies*.

I was drawn to Steve Carlton because of that success, but there was a deeper connection. He was a left-handed pitcher just like me! I watched him, I emulated him, and I wondered what he was like. That's the mystique of an idol. The way he went about his business on the mound—his focus, his competitiveness—and the respect he seemed to have for the game were examples to me, and it is something that has stayed with me to this day. Having respect for the game has been very important to me throughout my career.

I got to meet Steve by chance when I was playing college ball at Saint Joseph's University. My coach at Saint Joe's arranged for me to have a private tutoring session with Claude Osteen, the former big league pitcher who was then the Phillies' pitching coach. On an indoor mound at the Vet, Claude was talking to me about pitching and demonstrating to me, when all of sudden, Steve Carlton walked over. He said hello and we shook hands. It was a brief meeting, but I'd thought I'd died and gone to heaven.

That encounter came full circle in 1986. I was playing in the Chicago Cubs organization when, in a complete surprise to me, I got called up to the majors. The Cubs happened to be playing the Phillies at Wrigley Field. I was told by the Cubs that I'd be pitching the next day. I thought to myself, "Wouldn't it be cool if I'm pitching against Steve Carlton?" I looked through the newspaper and discovered that I'd miss Carlton by one day...

oh well. But at the end of the night I was told, "Uh, no, you're not pitching tomorrow; we're pushing you back to the next day." I'm going to pitch against Carlton! I was scared to death. I didn't know what to do.

I was in trouble throughout the game. But we scored enough runs and managed to win. I actually struck out Steve, which I thought was the coolest thing. And that was my first major league victory. I was on cloud nine. My career could've ended right there. I had made it to the major leagues, pitched against my boyhood hero, and won!

Having spent over four seasons as a Phillie, I've run into Carlton around the ballpark many times. Whenever I see him now, I'm brought back to my childhood again. He knows that he was my hero. I don't know what he thinks about it, but whether he realizes it or not, he had an impact on my life just by being the pitcher that he was.

Steve's retired number 32 hangs on the wall outside our clubhouse. Sometimes I'll stop by the wall and look at his statistics, and it boggles my mind because the game was so different in his era, compared to the one that I'm in. I marvel at the numbers because I know I can't do what Steve did. I wonder how he managed it. Especially in 1972, during a season that was pretty miserable for the Phillies. Because I've played on teams like that, I know what it can be like. And I wonder how Steve made it happen. The answer can be found in the pages of this book.

Jamie Moyer
Philadelphia Phillies
July 2010

Introduction

The idea for this book was born over a couple of beers at The Bishop's Collar, a popular tavern in the Fairmount section of Philadelphia. Naturally, we were discussing baseball, and the name of Hall of Fame pitcher Steve Carlton cropped up in our conversation. We talked about his phenomenal career and his place as one of baseball's best pitchers ever. As the bartender refilled our mugs, we zeroed in on Carlton's fabulous 1972 season when he won 27 games for the last-place Phillies, which won only 59 games.

It might have been the alcohol talking, but the more we marveled at Carlton's '72 season—his 15-game winning streak, 310 strikeouts, 1.97 ERA, all for a bad team—the more convinced we became that this was a compelling subject for a book. It seemed to us that a case could be made that it was the greatest single season by a pitcher in the modern era. We felt it was time that people were reminded of it. So we got right to work.

We were interested in interviewing Carlton to elicit his recollections about that magical season, his first in Philadelphia. Given his unwillingness to talk to the media during the last several years of his career, we weren't holding our breaths. Numerous attempts were made to contact Lefty and request his participation. Through his representative, not surprisingly, he declined. But we were undaunted—we were going to write the book, with or without him.

Although Steve Carlton had no involvement, many of his teammates, coaches, and opponents were amenable to interviews and shared their memories of Lefty that season. We also picked the brains of writers who covered the Phillies that year as well as members of the team's public relations department. In addition, we pored through box scores and newspaper accounts of games that Carlton pitched in 1972. Through our extensive interviews and research, we were able to piece together the details of Lefty's extraordinary and historic season.

Carlton declined our requests to be interviewed, but he sat down with veteran baseball writer Hal Bodley in the summer of 2009 and looked back at the '72 season.

"That season was amazing," he told Bodley, who covered the Phillies in the early '70s. "I was being taught how to think about the concept of reality. When I started thinking about that in 1970, my performance went way up. After the fall of '70, I started thinking about winning 20 games the following year and I was able to do that [20-9, 3.56 ERA] for the first time.

"After I won 20 games for the Cardinals in 1971," Carlton continued, "I started thinking about winning 25 games. That was my new goal. I had four months of down time—no pitching. I was preparing for the next season mentally. The Cardinals were a very good team at that time, winning 90 to 100 games.

"I felt if it [my mental approach] works this well, let's push it to 25... with the Cardinals. But on opening day of spring training I got traded, and I said to myself, 'Holy shit!' That team [the Phillies] wasn't winning very much.

"I had four months invested in this intellectual project and said to myself, 'If this works, let's make it work here [with the Phillies].' I spent a whole week [after the trade] fighting with this. I finally decided if it works, I'll dig in harder. My reality became more intense in '72 than it was in 1971 with a team that wasn't perceived to win 90 to 100 games like the Cardinals.

"I had created my reality around a team that was going to win, so my odds seemed to be better there [in St. Louis]. The effort was to increase last year's performance and I had invested four months [preparing for that]. I said, 'Well, if it works, we'll make it work here.'"

Carlton told Bodley that the whole year was "extreme focus and intent. I have never been through that before. It was such an elevated level. And what happens when you're like that, you control your environment. Everybody around me was more elevated. When that happens and you start to control the elements around you, and science knows this, it works. This was a strike-shortened year and I missed three starts. I might have won 30 games."

When Lefty went to the mound, "I had already won the game. Today, that's called quantum entanglement. You're entangling a thought into the future. As you go through the linear concept of that reality, it has already unfolded for you."

Carlton is a deep thinker, no question about it. He was and remains eccentric, and it is Steve's eccentric mentality that heightened his focus and concentration as a pitcher and helped him achieve tremendous success over a career spanning more than 20 years. He enjoyed no greater success than during his super-season of 1972.

As for the title, *Drinking Coffee with a Fork*, at first glance you may say, Wait a minute. Didn't the late Willie Stargell say that about facing

Sandy Koufax? If so, you'd probably be right. Stargell is widely considered to have said that about Koufax. But he offered the same analysis in regard to Carlton following a game against him on August 9, 1972. The direct quote, "Hitting him [Carlton] tonight was like trying to drink coffee with a fork," was attributed to Stargell in the August 10, 1972 edition of the *Philadelphia Daily News*. Eating *soup* with a fork might have been a better analogy, but then, who are we to argue with a Hall of Fame slugger like Stargell?

So pour yourself a cup of coffee, use a fork if you wish, sit back, turn the page, and read the story of one of the greatest and most improbable seasons that a pitcher has ever had.

DRINKING COFFEE
WITH A FORK

CHAPTER 1

The Trade

It was February 23rd, Paul Owens' wedding anniversary. Phillies general manager John Quinn always took his farm director and their wives out to dinner to celebrate the Owens' anniversary. Spring training was just under way for the Phillies in Clearwater, Florida, the site where the club still trains and has for decades, and the two men had been in town for a couple of days. It always felt good to get out of the bone-chilling Philadelphia winter and be back in Clearwater, where the new baseball season beckoned.

Quinn and his wife met Paul and Marcelle Owens that night at Heilman's Beachcomber Restaurant in Clearwater Beach. The Beachcomber on Mandalay Avenue was a popular eatery among the Phillies players, staff, and media. For years, it was one of the few night spots in town, and you could always find the players at the bar, or Phillies broadcaster Bill Campbell at the piano regaling folks with his rendition of "Fly Me to the Moon."

Or, did the Quinns and Owenses dine that night at the Island House, which was across Mandalay from the Beachcomber? Others who were close to the situation say it was probably the Island House, because Paul Owens loved that place. "It couldn't have been the Beachcomber," says one veteran Phillies staffer. "Quinn never went there." No, no, says another person who's been with the organization since the 1960s. "I think it was a place called the Garden Seat, or the Garden's Eat, something like that," they surmised. "It was down by the hospital. It's not there anymore." The details grow blurry when viewed across the distant plain of 39 years; the memory goes fuzzy. But suffice it to say that at the Beachcomber, or the Island House, or the Garden Seat/Garden's Eat (or someplace else), Quinn, Owens, and their wives had dinner, and at this dinner the trade was first discussed.

Quinn never liked to talk business at the dinner table, not in front of the wives. He didn't think it was particularly polite. John was gentlemanly and old school. Always dressed to the nines, he wore a suit and tie with suspenders and a white-starched collar everywhere. And he always smelled like "your father's after shave," as one Phils employee put it. A baseball lifer, Quinn grew up in the game. His father, Bob, was the president of the Boston Braves and shortly after the younger Quinn graduated from college, he joined his dad in the Braves organization. Soon he became the team's general manager. Quinn quickly earned a reputation as a shrewd dealer, engineering some of the bigger trades of the 1940s. He guided the Braves to the World Series in 1948, their first in 34 years, and later built the great Milwaukee Braves teams of Hank Aaron and Eddie Mathews, which won it all in '57. In 1959, Phillies owner Bob Carpenter signed Quinn as his GM. Why? "Because," Carpenter said at the time, "I wanted the best."

Old J.Q. may not have liked to talk baseball in front of the ladies, but on this night he must've been busting. He couldn't help it, he had to talk to Owens about a little piece of business he was working on. If anything, he wanted Owens' opinion. Quinn knew that Owens was one of the sharper baseball minds in the Phillies organization. If Owens agreed that it was a good deal, then that was all the confirmation that J.Q. needed.

Over the couple's first round of drinks, Quinn leaned in toward Owens. Whispering in his ear in an attempt to avoid talking business at the table, the Phillies GM said three words to his farm director: "Wise for Carlton." Owens, whom Dick Allen would later nickname "The Pope," because he bore a striking resemblance to Pope Paul VI, must have thought he was hearing the voice of an archangel from above. Wise for Carlton? Steve Carlton? The Cardinals' young left-hander? For Rick Wise? Wise was without question the pitching star of the beleaguered Phillies and a favorite among the fans, but surely Quinn was joking. If an archangel had appeared to the Pope at that moment, it would have said, "Behold, I bring you great tidings of joy, for the savior of your franchise is about to be born."

"Even up?" Owens asked Quinn incredulously.

"Yeah," whispered Quinn.

Well, Owens didn't have to think twice about it. He didn't need to think about it over dinner, he didn't need to sleep on it once they returned to the hotel. "Do it," Owens said immediately and without hesitation. "Do it in a minute." His advice to the veteran general manager? "Run to the phone and do it."

Quinn was surprised at how adamantly Owens felt.

"Should we check with your scouts to see what they think?" asked Quinn.

"No," Owens replied, "He's going to be a great one."

Owens himself had scouted Carlton and loved him. What wasn't there to love? Carlton was coming off his first 20-win season. He had once struck out a record 19 batters in a game. He'd already pitched in All-Star Games and the World Series. And having just turned 27, he had yet to reach his prime.

Quinn, fully satisfied by the Pope's blessing, said, "We'll call Bing Devine [the St. Louis Cardinals' general manager] when we get back to the hotel." At 9 p.m. that night, following the Owens' anniversary dinner, when John and Paul and their wives got back to their hotel, the call to Devine was made.

"OK, we'll make the deal," Quinn said to Devine.

"I want to run it by Red [Schoendienst, the Cardinals' manager] first," Devine said. "Let me call you back at 9 tomorrow morning. But as far as I'm concerned, we have a deal."

Two days later, on Friday, February 25th, the trade was official. Steven Norman Carlton, the man they called "Lefty," was a Philadelphia Phillie.

Whenever you hear athletes say, "it's not about the money," don't believe them. It's always about the money. If there's a 2000-year-old Tibetan monk somewhere in the Himalayas, who's plugged into the mysteries of the universe, when asked he'd probably tell you that the answer to all of your questions, my son, is "the money." And "the money" is the reason for the trade that not only changed the course of one pitcher's career, but also helped to change the course of a franchise for the next decade.

Both guys wanted more money. Simple as that. And their teams didn't want to give it to them. If Rick Wise and Steve Carlton had been happy with their contracts with the Phillies and Cardinals respectively, the trade would never have happened.

Carlton had held out before. In 1970, he failed to report to spring training in a contract battle with August Busch, the Budweiser beer baron who owned the Cardinals. Lefty was coming off the best season of his young career and was determined to cash in on it. In '69, in just his third full season in the majors, Carlton went 17 and 11 (the second highest win total on the Cardinals staff behind the great Bob Gibson's 20 victories), with a 2.17 ERA. He pitched 236 and a third innings, striking out 210. He was the starting, and winning, pitcher in the All-Star Game, his second consecutive All-Star selection. He also hit a double in the game, becoming the last pitcher to get an extra-base hit in an All-Star Game. And in September of that year, the young, gangly left-hander turned in one of the more amazing efforts in baseball history. Carlton struck out 19 New York Mets at Shea Stadium, the first pitcher to strike out 19 batters in a game in the modern era. Twice that night he got Ron Swoboda out on strikes. But Swoboda also managed two hits. And they were huge. The Mets outfielder drilled a pair of two-run homers, handing Carlton a 4-3 loss in a game in which he struck out 19.

Nonetheless, how would you like to go into free agency or arbitration today with those kinds of numbers? But, of course, there was no free agency or arbitration. Carlton was making $25,000. He wanted $50,000. Carlton was quoted at the time as saying that he "was just negotiating for what I was worth." According to the *New York Daily News*, an incensed Busch replied, "I don't give a damn if he never pitches another ball for the Cardinals." The Cardinals offered $30,000. They settled on $40,000.

Now, two winters later, they were at it again. This time, Carlton had gone 20-9 in the previous season, leading the Cardinals pitching staff in victories, and was once again named to the NL All-Star team. This time he wanted $65,000. After all, he was a 20-game winner. While winning 20 was, at the time, a more common occurrence than in today's game, it was still a benchmark of success. For Carlton, it was an even more significant milestone. It meant that he had reached the top echelon of his profession, and why shouldn't he be paid like it?

Of course, August Busch saw things differently. Players would get what *he* thought they deserved, or they wouldn't play for the Cardinals. Wasn't that how it always worked in baseball? The world around Busch was changing, and he could barely recognize it anymore. Players were sending lawyers and representatives to do their negotiating. Unheard of! Worst of all, and particularly galling to the Cardinals owner, his own player, Curt Flood, was challenging the legality of baseball's age-old reserve clause. The reserve clause was a provision in every major leaguer's contract that gave teams the right to keep players and to prevent them from pedaling their services on the open market. If a player's contract expired, and he and the club could not reach agreement on a new set of terms, then the player was bound by the club to play under the previous terms and conditions. The expired contract would essentially roll over to the next year. He didn't have to sign a new deal. He was still the property of that club. This meant that players had virtually no say as to where they played, and were, in effect, bound for life to the teams that originally drafted and signed them.

Why did Flood take the bold step of challenging the reserve clause? Because he didn't want to become a Philadelphia Phillie.

Flood was a Gold Glove center fielder and a mainstay on the Cardinals' championship teams of the '60s. Following the '69 season, Flood, who was earning $90,000 but seeking a contract worth $100,000, was shipped, along with catcher Tim McCarver, outfielder Byron Browne, and pitcher Joe Hoerner, to the Phillies. Flood refused. He didn't want to play for the sad-sack Phils in decaying Connie Mack Stadium. Furthermore, he felt that having no say in the matter was not only unfair, but in violation of federal anti-trust laws. He wrote a letter to Commissioner Bowie Kuhn indicating how he felt and demanding that Kuhn declare him a free agent. Kuhn would not. So…Flood sued baseball. He took his battle all the way to the U.S. Supreme Court. But that's where he ultimately struck out. In 1972, the same year that Carlton would become a Phillie via a trade with the Cardinals, the U.S. Supreme Court ruled against Flood in a 5-3 decision. (Justice Lewis Powell was not involved in the case because he owned stock in Anheuser-Busch, the Cardinals' parent company.) While Flood may have lost in his bid to challenge the reserve clause, the icy winds of change were rattling the owners' windows. Soon they agreed to add arbitration as a means of settling disputes. And arbitration was the key that unlocked the door to free agency. Three years later, an arbitrator's ruling allowed pitchers Andy Messersmith and Dave McNally to walk through that door as free agents, forever transforming the business of sports.

For the time being, however, owners like Busch still held all the cards, and they were going to use them. "You weren't going to tell Gussie Busch what to do," recalls Joe Torre, who was a teammate of Carlton's in St. Louis. Lefty earned $45,000 in 1971, and was now looking for a $20,000 increase. The Cardinals' final offer was $60,000. Busch's Cardinals were digging in their heels over a mere five grand.

Meanwhile in Philadelphia, a salary dispute of similar proportion was raging. Star hurler Rick Wise also wanted a raise. "I had made $25,000 in 1971," Wise remembers, "and wanted my salary doubled to $50,000."

In '71, Wise won 17 games. Had a 2.88 ERA. Pitched 17 complete games, and 272 and a third innings. He wasn't too shabby with the bat either, hitting six home runs. (That was as many home runs as outfielder Oscar Gamble hit, and Gamble had 183 more at-bats.) Wise made the All-Star team that season, too. "I was head and shoulders above anybody else on the staff," Wise says, looking back on it now. "A season like that, nowadays, would be worth 10 or 12 million."

In addition to his statistical line, on June 23rd of that season the right-hander pitched one of the most memorable games in Phillies history. It was a Wednesday night, and the Phils were at Cincinnati's Riverfront Stadium to play the Reds. An announced crowd of little more than 19,000 fans were on hand for what was the third game of a four-game series, Wise facing the Reds' Ross Grimsley. It was a hot, humid night in Cincinnati, with the temperature on the stadium's AstroTurf hitting over 100 degrees by game time. "I was coming off the effects of the flu," said Wise. "I was very drained. I knew if I didn't locate my pitches, I wouldn't be around very long. It was so hot it sweated out the remnants of the flu in me."

Wise set the Reds down in order in the first inning, thanks to a defensive gem from shortstop Larry Bowa on the game's opening play. Pete Rose led off with a sharp grounder in the hole, which Bowa fielded splendidly. He made the stop, then fired a bullet to first baseman Deron Johnson to get Rose by a step. The Phillies also helped Wise by putting an early run on the scoreboard in the second inning. It would be the only run he needed, but in the fifth, the pitcher added his own insurance. With one out, and Roger Freed on second base following a leadoff double, Wise, a very good hitting-pitcher, took Grimsley deep. A two-run shot from the pitcher who was working on a no-no! How amazing is that?! Actually, at that point the no-no was a perfect game. Wise had retired every Reds batter he'd faced, and now he had a comfortable 3-0 lead from which to work.

In the bottom half of the fifth, Wise got Johnny Bench, Tony Perez, and Hal McRae, 1-2-3. Reds second baseman Tommy Helms led off the next inning. Five years earlier, Helms had been named NL Rookie of the Year, and some three decades later his nephew, Wes, would play briefly for the Phillies. Helms hit a come-backer that bounced above the mound. Wise took a few steps backward, jumped up, gloved the ball out of the air, and threw to Johnson at first to nail Helms. Every no-hitter has a couple of terrific defensive plays, and this one was no different.

Wise was still perfect, but up to the plate next stepped Dave Concepción, a light-hitting shortstop from Venezuela, and that's where the string of perfection ended. Concepción, who would become a nine-time All-Star and develop into a quality batsman, hit .205 for the year, his second with the Reds. But Concepción artfully worked a five-pitch walk. He turned out to be the only Red to reach base that night. "I tried to put something extra on a 3-1 fastball and overthrew it," Wise lamented 38 years later. Now his goal was to keep the no-hitter intact.

By now, everyone in the dugout was aware of what was happening, but, of course, in keeping with baseball protocol, no one mentioned it. You never mention when a guy is throwing a no-hitter for fear of jinxing it, and that was certainly the case in this one. Wise chuckled at the thought of Phillies manager Frank Lucchesi, who was "a bundle of nerves," as the game progressed. "Nobody wanted to look at me in the dugout," he added.

Wise was the first batter of the eighth inning, still with his no-hitter, and about to face Reds reliever Clay Carroll, who had just entered the ballgame. As the Phillies starter strode to the plate, the Cincinnati fans rose in unison and gave the opposing pitcher a standing ovation. They certainly appreciated what Wise was doing, and what they were lucky enough to witness, albeit at the expense of their own team. The Phils starter was clearly moved by the sentiment. "I thought that was very classy," he said.

So…he promptly hit another homer—two home runs on the night. Incredible! He had now driven in three of his team's four runs. And he was six outs away from a no-hitter. Future Hall of Famer Tony Perez began the Reds' half of the eighth with a slow bouncer to third base. Phillies rookie John Vukovich, who would later spend over 20 years with the organization as a beloved coach, began to charge the ball, then wisely stopped, and with textbook precision, fielded the ball on a big hop. Vuk's throw narrowly beat Perez to first base in a close play for the inning's first out. A fly ball caught by Willie Montañez in center and a 6-3 ground out followed, ending the frame.

Wise was now just three outs away. He'd have to face batters 8, 9, and 1 to try and close it out. "[Reds third baseman] Jimmy Stewart led off the ninth inning," Wise recalls, rattling it off as if it had happened that morning. "He was called out on strikes on a pitch that was on the inside corner. Years later Stewart would kid me that the pitch was inside [and should've been called a ball]. I got the second out [Ty Cline, on a ground-out to second baseman Terry Harmon, with Wise hustling over to cover first base], and then Pete Rose came up."

Fourteen years later, Rose would pass Ty Cobb as baseball's all-time hits king. No major leaguer has ever gotten more hits than Pete Rose. However, on this night, Rose was unable to add to what would become a record total. "Rose was a great hitter and a tough out," Wise says with understatement. "I wasn't going to get beat on a curveball or change-up, so I threw him nothing but fastballs."

From a left-handed, crouching stance, the switch-hitting Rose deftly worked the count full. Wise was one pitch away. Too close to lose it now. He delivered another fastball. Rose swung and made contact, lifting a harmless humpback liner to third base. There Vukovich's reliable glove awaited. He easily put it away to end the ballgame. Rick Wise had pitched a no-hit, no-run game! Wise raised his arms in celebration as his teammates sprinted over to congratulate him. The final score was 4-0, Phillies. "I threw 95 pitches. Struck out three. Only about four balls were hit out of the infield. There were two good defensive plays. I made one and Bowa made one," said Wise, summing up the best night of his baseball life. In one hour and 53 minutes, Wise had pitched the Phillies' first no-hitter since Jim Bunning's famous Father's Day perfect game in 1964. And he hit *two home runs* in the process! It is the only time a pitcher has hit multiple home runs while tossing a no-hitter. It was easily and without question the highlight of a mostly forgettable season in which the Phillies won only 67 games and dropped 95, finishing dead last in the NL East, some 30 games out of first place. No wonder Wise wanted a sizable raise. Getting one, however, would not be easy.

"The Phillies had a reputation for stinginess," says Stan Hochman, the longtime sports columnist for the *Philadelphia Daily News*. In 1972, Bowa, one of the best shortstops in the franchise's history, was heading into his third full season as a big leaguer. He remembers that the Phillies did not have a particularly large payroll. "We had a lot of young kids who were making the minimum or a little above the minimum. Wise probably made the most money. I know he was asking for a big raise, although today you'd probably laugh at it," Bowa joked. Wise knew the circumstances going into the negotiations. He also knew that Quinn was "a tough Irishman," as Wise puts it, a strong, stubborn, intimidating personality who was known to low-ball players.

After the season, Wise went to see Quinn at his office in the state-of-the-art Veterans Stadium, the Phillies new home, which had opened for business the previous April. Quinn, in suit, tie, suspenders, white starched collar, and smelling of your father's after shave, listened as Wise demanded the whopping sum of 50 grand. The Phils' GM thought his ace was worthy of a reward for an outstanding year, but hell if he was going to double the guy's salary. J.Q. offered him a $10,000 raise, far below what Wise was seeking. "I said, 'no way,' and he wouldn't budge," Wise recalls.

Hal Bodley was the Phillies beat writer for the Wilmington *News Journal*, and he remembers the salary impasse well. "John Quinn was adamant about not giving Rick Wise what he wanted even though he had had a fantastic 1971. This was before free agency; Quinn had the hammer. He could do whatever he wanted to do." As Wise says, "We had no power. No leverage. No arbitration." Rick loved playing in Philly, but he felt strongly about his position. He went to spring training that February without signing a contract.

It was at about this time that Gussie Busch learned the Phillies themselves had a disgruntled pitcher on their hands. In St. Louis, talks with Carlton were going nowhere. Might the Phillies be interested in making a deal? Busch instructed Bing Devine to approach the Phillies about a straight-up, disgruntled-pitcher-for-disgruntled-pitcher trade. "It was more Gussie Busch telling you who the boss was more than anything else. He wasn't going to be held hostage," notes Torre. The owners still had their mighty reserve clause. The players had no freedom. It was take it or leave it. In those days, if a player fought the front office over salary, he might very well find himself with a new team. "It was well-documented," says Bowa, "that if you didn't go along with John Quinn, he was going to find a way to move you. That was the reputation he had. If you couldn't come to terms, he'll find a way to resolve the problem."

The Cards and Phils resolved their problems by swapping them. Carlton fumed. Sure, he was having trouble ironing out a contract agreement with the Cardinals, but he never expected to be traded because of it. That was the last thing he wanted. He had come up through the organization and couldn't have imagined ever leaving. What angered Steve most was that he had no say in the matter. "All of a sudden," he said at the time, "you're traded, cold turkey."

The first thing Carlton did upon hearing the news was to call Marvin Miller, the head of the Players Association. "What rights do I have?" Carlton asked Miller. "Well, you have two alternatives," said the union chief. "You can go play for Philadelphia, or you can quit." Unlike Curt Flood before him, Carlton chose to go play for Philadelphia.

Rick Wise was in his condo in Clearwater Beach early on February 25th when he heard a knock at the door. It was Eddie Ferenz, the Phillies' traveling secretary. "You have been traded to the Cardinals," Ferenz told him. Wise was stunned. "Quinn never talked to me. I packed my bags and left," he said.

Over at the Ft. Harrison Jack Tar Hotel that morning, Larry Shenk, the Phillies' public relations director, went looking for his young PR assistant, who was grabbing some breakfast at the hotel's coffee shop. "It was my first spring training with the Phillies," says Chris Wheeler. "Wheels" has been a Phillies broadcaster for more than 30 years, but in the spring of 1972, he was Shenk's assistant and had only been on the job since the previous July.

Shenk's day began with an early morning phone call from Paul Owens.

"John Quinn needs to see you."

Shenk knew something was up. He went to Quinn's room at the hotel (everyone in the organization stayed there during spring training—front office personnel, team staffers, as well as the members of the media) and the general manager informed him of the trade. Shenk went downstairs and found Wheeler about to dig into his bacon and scrambled eggs with an English muffin on the side.

"Well, J.Q. made a deal," he told his assistant.

"You've gotta be kidding me," Wheeler replied.

"What do you think of Steve Carlton for Rick Wise?"

Wheeler could not believe it. "I bet you we get killed for this," he said.

Thanks, in part, to the two homer no-hitter, there may not have been a more popular Phillie in the winter of 1972 than Rick Wise. He was the team's best pitcher. And…he could hit! Some would say that with Wise in the batting order it was like having an extra position player. "The fans had so little to latch onto, and they had come to like Wise," recalls the *Daily News'* Stan Hochman.

The entire Phillies public relations department was made up of Shenk and Wheeler. Their spring training office was in the hotel. The Jack Tar was in downtown Clearwater, not far from Jack Russell Stadium where for decades the team trained and played Grapefruit League games. Today the Church of Scientology is headquartered at the site of the hotel. The public relations duo had no time for breakfast; they had to hurry back to the office, where they would hastily prepare for a press conference. Shenk's head was swimming with the details. He had to get hold of the writers. There was Bill Conlin of the *Daily News*, Ray Kelly of the old Philadelphia *Bulletin*, the *Inquirer*'s Allen Lewis, Bus Saidt of the *Trenton Times*, and Hal Bodley of the Wilmington paper. That was the main corps that followed the club. There were also the wire services (the Associated Press and United Press International) to call. Quinn handled the press conference, and in suit, tie, suspenders, starched collar, and after shave, he revealed the details of the trade to the world.

It was not met with celebration.

The headline in the next morning's *Philadelphia Daily News* read, "No-Hit, No-Run, No Longer a Phil." The *Inquirer*'s analysis—next to the news that the 76ers had beaten Pete Maravich and the Hawks in Hershey behind Fred Foster's 15 fourth-quarter points, and the details of how Penn's Bobby Morse had scored 24 points in 24 minutes for Chuck Daly's 19-2 Quakers in a win over Cornell, and advertisements touting the Boat Show at the Civic Center and the Ice Capades in their "last three days" at the Spectrum—was this: "If there is a long-range edge in this trade, however, the Cardinals are likely to have it. Wise, with his excellent control, could be a big winner for many years to come."

"I don't think many people liked the trade, or thought it was a good trade," Bodley remembers. Frank Bilovsky was a *Bulletin* sportswriter who helped out with the Phillies beat. "You have to remember," as Bilovsky puts it, "they were equally as bad the year before, and Wise was all they had."

"I'm telling you," says Wheeler, "people loved him. And what else did they have to root for? A guy pitches a no-hitter and hits two homers in the game? It doesn't get any better than that."

Phillies fans didn't know it at the time, but it *would* get better. In Steve Carlton, the club had the foundation on which it arguably would build its best teams, eventually earning the franchise its first World Series title. But in late February of '72, few could see that far into the future.

following season, helping the BoSox win the pennant, and both players were instrumental in the now-famous sixth game of the 1975 World Series between the Red Sox and Reds. Carbo will forever be remembered for hitting the game-tying, three-run homer, while Wise pitched a scoreless top half of the 12th inning (before Carlton Fisk's dramatic home run) to become the game's winning pitcher.

Wise enjoyed a successful career, however paling next to Carlton's. (Incidentally, Carlton was not the only Hall of Famer for whom Rick Wise would be dealt. In 1978, Boston traded Wise, future Phillies catcher Bo Diaz, and two others to Cleveland in the deal that brought the Red Sox pitcher Dennis Eckersley.)

Carlton went on to become one of the greatest pitchers of all time, a 300-game winner, and the first four-time Cy Young Award-winner in baseball history. But no one would dare predict that in the spring of 1972. He was just a guy with great stuff who was coming off his best year to date. Says ESPN.com's Stark, "The Cardinals never would have traded him if they thought he would become that guy. Nobody thought of him as superhuman before. That all changed in 1972."

Little did anyone know, but they were about to find out. And it surely exceeded the wildest of expectations. With as bad a major league team as has ever suited up playing behind him, Steve Carlton was about to accomplish in the 1972 season what can only be described as "superhuman." He would become "Super Steve." With the passage of time his achievement has been consigned to the dusty pages of the record books. It has become franchise folklore, bearing an almost mythic quality.

In 1972, the legend of Steve Carlton was born.

CHAPTER 2

The Strike

Carlton was surprised by the trade, even a bit upset over it, but having reached a contract agreement with the Phillies, he reported to Clearwater the next day to join his new team. Milling about outside the clubhouse at Jack Russell Stadium, along with the rest of the press contingent, was Hal Bodley, the Phillies beat reporter for the Wilmington *News Journal*. Like everyone, Bodley was anxious to get a look at the new left-hander in a Phils uniform. He had seen Carlton pitch against the Phillies, but the two men had never met. That was about to change.

The clubhouse doors swung open and out popped catcher Tim Mc-Carver, who was headed to the playing field for that day's workout, Carlton's first as a Phillie. By the catcher's side was the newly acquired ace. McCarver called Bodley over.

"I have someone I'd like you to meet," Tim said to Hal. It was Steve Carlton. Timidly, the pitcher greeted him with a "Hello" and an extended hand.

"Hi Steve," Bodley said as he shook hands with Carlton. "Welcome to the Phillies."

Today, the first workout by a star player acquired in a blockbuster trade would induce a shark-like feeding frenzy from the media. But in those days it was met with nothing more than standard coverage. Just the usual suspects from the Phillies press corps were there to witness Carlton for the first time, in a white, burgundy-pinstriped Phillies uniform with the fat, circular "P" over the left chest.

In St. Louis, Steve had always worn number 32. But in Philadelphia number 32 was already taken. Fellow pitcher Darrell "Bucky" Brandon, a

right-hander from Nacogdoches, Texas, was in his second season as a
Phillie, and 32 was his number. It would not be his for long. Shortly after
the new pitcher arrived at the Phillies camp, PR director Shenk pulled
Brandon aside.

"Steve would like to wear number 32 for the Phillies," Shenk told
him. Brandon thought about it for a few moments.

"Well, he won 20 games," Brandon replied. "He can have it."

That season Bucky became number 30 in the Phillies program.

Some years later, his and Carlton's paths crossed at a baseball card
and memorabilia show. As Brandon's ex-teammate signed photos of himself wearing a number 32 Phillies uniform in various stages of his Hall of
Fame glory, and for top dollar at that, Bucky shouted over to Carlton.
"Hey Lefty, I gave you that number," he said in jest. "And it's about time
you paid me back." Carlton laughed. He never did pay him back.

Most could tell from that first workout that the trade had yielded a
special player. "I'll never forget the first time I saw him," said Chris
Wheeler, the PR assistant and future broadcaster. "He just stood out so
much. There was something about the way the mitt popped when he threw
the ball. It was different."

There was something different about Carlton; something different
about the way he carried himself. It was as if he knew, correctly, that how
one carried oneself in the world was of vital importance, especially for a
big league ballplayer. He had a proud walk. Shoulders back. Head up.
Wherever he was going, it was with a purpose. Lefty had matinee-idol
good looks—dark, wavy, brown hair, worn fashionably long in the popular style of the times, with long sideburns. He had small, handsome, hazel
eyes.

Carlton was tall and thin, standing six feet five and weighing 210
pounds. He was blessed with impressive size and strength, but his was an
unusual body. He was all arms and legs. His torso was rather short. The
parts didn't seem to fit. Long arms and long legs connected to a short torso
as if intended for another man. His neck was also long, with a conspicuous
Adam's apple.

Carlton hated to run wind sprints; didn't think they were necessary.
In subsequent years, he refused to run them, adhering instead to the rigors
of his own unique training regimen, spiced with martial arts exercises.
Some observers have guessed that his aversion to wind sprints was because he wasn't very adept at running. Carlton on the base paths wasn't a
pretty sight, and he often clogged the bases, impeding the fleeter players
behind him. He was a superb athlete, but he couldn't run. It was as if his
legs were almost too long. Ah, but they were perfect for his left-handed
throwing motion.

To watch Steve Carlton throw a baseball was like watching Rembrandt paint, or Perlman play the violin. It was a virtuoso performance. His mechanics were perfect. There was no wasted motion. Every movement had a purpose. His arms and hands, together, swing upward above his head as his right foot steps backward. Rotating his hips, and his weight, he pivots on his left foot, which is flush against the pitching rubber. His long right leg swings across his body, kicking above his waist, his knee slightly bent, as his hands and glove drop down. Then, in an explosion of power, the right leg strides forward. His gloved hand pulls his front shoulder toward the plate as that glorious left arm is cocked at roughly a 90-degree angle. The clean, white, horsehide ball is nestled in his large left hand. His back remains straight. In whiplike fashion, the arm, hand, and back rocket forward as he pushes off the rubber with his left foot. The right foot lands, the left arm comes forward, and the fingers release the ball as the back bends in perfect unison on the follow-through. Every motion, every body part flows smoothly. Nothing creaks, nothing jerks. Each pitch is delivered identically with the last.

The pitching coach for the '72 Phillies was Ray Rippelmeyer, who was in his third season with the club. As a player, Rippelmeyer pitched for 10 seasons in the minors, finally reaching the big leagues in 1962 with the Washington Senators where he had little more than a cup of coffee, appearing in just 18 games. In 1966, he joined the Phillies organization as the pitching coach of their triple-A farm team in San Diego. That's where he got his first glimpse of a raw talent named Steve Carlton. The young Lefty was pitching for Tulsa, the Cardinals' triple-A club. At that time, Carlton had three pitches: a fastball, a slider, and a curveball. When Ray became the Phillies' pitching coach in '70, he noticed that as a Cardinal, Carlton had abandoned the slider. He was throwing the fastball and curve almost exclusively.

Rippelmeyer always liked to catch the pitchers in spring training, and he did so with his new staff ace on Carlton's first day in camp. After a few minutes catching Carlton, the pitching coach stopped his new charge.

"Where's that sharp breaking ball I saw in Tulsa?" Ray asked.

"The Cardinals wouldn't let me throw it," Steve replied. "They told me, if I throw the slider, I'll lose my curveball."

"There's no reason you can't throw both," Rippelmeyer assured him.

The two men went back to their game of catch. Carlton threw about a half-dozen sliders in a row, and Rip was impressed. "That's the pitch," he yelled. "That would be the biggest crime since the Brinks robbery if you don't throw that pitch. That's the best slider that I've seen in the National League." Rip didn't insist, but the pitching coach strongly suggested that now that Carlton was a Phillie, he should throw the slider, and at the rest of the league's peril.

Rippelmeyer remembers seeing that slider when Carlton was a minor leaguer. However, Carlton, at his Hall of Fame press conference in 1994, told reporters that he developed the pitch in 1968 during a Cardinals off-season exhibition tour of Japan. He had been trying to throw the pitch while limiting the wrist turn so he wouldn't hurt his elbow. Imagine the position one's wrist is in when pulling down a window shade. That's similar to the wrist action in delivering a slider; the wrist and hand turn down and away, which creates the necessary spin that makes the pitch break. A pitcher "pulls the shade" with a slight turn of his wrist, which turns the forearm and rotates the elbow, and also happens to put a fair amount of pressure on the elbow. Carlton said that he'd been tinkering with the pitch, but after Sadaharu Oh, the legendary Japanese slugger, tagged him for two home runs, he decided to throw it to the left-handed-hitting Oh. The next time Oh came to bat, Carlton threw him his slider. The Japanese star, obviously fooled by the pitch, backed away as the ball crossed the plate for a strike. It was then that the young Carlton realized he had an effective pitch (at least that's how the story was reported in *Sports Illustrated* in 1994). Carlton was able to throw the slider without rotating his elbow and as a result, he was able to keep from developing elbow problems. It may also have been why his slider had such unparalleled action. Tim McCarver has said that he's never met a guy who is stronger, from fingertips to elbows, than Steve Carlton. Undoubtedly, his freakish physique gave him an advantage in throwing his signature pitch.

The slider was a key pitch for Carlton in '69, yet not so much in '70. But it apparently had nothing to do with the Cardinals' wishes, as Rippelmeyer remembers Steve telling him in spring training. He felt his release was off and he wasn't throwing it right. At least, that's what Carlton told Philadelphia reporters early in '72. He reportedly said that in 1970, he had thrown the pitch so improperly that by the end of the season he had a sore arm. Remember, he went a dismal 10-19 that year. So the following season, he abandoned the slider. Using a two-pitch repertoire of fastball and curve, Carlton went 20-9.

It may have been McCarver who convinced Lefty that the slider was his best pitch and encouraged him to make more use of it. The trade to the Phillies reunited Carlton with his old Cardinals teammate. McCarver caught Carlton when the latter was just a teenaged rookie. Even as a callow youth, he would fight the veteran catcher on such baseball points as pitch selection. But McCarver stayed after him, and Carlton developed an enormous amount of respect for Tim, which later blossomed into a wonderful friendship. No teammate would grow closer to Steve Carlton, both on the field and off, than Tim McCarver. "Those two were great together," said a friend of both men. "Total polar opposites, but great together," he continued. "They would have the damndest arguments and Timmy would get mad, and he'd get loud arguing his point. Lefty would say, 'Timmy, you're losing the argument, the volume just went up.' Timmy would get even madder. Those two were wonderful together." A few years later, during a second tour of duty for McCarver with the Phillies, Tim became Steve's "personal catcher." They were battery mates for each of Lefty's starts. That prompted McCarver to once famously joke that upon their deaths he and Carlton would be "buried sixty feet, six inches apart."

Carlton's slider became virtually unhittable. It was the pitch that would one day land him in the Hall of Fame. It came off his fingertips, spinning much like a fastball, until the bottom dropped out of it. It approached the batter waist-high, and then went straight down. Carlton threw it down and away to left-handed hitters and watched them chase it. And he wasn't afraid to throw it in the dirt. "He didn't always throw it for a strike," former Pirate star Al Oliver says. "Guys would chase it down in the dirt." Carlton threw it down and in to right-handed hitters and watched it baffle them. To a righty, it started looking much like a belt-high fastball, but once the batter began to swing, to his consternation, the ball was gone, winding up on his right shoe-top. "If he hit one right-handed batter on the back foot with his slider, he hit fifty, and for strike three," says Larry Bowa. As the Phillies' shortstop, Bowa had a front-row view of how devastating Carlton's slider could be. "When you play shortstop, you're lined up right behind the pitcher. You really get to see pitches," the former Gold Glover says. "To this day I have never seen so many batters swing at so many bad pitches in my life. You would almost get hypnotized out there. You never expected anyone to hit the ball hard." Most lefties will keep the ball outside when facing a right-handed hitter. But Carlton wasn't afraid to pitch inside to righties.

Baseball people will tell you that the key to any breaking pitch is the spin. Batters look for the spin action to recognize the pitch. But Lefty's slider had no breaking ball spin. It looked like a fastball, until zoom, it dived completely out of the strike zone. It never stayed in the strike zone for very long, fooling batters with great regularity. The slider was Carlton's "out" pitch, the one he used to close out an at-bat, and when he did, opposing hitters were helpless. What was it that made that pitch so great? Was it the way he gripped it? The slider is gripped with the index and middle fingers across the widest seam and the thumb positioned underneath the ball. The pressure Carlton applied to the seam with his middle finger gave the pitch its bite. Could it have been his arm action that made the pitch so special, the strength of his hand, wrist, and forearm enabling him to deliver it with minimal stress on the elbow? As his front shoulder opened toward the plate, he kept his left elbow above his back shoulder, fingers on top of the baseball, in textbook fashion. Location, certainly, was a factor. Carlton had impeccable control. The Carlton slider wasn't over-powering, it was simply unhittable.

Former Pirate Manny Sanguillen remembers some sage advice he received from a baseball legend. "Roberto Clemente once gave me advice on hitting Carlton. He said, 'Look for the fastball, try to adjust to the curve, don't swing at the slider.'" That may have been easy for the great Clemente, but who could tell the difference between Carlton's fastball and his slider? "It was very hard to lay off his slider," says former Cardinal and Brewer Ted Simmons. "It came in looking like a strike. It took a lot of discipline at the plate to lay off it." Most swung at it and missed. Many swung at it and tried to stop. "Umpires would look down to first and third all the time to appeal," Wheeler recalls, "because there were so many checked swings." The home plate umpires needed help from the umps at first and third to determine if the batter had swung around.

Other pitchers tried to unlock the mystery of the Carlton slider, but none were successful. Not that Lefty was much help. Dick Ruthven was a young pitcher for the Phillies in the early to mid-'70s. One night he approached Carlton in the Phillies clubhouse. "Hey Lefty, how do you throw your slider?" asked Ruthven, no doubt hoping for the kind of advice that might potentially change his career. Carlton picked up a baseball and looked in Ruthven's direction as the young hurler waited in anticipation for the great master's words of wisdom. "I grip the ball like this," Carlton said, "and I throw the shit out of it." That was about as detailed an explanation as he was going to give. A perplexed Ruthven shook his head and walked away. "I can't throw the shit out of it," he was overheard saying to himself. So much for a serious discussion from Carlton on the art of throwing the slider.

You noticed Lefty, and you noticed his talent on day one with the Phillies. His new teammates certainly did. Most did not know him. Oh, they knew *of* him, but they didn't *know* him. "He was a competitor, had good stuff, was tough to hit," notes Bowa, "but that was all I knew about him." They certainly didn't know how good a teammate he would become. "You never know from the other bench what a guy's going to be like until he's on your team," says Terry Harmon, an infielder for the '72 Phillies, who played his entire 10-season career in Philadelphia. Harmon was there before the Carlton trade and was a teammate of Carlton's until 1977. "Is he friendly or stand-offish?" Harmon mused, rattling off the questions one might have regarding a new and unknown teammate. "What's he like in the clubhouse? What's he like on the road? You don't know any of those things until he's in your clubhouse." It didn't take long for his new teammates to find out what Carlton was like. "There are so many examples of guys on other teams whom you hated until they were on your team," Harmon continued. "Then they turn out to be the best guys in the world. Carlton was surely one of the best guys in the world, a great teammate." That sentiment is quickly echoed by those in the organization who came in contact with the new pitcher that season, and throughout his stellar career, for that matter. On one point there is no debate. Carlton was a great teammate. "The misperception about Lefty," Wheeler says, "is that he was this sullen, solitary figure that just went along by himself. No, he blended right in. He was one of the guys."

Second baseman Denny Doyle sums it up this way: "Carlton was a happy-go-lucky guy. He was all business on the field—a fun guy off the field."

It didn't take very long for Steve Carlton to become the leader of the '72 Phillies, especially when his new teammates found out what a good guy he was and what wondrous talent he possessed. However, seeing that talent on display in a regular season game would take a little longer than anyone had thought.

Marvin Miller, Executive Director of the Major League Baseball Players Association, always liked to sit in the grandstand and bask in the sunshine during his trips to spring training. Once, while in Scottsdale, Arizona, at the Chicago Cubs facility, as he sat in the warm afternoon sun, Miller chatted with a group of players who had just completed a workout. One of the Cubs, infielder Glenn Beckert, distinctly remembers Miller's message that day. "He said," recalled Beckert, "someday major league players will make a million dollars a year."

Miller could see into the future, and it was just over the not-too-distant horizon. Since taking on the job as union boss in 1966, the Bronx native visited every team, every spring. He was a labor economist by trade, rising to become the chief negotiator for the United Steelworkers Union. Ironically, it was a pair of former Phillies pitching greats who were instrumental in Miller's becoming the head of the MLBPA. Robin Roberts and Jim Bunning, along with Harvey Kuenn, made up the committee that interviewed Miller. Roberts and Bunning, acting on the recommendation of a University of Pennsylvania labor professor, presented Miller's name to the players' union. In the spring of '66, he was elected its executive director.

Miller negotiated the union's first collective bargaining agreement with the owners. He got them to raise the minimum salary for a player from $6,000 to $10,000. He also was able to get the owners to agree to binding arbitration, which he considered to be the union's greatest early achievement. Under Miller's stewardship, the MLBPA was on its way to becoming one of the strongest unions in the country. In the spring of '72, free agency was still an ideal, perhaps a future goal. At issue for Miller as he visited players at the major league camps that year was the players' pension benefits and the owners' refusal to increase payments to the plan.

From 1959 through 1962, baseball played two All-Star Games from which 95 percent of the proceeds went to the pension plan. But the second game had been eliminated, starting in 1963. There was also a tie-in with TV money, which the owners also tried to eliminate. Cubs pitcher Milt Pappas was a player rep for 10 years and still remembers what it was like dealing with the owners in those days. "The owners walked all over us. They treated players like cattle," he says. In February of '72, the players union asked the owners for an immediate 17 percent increase in pension benefits in a one-year contract, which would cost the owners a million dollars in increased contributions. What was the owners' reaction? In the words of August Busch, boss man of the Cardinals, the owners wouldn't contribute "another damn cent" to the pension plan.

It was clear that both sides were preparing for a fight. That was also going to make 1972 the wrong year, you might say, to be elected as a player representative to the union. Unfortunately for Terry Harmon, it was his first as the Phillies rep. Apparently, no one else wanted the job. "I think I was the last guy to the ballpark that day, that's how I got it," jokes Harmon. Normally, the job as the team's representative to the players association is titular in nature. In reality you have little responsibility. Make sure everyone gets the information they need from the union, whenever there is pertinent information to pass along from the union, and that's about it. But times were changing. The union was beginning to kick up its heels. Most players had followed the Flood case, and Curt's stance against the reserve clause had energized the troops. Now, for Harmon and the others elected by their teams, the role of player rep would hardly be a do-little job. In one of his first meetings, Harmon had to travel to New York to meet with Marvin Miller and the other player reps. "I'm thinking it's just going to be a quick trip, up and back. I didn't bring anything with me, just the clothes I was wearing," remembers Harmon. "The meeting lasted for three days. I had to go out and buy a toothbrush and toothpaste and lived in the same clothes for three days."

Meanwhile, a salary dispute involving one of the game's brightest young stars was making front-page news. Vida Blue of the Oakland A's had captured the American League by storm in 1971. The 21-year-old pitcher won 24 games and had a league-best 1.82 ERA. With style and flair, the colorful Blue helped the "Swingin' A's" win the AL West by 16 games before eventually being swept by the Orioles in the League Championship Series. He not only captured the Cy Young Award that season, but was also voted the league's MVP. All while earning $14,000. In the off-season he went looking for a substantial raise. "I thought I should have been rewarded," Blue says, "I wanted $80,000." He wasn't going to get it, not from cantankerous A's owner Charlie Finley. "He was a combination of George Steinbrenner, Ted Turner, and Al Davis," Blue says of Finley. "He knew his rights as an owner. If it wasn't his idea, it wasn't right." The A's star retained the services of a Beverly Hills lawyer to help him negotiate, making Blue one of the few players back then to use an agent. This did not sit well with Mr. Finley, who, according to Blue, was offended that his player had a representative. The contract talks did not go well, resulting in a lengthy impasse. Vida decided to boycott spring training. His lawyer had a friend who owned a company that manufactured bathroom and plumbing fixtures, so while Blue tried to stay in shape by training on his own, he also went to work at the plumbing fixture company. He lasted one week on the job. Blue wasn't about to quit his day job, and so his hold-out ended up exceeding his stint as a plumbing executive.

On March 8th, players around the majors began voting team by team on whether to authorize a strike. The majority of the Phillies were behind it. They knew the stakes. Miller had laid out the information clearly and concisely. He presented the issues and options and let the players decide. For most the decision was easy. A week later, the owners offered to contribute over $400,000 to the health-care portion of the plan, but nothing more. On March 29th, in a final attempt to engage the owners at the bargaining table, the players lowered their demand to an $800,000 increase. The owners balked. On March 30th, the strike authorization vote was returned. The players voted 663 to 10 in favor of authorizing a strike.

The next day (which happened to be Good Friday for the world's Christians; the strike poised to begin Easter weekend), the player reps and their alternates met with Miller in Dallas. The meeting lasted for four and a half hours, and upon its conclusion the union had officially voted to stage the game's first-ever work stoppage, effective the next day. On Saturday, April 1st, the Phillies were scheduled to play a Grapefruit League game with the Pirates, but that was now canceled. The players were on strike, putting the remainder of the exhibition season, as well as Opening Day, in jeopardy. This was no April Fool's Day joke. The vote had been 47-0 with one abstention. While neither side wanted it to come to this, both were steadfast in their positions.

"Major League Ballplayers Walk Out" screamed the headline in Saturday morning's *Philadelphia Inquirer*, stealing the spotlight from the Vietnam War and a story headlined "Reds Rout South Viets at 5 Bases." Commissioner Kuhn said he felt for the sports fans of America, stating that they were "the real losers in the strike action." In Clearwater, some of the Phillies claimed they were caught by surprise. They said they thought Friday's meeting was simply for informational purposes, and that another vote of the union's rank and file would be taken before calling a strike. Now, suddenly, there would be no baseball, and for how long, no one knew.

Joe Torre and Dal Maxvill were the Cardinals' player representatives. "We went in to Gussie Busch and told him we were going to strike," remembers Torre. "He took it very personally." Torre looks back across the years from the visiting manager's office at, ironically enough, the new Busch Stadium in St. Louis. It's a July afternoon in 2009, and he is now managing the L.A. Dodgers, who are about to play the Cardinals. The Dodgers lost the previous night's game 10-0, but their 62 wins to that point are the most in baseball. Come October, they'll advance to their second consecutive LCS, where, also for the second consecutive year, their season will end at the hands of the Phillies. But, on this night, the Dodgers are mired in their first three-game losing streak of the year, and the season's finish line seems light years away. Torre may be famous for his exploits as a manager, especially for the championships he won as skipper of the Yankees, but in 1972 he was in the midst of a stellar playing career. The catcher/first baseman showed up at spring training as the reigning NL MVP. Torre was coming off a '71 season in which he hit .363 to win the batting title. His 230 hits and 137 RBI in '71 also led the league. And he was the Cardinals' player rep who had to tell the volatile Busch that his players weren't going to be playing. "The strike probably hurt our ball club more than any other team because he treated us so well," says Torre. "We had a lot of perks that other teams didn't have. So when we went on strike, Gussie took away a lot of the little perks he had given us."

The first strike in baseball history was now in full force. Many of the Phillies weren't quite sure what to do. Some, whose families were in town, took a couple of days to hit Disney World with their kids, or see the sights in Florida. Stadiums were silent, training facilities tightly locked. If players wanted to work out, they would have to do it on their own. While teams would not permit players to use their spring training sites, the Phillies players continued to work out as a group. They found a city park with a large enough baseball field about a half-hour north of Clearwater and scheduled informal workouts for whomever wanted to attend. They took batting practice, took grounders, and shagged flies—the usual spring training routine. But as the strike progressed, a lot of the players decided to head home, train there, and wait. No one could tell how long this thing was going to last, and uncertainty filled the springtime air. Would it be a few days? A few weeks? Was the whole season in jeopardy? "I thought it's just my luck," recalls Tommy Hutton, a first baseman/outfielder who spent six seasons as a Phillie, but who was a rookie that year. "I'm finally going to make a big league club, and there's a work stoppage."

Opening Day quickly became a casualty of the strike. The Phillies were scheduled to open the season in St. Louis on Friday, April 7th, in the first game of a three-game series. The home opener at the Vet was set for the following Monday night versus Montreal, and that now seemed wishful thinking. The strike did indeed last into the first weekend of the regular season. The 24 major league clubs estimated they lost $2.5 million in revenue by not playing that weekend. The average player, making $22,500, was losing about $140 a game in salary. Throughout that first week of the strike, Marvin Miller continued to meet with John Gaherin, the owners' chief negotiator, in New York. But they were not close to reaching a settlement. Said Phillies executive Ruly Carpenter, "This strike is taking all the fun out of the game; it will never be the same."

Harmon, the Phillies' rep, along with all of the team reps, traveled back and forth to New York to meet with Miller. There were meetings and conference calls as the union hunkered down, remaining resolute in their solidarity. Hard feelings were developing on both sides, and the players realized that the only way something would get done was if they held together. Phillies management was not happy about the situation, but to their credit, Harmon says, they never held it against the player rep. "They never said, 'Terry if you don't see it our way, you're going to get released or traded.' If I'm not mistaken, some player reps did get traded." Instead, they maintained a constructive dialogue as baseball's first-ever strike entered its second week. "They were not confrontational," says Harmon. "Their attitude was, 'let's try and work through this thing and get it done,' because Bob Carpenter [the Phillies' owner] and Ruly Carpenter wanted to play baseball."

The date of the home opener at the Vet passed without baseball. On April 10th, the owners offered to contribute $400,000 in "surplus funds" to the pension plan. The next day the players countered, asking for $500,000 in "surplus funds." On April 13th, at a meeting in Dallas, the owners agreed to the players' wishes. The strike was over. The season would begin two days later. Everyone involved breathed a sigh of relief, although, as Ruly Carpenter observed, things would never be the same. The labor landscape had been altered forever and a seismic shift was on the way. Miller refrained from calling it a victory for the players. "I'm just happy to announce that a settlement finally has been reached so that the season can start this Saturday," he was reported to have said at a press conference. "The real issues were never a question of pension or money," Miller went on. "They were more a question of human dignity. The central issue had to do with the importance of players being treated as adult human beings. We are not about to claim victory even though our objectives were achieved."

Back in Oakland, at some point during the strike, Vida Blue and the A's came to an agreement on a new contract, worth approximately $60,000 a year. "The dispute soured my stomach," Blue says. "My heart and soul got nibbled away. It hurts to this day. I became a public spectacle."

Had the owners wanted, they could have shut down for the entire season. That almost certainly could have broken the union. They could have used replacement players, as would be the case in the spring of 1995, but things never got to that point. The strike didn't last long enough. After all, this strike business was costing the owners money; the quicker it was resolved, the better. "If the owners wanted it to be long, it could've been long," says Harmon. "But they decided to get it settled and move on." And had the strike lasted a couple of months or longer, would the players have been able to stand their ground? "I don't know, I doubt it," he says. "It probably lasted about as long as it could have before something might've happened that would've been detrimental to us."

On Friday, April 14th, the Phillies players who were back in Philadelphia held a final workout at the Vet before catching a flight to Chicago where they would finally begin the season the next day. Carlton was not at the workout. He was back at his home in St. Louis, as was pitcher Joe Hoerner. Also among the missing were pitcher Woodie Fryman, who was home in Kentucky, and Tommy Hutton and another pitcher, Dick Selma, who both lived on the West Coast. They'd join the club in Chicago later that night.

The first work stoppage in baseball history lasted 13 days. It cost the owners roughly five million dollars in lost revenue. For the players, five percent of their salaries was gone. The strike claimed 85 regular season games, none of which would be rescheduled. The game's powers felt that it was a logistical impossibility to make up each game. As a result, the 1972 season was played with an unbalanced schedule. Some teams played 153 games, others 156. The Phillies would play a 156-game schedule rather than the customary 162. The first was played on Saturday, April 15th versus the Cubs at Wrigley Field. It was Steve Carlton's debut as a Phillie.

CHAPTER 3

Opening Day...
at Last

When Steve Carlton looked around Wrigley Field's visitors locker room, it could not escape his notice that the Phillies team which he had joined was considerably less talented than the Cardinals team that he had departed. All-time great Bob Gibson anchored the St. Louis pitching staff. Winner of two Cy Young Awards, Gibson had posted a microscopic 1.12 ERA in 1968 when he won the award unanimously. Left fielder Lou Brock was in the middle of a Hall of Fame career in which he would break Ty Cobb's stolen base record (Rickey Henderson would later break Brock's record) and would also become a member of the exclusive 3,000-hit club. Right fielder Matty Alou was a perennial .300 hitter and former batting titlist. Reigning MVP Joe Torre held down third base. Catcher Ted Simmons was coming off a .300 season in his sophomore year; he would go on to amass nearly 2500 hits.

Carlton had grown accustomed to playing for a winner in St. Louis. In 1967, his rookie season, the Redbirds won the World Series, and the next year they came close again, losing the seventh game of the Series to the Tigers.

On the other hand, the Phillies had never won a World Series and had not been to the Fall Classic in more than 20 years. They were composed predominantly of young, unaccomplished fringe players who would have short and undistinguished major league careers. A handful of young Phillies were blessed with talent, but by and large they had not yet come into their own. Some of those players would find their niche for another team after the Phillies lost patience and traded them, while others, despite potential, fizzled out quickly. A couple, notably Larry Bowa and Greg Luzinski, went on to enjoy long and productive runs for the Phillies.

Catcher Tim McCarver was one of the few veterans on the roster. Before he came to Philadelphia in the Curt Flood trade, he was the starting backstop in St. Louis for seven years. McCarver earned World Series rings for the Cardinals' triumphs in 1964 and 1967; in '67, he finished runner-up in the MVP vote to his teammate Orlando Cepeda.

Deron Johnson was the club's starting first baseman. He was a journeyman whose first taste in the majors was with Mickey Mantle and Yogi Berra's Yankees in 1960. Philadelphia was Johnson's fifth stop in a nine-city major league career. He had been the Phillies' top power hitter in each of the two previous seasons, smacking 27 and 34 home runs. But an early season leg injury landed him on the disabled list and significantly diminished his playing time and production. Rookie Tommy Hutton, obtained from the Dodgers in an off-season trade, handled the majority of the first-base duties in '72, and while he was a slick fielder, he didn't hit much.

Manager Frank Lucchesi platooned left-handed-hitting Denny Doyle and right-handed-hitting Terry Harmon at second base. Baby-faced Doyle played good defense, but hit .219 his first two seasons for the Phillies, with little power. He did better in '72, but not much. Doyle would have his best days with the Red Sox. Acquired from the Angels in the middle of the 1975 season, Doyle hit .310 and put together a 22-game hitting streak to help the Sox avoid one of their patented late-season collapses, and fend off the Orioles to win the division. In 1975, Doyle, along with his brothers Brian and Blake, founded the Doyle Baseball Academy in Winter Haven, Florida, which they own and operate to this day. The Doyles have coached roughly a million youngsters through their academy, some of whom, like Gary Sheffield, Paul Konerko, Derrek Lee, Tim Wakefield, Walt Weiss, and J.D. Drew, went on to enjoy stellar major league careers. Harmon was a utility man throughout his career and welcomed the opportunity to get into the lineup against lefties.

Shortstop Larry Bowa made the majors more because of his persistence and fire than his natural ability. Cut from his high school team three straight years, Bowa persevered, made the team his senior year, and the Phillies signed him after he graduated. He worked his way up the minors and in 1970, Lucchesi, who liked Larry's tenacity, gave him the starting shortstop job. He had a good glove and strong arm—he would lead National League shortstops in fielding percentage in '72. He was also one of the few players on the team with any speed; 1972 would be the third straight season in which Bowa was the only Phillie to reach double digits in steals.

Hitting, however, was not Bowa's strong suit. He was a natural right-handed hitter, but in the minors he had considerable difficulty hitting the breaking ball of right-handed pitchers. As one Phillies coach observed, Bowa had a tendency to put his foot in the bucket and couldn't hit the ball if he had a tennis racquet. So he became a switch-hitter. Initially, his left-handed swing was decidedly weak. His speed helped him to hit .250 and .249 his first two seasons for the Phillies, but he displayed no power. Bowa hit no home runs either year, and it wasn't until August '72, after more than 1500 career at-bats, that he finally circled the bases. And it was an inside-the-park homer; his first home run out of the ballpark wasn't until 1974. Despite his offensive struggles early in his career, Bowa went on to accumulate almost 2200 hits.

Don Money came up as a shortstop, but moved to third in 1970 to make room for Bowa. Money's defense was consistently solid, but the Phillies brass was still trying to figure out if he could hit. He showed promise in 1970 by hitting .295, but the year before and year after, his average was in the .220s. In '72, he would have another dismal offensive season, finishing in the .220s again, and less than a month after the Phillies' last game, he was sent packing to Milwaukee in a seven-player trade. The change of scenery worked wonders for Money's game. He spent more than a decade with the Brewers, and he was a four-time All-Star.

Colorful Willie Montañez was Philly's everyday center fielder. When Flood refused to report to Philadelphia after the trade, Montañez was one of two players whom the Cardinals sent to the Phillies as compensation in 1970. He cracked the starting lineup in 1971 with a bang by finishing second to Atlanta's Earl Williams for the National League Rookie of the Year Award. It did not take long for him to earn the "hot dog" label for flipping his bat as he walked to the plate and catching flyballs with a showy snap of the glove.

Montañez was flanked by a pair of 21-year-olds, Greg Luzinski and Mike Anderson. Both had fine minor league credentials, and the Phillies were expecting big things out of them. Luzinski delivered; Anderson did not. The strong, stocky Luzinski, nicknamed "Bull," would develop into one of baseball's premier sluggers of the 1970s—he finished second in the National League MVP vote in 1975 and 1977. In '72, though, he was learning to hit big league pitching, and while his 18 home runs and 68 RBI were good enough to lead the lowly Phillies, the numbers were modest for an outfielder. Anderson played an excellent right field and had a rifle arm, but he never hit a lick in the majors. With a measly two home runs and five RBI a month and a half into the '72 season, he would be sent back to the minors.

The scary part is that the pitching staff, aside from Carlton, was even worse. As a result of a decision made in spring training, Carlton pitched more frequently than he did in St. Louis. With the Cardinals, he pitched every fifth day. "That was because everything revolved around Bob Gibson," Carlton told Jack Lang of the *New York Times* in 1972. "He was the ace of the staff and Gibby required four days' rest between starts. So to set up a rotation, the rest of the staff had to give way." Soon after the trade, Lucchesi called Carlton into his office at the Phillies' complex in Clearwater and asked him about pitching every fourth day instead of every fifth. Although Carlton had not done it before, he agreed. After the season, Carlton told Lang that pitching every fourth day helped him to develop a high rate of consistency and develop a good rhythm. The three pitchers whom Lucchesi picked to follow Carlton in the rotation were Woodie Fryman, Dick Selma, and Billy Champion. The trio would win 10 games for the '72 Phillies—*combined.*

Southpaw Fryman had achieved some success in Philly. He had averaged 10 wins a season his first four years in town and made the All-Star team in 1968. Selma was a hard-throwing and hardheaded righty whom Lucchesi used solely in the bullpen in 1970 and 1971. He had a strong season in '70, saving 22 and striking out more than a batter an inning. But arm injuries sidelined him for most of '71, and he saved just one game. Selma had been a starter for the Cubs and Mets in the late 1960s, and Lucchesi, with a pitching corps scarce on talent, returned Selma to that role in '72. Selma wasn't crazy about the move, and his performance reflected his displeasure; by June 1st, he would lose his job as a starter.

Seemingly by default, the freckle-faced, 24-year-old Billy Champion, a spot starter in '71, was given the fourth place in the rotation. Barry Lersch and Ken Reynolds, two more young arms, had been starters at times in 1971. But an 11-game losing streak by Lersch and erratic pitching by Reynolds prompted Lucchesi to relegate them to middle relievers as the '72 season opened.

The longest-tenured Phillie by many years, Chris Short, also failed to dazzle opponents when he started in '71. In his prime, Short was one of the National League's best lefties, winning 83 games over a five-year stretch in the 1960s. But age and injuries had worn Shorty down, and he was nearing the end of the line. He, too, was dispatched to the bullpen in 1972, which would be his 14th and final season in Philadelphia.

Jim Bunning had also started periodically in 1971, but he got hammered routinely. He finished the season with a 5-12 record and a 5.48 ERA. He was at the top of his game during his first tour of duty with the Phillies in the mid-'60s when he won 19 games three times and pitched a perfect game in 1964. When the man destined for the Hall of Fame and the United States Senate returned to Philadelphia in 1970, he had lost his stuff. He retired after the '71 season.

Joe Hoerner, another teammate of Carlton's on the Cardinals, also came over in the Flood deal. He replaced Selma as the Phillies' top reliever in 1971. The sidearm-throwing lefty was one of the bright spots on the '71 pitching staff besides Rick Wise, as his ERA was an impressive 1.97.

The man entrusted with the daunting task of trying to win games with this motley crew was, of course, Frank Lucchesi. Son of Italian immigrants, Lucchesi grew up in San Francisco; he graduated from the same high school (Galileo) that Joe DiMaggio attended for a year before dropping out. Five feet seven, slightly pudgy, and effusive, the 44-year-old Lucchesi was starting his third year as the Phillies' pilot. He managed the team to a fifth-place finish in the six-team National League Eastern Division in 1970, and then his Phils dropped into the basement in 1971. It was going to take some doing for his club to escape that fate in '72.

Lucchesi paid his dues to become a big league skipper. He spent 25 years in the minors—six as a player, seven as a player-manager, and 12 as a manager—before he was offered the job to replace the Phillies' interim manager, George Myatt, at the end of the 1969 season.

Affable, kindhearted, and generous, Lucchesi welcomed the opportunity to serve as a community ambassador while he managed the Phillies. He frequently visited area hospitals, spreading good cheer to sick patients, especially children and the elderly.

So what kind of team did the Philadelphia Phillies have as they embarked on the 1972 season? Phillies personnel, writers, players, and coaches all were in agreement: downright shitful. "The team was terrible," said Chris Wheeler. "There was a lot of deadwood." Frank Bilovsky agreed that they were very bad: "Carlton was the only player worth seeing on that team." Jayson Stark, a teenager at the time, would soon become one of the team's beat writers. His characterization of the '72 Phillies: "Awful."

The players acknowledged that their fate was sealed. Money: "Each year, you start out the season with aspirations for the World Series. And then you look around." Bowa: "We were a *bad* team. We were young. We were green. We were glad to be in the big leagues." Luzinski: "You could tell [it was going to be a bad year.] You'd see other teams, other lineups, and you just knew, we didn't have the ability that other teams had; it was that simple." Ray Rippelmeyer recalled his feelings when the strike ended and the season got under way. "I knew it was going to be a long, tough year." And it was. Except when Steve Carlton took the hill.

The opening two-game series against the Cubs was a microcosm of the Phillies' season, as Carlton's superb pitching and the team's paltry hitting were exemplified. It was Carlton's first Opening Day assignment—Bob

Gibson always had the honor when they were teammates with the Cardinals. Carlton would make 13 more Opening Day starts for the Phillies. His mound opponent that day was Fergie Jenkins, the National League's Cy Young Award winner in 1971. Jenkins was a pitcher that John Quinn wished he had *not* traded. Jenkins was signed by the Phillies and had pitched just eight games for the major league squad when Quinn dealt him and two players to the Cubs in 1966 for veteran pitcher Larry Jackson and a second pitcher. While Jackson turned in three solid seasons in Philly, he didn't pay nearly the dividends for the Phillies that Jenkins did for the Cubs. In 1972, he would win 20 for the sixth straight year; he would go on to win 284 games and earn induction into the Hall of Fame.

Jenkins was the first of six future Hall of Famers whom Carlton squared off against in '72. He also went head-to-head with Gibson, Tom Seaver (twice), Juan Marichal, Don Sutton, and Phil Niekro. Carlton also faced four other 200-game winners: Jerry Reuss (twice), Jerry Koosman (twice), Tommy John, and Milt Pappas, as well as Steve Blass, the runner-up in the 1972 Cy Young Award voting, and Jon Matlack, the National League Rookie of the Year. To say the least, in 1972, Carlton had a penchant for drawing outstanding opposing pitchers.

It was a chilly Saturday afternoon, and the stands at venerable Wrigley Field were only half full. The cold weather and sour taste in fans' mouths from the strike kept the attendance down. Carlton faced a formidable Cubs lineup. "Sweet-swinging" Billy Williams was on the verge of a standout season, as he won the National League batting title and finished second to Johnny Bench for the MVP award. Ron Santo, Joe Pepitone, and Rick Monday were legitimate home run threats.

After Carlton opened the game with two perfect innings, the Cubs nicked him for a run in the bottom of the third. An inning later, Luzinski evened the score with a home run off Jenkins over the ivy-covered left-field wall. Bill Hands, normally a starter, relieved Jenkins in the seventh inning. Carlton helped himself by sacrificing Doyle to second, and McCarver singled Doyle home. In the bottom of the eighth inning, with the Phillies and Carlton clinging to a 2-1 lead, José Cardenal reached base on a forceout and stole second. With two outs, Glenn Beckert dug in against Carlton. The Cubs' second baseman was a pesky hitter who was extremely difficult to strike out—he was the league's toughest to fan in five different seasons. Beckert swatted a single to chase Cardenal home and tie the score.

Beckert recalled the story of running into Carlton at a card show years after they had both retired. Beckert had a solid career, but it was pedestrian compared to Carlton's, and he didn't think that the legendary lefty would remember him. "You don't know who I am, do you?" asked Beckert.

Carlton snapped, "Yeah, you're the sonofabitch who broke up my no-hitter."

Sure enough, in June 1968, Carlton's second full year with the Cardinals, he threw a one-hit shutout against the Cubs; Beckert's fourth-inning single was the lone hit. While Carlton threw six one-hitters in his career, the no-hitter eluded him. In 1965, Beckert's rookie year, he was not able to break up an opposing pitcher's no-hitter; in fact, the hurler, Sandy Koufax, threw a perfect game that night. "Koufax was the best pitcher I ever faced," said Beckert, "but Carlton was right up there."

With the Phillies just four outs away from an Opening Day win, Beckert played the spoiler again against Carlton by plating the game-tying run. The game went to the ninth, and Hands retired the first two Phillies. With Carlton due up next, Lucchesi opted to send up a pinch-hitter. Reserve outfielder Ron Stone came through with a single to right, and Bowa followed with another single to right, sending Stone to third. Cubs manager Leo Durocher, Willie Mays' first big league skipper, called in left-hander Steve Hamilton to face the left-handed-hitting McCarver. Cardenal, who had just scored the tying run, proved to be the goat as he botched McCarver's flyball to right field, which allowed two unearned runs to score. Joe Hoerner came out of the bullpen and set the side down in the ninth for the save. It was one of just three times that year in which a reliever saved a game for Carlton. He went the distance in his other 24 wins.

So the Phillies prevailed 4-2, and Steve Carlton won his first start as a Phillie. Although Carlton only struck out five hitters—one of his lowest K totals of the season—he was sharp, relying on his fastball and newfound slider, and mixing in an occasional curveball. He allowed only six Cub baserunners—four hits and two walks.

The Phillies banged out 10 hits in the opener, but they showed their true colors the next afternoon against rookie Burt Hooton. The Cubs had drafted the highly touted Hooton out of the University of Texas the previous June, and after just a dozen starts in the minors, he was promoted to the majors and made three starts late in the 1971 season. So this was just his fourth major league start. While his control was spotty—he walked seven—Hooton's specialty pitch, the knuckle-curveball, baffled Phils hitters all afternoon. He carried a 4-0 lead and a no-hitter into the ninth inning, but the Phillies sent up the heart of the order to try to foil the no-hitter and get some runs on the scoreboard. But Montañez grounded out to Beckert, and Hooton struck out Johnson and Luzinski to preserve the no-hitter. With a win and a loss, the Phillies headed home to face the Cardinals in their home opener the next night.

CHAPTER 4

The Showdown with Gibson

On Monday, April 17th, baseball returned to Philadelphia. It was finally the night of the home opener, a week late thanks to the players strike. Veterans Stadium had awakened from its winter slumber and was alive with anticipation for the start of the new season, the second in its history. The stadium had been primped and primed for the occasion. Both dugouts were freshly painted. The seats and walkways power-washed clean. The red, white, and blue bunting—customary for season openers—hung from the railings and the stadium's facade. The Phillies home opener is one of the highlights of the year, and is always well attended. That wasn't always the case, but more than 38,000 passed through the turnstiles for the 1972 edition, which would prove to be one of the larger crowds of the season. Especially considering that Steve Carlton was not pitching. Baseball was back, and all was right with the world.

The 56,000-seat facility, state of the art at the time and the prototype for the "cookie cutter" multi-purpose venues of the era, was home not only to the Philadelphia Phillies, but also to the Philadelphia Eagles of the NFL. By the time it was razed in 2004, "the Vet" had become notorious for its unforgiving artificial turf as well as its equally unforgiving fans, the denizens of the 700 level, which was the stadium's uppermost section. Sometime during the late 1990s, a makeshift courtroom and holding cell were erected in the bowels of the building for use primarily during Eagles games when drunken rowdies would run afoul of the law. A judge was always on duty, and he was generally busy. The accused, restrained and handcuffed, had only to be taken downstairs, rather than downtown. It proved to be an effective means of maintaining law and order, and only enhanced the tough, snarling reputation of the stadium and its fandom.

Many special festivities were planned to mark the return of baseball to the Vet. Mayor Frank Rizzo tossed the ceremonial first pitch. The city's famed Mummers, the costumed string bands whose parade down Broad Street is an annual New Year's Day tradition, entertained with a pregame strut on the stadium turf. And, last but not least, the immortal "Kite Man" performed his act of derring-do.

Kite Man was one of the brainchildren of Phillies promotional wiz Bill Giles. Giles, the son of ex-National League president Warren Giles, grew up in the game, and it has been his life's work. He joined the Phillies from the Houston Astros in 1969 as a club vice president, and helped the franchise transition into its new stadium. Giles later headed up the ownership group that bought the team from the Carpenter family, and today remains the club's chairman. As a member of baseball's rules and television committees, his contributions to the game have been many. But back in those days he was famous for his promotions. "We weren't drawing many people in the early '70s," Giles recalls. "My whole concept was to do crazy things all the time in order to get people to come out once, and hope that they enjoyed the ballgame enough to come back when there wasn't a stupid promotion."

The Phillies were known for their "inspired" promotions at the Vet. There was Karl Wallenda, who twice walked a tightrope across the top of the concrete, bowl-shaped stadium. There were Phil and Phillis, the mascots in colonial costumes. There was the ever-popular Hot Pants Patrol, which was a team of ball girls decked out in short-shorts. And of course, there was the one and only Phillie Phanatic. That fuzzy green mascot now tears around Citizens Bank Park on his all-terrain vehicle, still delighting millions of fans every season. All were ideas that came to fruition under Giles' stewardship.

Kite Man was actually Richard Johnson of Cypress Gardens, Florida, although he was not the first man hired to strap himself to the kite. It turned out the original Kite Man had a scheduling conflict. Because the season opener was pushed back a week due to the players strike, that Kite Man couldn't make it for the new date. According to Giles, "He had to fly to Mexico to teach the President of Mexico how to water-ski."

So Giles found Johnson, who was willing to take the plunge, so to speak. He would earn $1,000 for his troubles. Kite Man flew a type of parasail contraption. It was a nylon kite, 16 feet by 23 feet, connected to a harness. A 100-foot-long plywood ramp was built in the right center-field seats; the yellow-colored seats in the Vet's upper section. The idea was for Johnson, on water skis, to ski down the ramp, take off, and fly onto the field, delivering the game ball. In order to reach the necessary speed for takeoff, about 40 to 50 mph, the ramp would be doused with water to gain the appropriate slickness.

A few days before the stunt was to take place, Johnson went out to the Vet. He took one look at the ramp and turned to Giles. "I can't water-ski down that thing," he said. "How about if I put on roller skates and have a car drag me around the parking lot? I'll get high enough to where I can fly into the stadium."

"Look," Giles replied. "How about instead of $1,000, I'll give you $1,500 if you go down that ramp?"

"OK, I'll do it," said the Kite Man.

"Do you want to take a practice run?" Giles asked.

"No, no," he said. "If I'm going to kill myself, I want more than just you watching."

A practice run probably would not have helped. The flight attempt was going to be challenging thanks to the swirling South Philadelphia winds. On the night of the big event, Johnson may have had a feeling it wasn't going to be easy when, minutes before the stunt, he tried to light a cigarette. The wind blew out his match.

Kite Man headed down the ramp erected in the yellow seats at the top of the stadium. He never actually became airborne. He got about halfway down the ramp, to the next section, the one with the orange seats, when just then a wind gust blew him sideways and off course. The gust sent Kite Man into a nosedive, and crashing into a railing below those orange seats. He never even made it to the end of the ramp.

"I thought the poor guy was dead," recalls Giles.

Actually, no one was injured. Kite Man was a little embarrassed, but OK. Unable to glide in with the game ball, he threw it instead onto the AstroTurf, about 200 feet below.

In one sense, Kite Man's crash was a fitting way for the 1972 Phillies to open the season. It was the perfect metaphor for what was to happen on the field that year. Except, that is, for when Steve Carlton pitched.

This was not one of those nights. It was Woodie Fryman's turn to start for the Phillies as they played host to the Cardinals. At age 32, Fryman was one of the oldest players on the '72 team. He would not spend the entire season in Philadelphia. After 23 games, he'd find himself placed on waivers. But things had a happy ending for the tobacco farmer from Kentucky. Detroit picked him up, and Fryman wound up starting two games for the Tigers in October in the ALCS, which the Tigers lost to Oakland.

Fryman pitched well in his first start of the year, giving the Cardinals three runs in eight innings of work. He even hit a home run, a two-run shot in the third inning off Cardinals starter Reggie Cleveland. When Fryman was lifted for a pinch-hitter to begin the bottom of the eighth, the score was 3-3. On came Joe Hoerner in relief to pitch the ninth. But Hoerner blew it, giving up two to the Cardinals in the last inning. Ted Simmons ripped an RBI double for the go-ahead score. The Phils got one run back in the home half, but that was it; they dropped the home opener, 5-4. The 38,000 fans went home disappointed, a scenario that would repeat itself often in '72.

The Phillies managed to win the next night's game, evening their record to two and two. And that set the stage for the rubber match, in which Carlton was getting the ball for the first time in front of the Philly fans. He was fresh off the season-opening victory in which he made a splash by outlasting Fergie Jenkins. Now here was the first chance for the home folks to see the new ace in person. He'd be facing his old team for the first time since the trade, and he'd be facing the league's most feared pitcher, Bob Gibson. And yet only 8,184 attended the Wednesday night affair at the Vet.

At 36, Gibson was headed for the last big season of his Hall of Fame career. He was coming off a no-decision in the season opener, a 3-2 loss to Montreal. Gibson went six innings and yielded two runs; a "quality start" by today's standards. "Gibby" would finish 1972 with a 19 and 11 record and an ERA of 2.46 with 23 complete games. Three seasons later he was finished, bowing out at the age of 39. While it may have been a last hurrah of sorts, Gibson was still as tough and intimidating as ever.

Larry Bowa remembers what it was like to face Gibson back in those days. "He would glare at you from the mound. If you squared around to bunt, he would yell, 'You better get it down.' Gibson was an intimidating pitcher. Because we were a young team, we probably focused more on how intimidating he was."

Gibson wasn't afraid to throw at you. He wasn't afraid to knock you down. He wasn't afraid to brush you back. Gibson owned the inside corner of the plate. "And in those days," observes Ruly Carpenter, "players didn't wear helmets. If Gibson would throw a few at your head, you would certainly be intimidated."

And he was a fast worker. Gibby never wasted time between pitches. Carlton admired Gibson, and was greatly influenced by him as a young pitcher. As teammates in St. Louis, Gibson became Carlton's role model. "Having Gibson around to observe," says Simmons, "had to be helpful to Carlton." Young Steve watched and learned from the great pitcher. In Gibson, he saw an example of what a big league pitcher was supposed to be. From Gibson he learned how to conduct himself on the field, how to take care of his business, and above all, how to compete. Bob Gibson was nothing if not a relentless competitor. There was a lot of Gibson that rubbed off on Carlton. "Gibson's personality was so strong, he exuded so much confidence, that just being around him had a positive effect on everybody," Simmons recalled.

Joe Torre caught both pitchers in his days with the Cardinals. "A great deal came from watching Gibby. Carlton learned to get the ball and throw it and dictate the pace of the game."Gibson was always in control on the mound. Just give him the ball, let him throw it, and get out of his way. And no one dared break his rhythm. Once in a tight situation during a game, Tim McCarver tried to go to the mound, as catchers often do, to settle him down. Gibson flashed the catcher a look that could melt an iceberg.

"What do you think you're doing?" asked the pitcher.

"What do you mean?" replied his catcher.

"Until there's a line in the box score that says 'Losing Catcher,' you get back there behind home plate."

Carlton was exactly the same way. He also worked quickly, and never liked to have his rhythm broken. The mound was his office, and it was a place where no one else was welcome.

Larry Bowa once made the mistake of approaching Carlton's mound space during a tense situation in a game. The six-foot-five Carlton shot the diminutive shortstop an angry stare.

"What do you think you're doing? Get back to your position and don't you ever come over here again," the pitcher bellowed.

"He used to scare the crap out of Bowa," says Greg Luzinski. "He didn't like people coming to the mound."

If Carlton had an extra adrenaline rush because he was pitching against his former team for the first time, and against Gibson, he didn't show it outwardly. But inwardly, those around the team could sense that it wasn't just another game. "It was a big game for him," says one member of the media. "I think you could tell that just wandering around the clubhouse before the game."

One thing the starting pitcher would not do was get caught up in the pregame hype. If the media wanted to make an overly big deal about the matchup, they would have to do so without his help. "He would never get involved in the buildup to anything," Hal Bodley noted. "He'd say, 'That's for somebody else to decide' or, 'That's for you people to talk about.' He never got caught up in that stuff." But, strangely, the newspapers did not make much pregame fuss over the matchup. The *Evening Bulletin* printed exactly one sentence under the headline, "It's Carlton vs. Gibson." The sentence read: "Steve Carlton against Bob Gibson should put some fans in the seats at the Vet tonight as the teams end their series."

That was it. But it didn't, judging by the attendance figure. The poor bastards who didn't buy a ticket were about to regret it, because this game would live up to a heaping helping of hyperbole.

It was a gorgeous night for baseball. While it was late April, the temperatures were more fitting for late June. The forecast that day called for sunny skies and highs in the upper 70s. Apollo 16, the 10th mission in the Apollo space program, launched three days earlier, was preparing to make its lunar landing. With the U.S. on a moon mission, the Phillies' starter was on a mound mission, and Steve Carlton embarked on it with his own retro-rocket burn of competitive fire.

Carlton had an easy first inning. He struck out Lou Brock to start things before setting the Cardinals down in order. He made quick work of them in the second inning, with another 1-2-3 frame. In fact, Carlton retired 10 of the first 12 Cardinals he faced. Bob Gibson was just as effective.

The Phillies threatened in the third, getting two singles, but Gibson got out of it, leaving two runners on base. The game was scoreless. The Phillies threatened again in the fifth inning. Denny Doyle rapped a one-out single. And Carlton, of all people, beat out a bunt. Bowa made the second out with a tapper in front of home that moved the runners to second and third. But the Phils failed to push a run across when Gibson got McCarver to ground out. It was still 0-0 after five, and a bona fide pitcher's duel as all had anticipated. Carlton and Gibson were working as if mirror images of one another; getting the ball, throwing the ball, and dictating the pace.

Things broke the Phillies' way in the sixth.

After another perfect inning from Carlton, who struck out Brock to end the Cardinal half, Willie Montañez led off for the Phillies in the bottom of the inning. Montañez hailed from Catano, Puerto Rico. He stood six feet tall and weighed 170 pounds. The onetime Cardinals farmhand came to the Phillies in place of Curt Flood in order to complete that 1969 trade. As a rookie in 1971, Montañez slugged 30 homers, still a franchise record for home runs by a rookie, although he never hit more than 20 again in a 14-year career. But the power he displayed that season, and his flamboyant style of play, quickly made the outfielder/first baseman a fan favorite. Willie would stroll to the batter's box by flipping his bat in the air, barrel over handle, and catching it. Little Leaguers throughout the Delaware Valley soon did the same. But Willie was just as showy in the field. He never made a catch routinely. It was never his style to use two hands to secure the ball in his glove. Willie would grab every fly ball with a one-handed wrist snap. He did that not only in the outfield, but also when playing first base. He always took infielders' throws with that one-handed snap action. It drove his managers crazy. Opponents, too. And sometimes even his teammates.

"Montañez was a hot dog," says Ray Rippelmeyer. "That was his biggest problem. He was not a good fielding first baseman or outfielder."

The pitching coach remembers a game in 1971, Willie's rookie year with the Phils. Rick Wise is pitching. The bases are loaded. The batter sends a long fly ball to right-center. Willie races over. He's in place to make the catch. But Willie tries to do his flashy wrist-snap thing. The ball hits his glove and bounces away. All three runs score. The batter winds up on third base.

"Wise just stood on the mound with his hands on his hips," Rippelmeyer recalled.

Montañez was just the kind of batter in whose ear Gibson wouldn't hesitate to place a pitch. But this at-bat was trouble for the nasty righty. The Phillies' center fielder, batting left-handed, roped a shot down the line that kicked into the Veterans Stadium corner, caroming off the green-painted wall and into right field. Montañez, who had good speed, motored all the way to third with a triple. "Gibson always pitches me inside, so I had to pull the ball," said Montañez after the game.

The Phillies were now in business. That brought up first baseman Deron Johnson. The 33-year-old Johnson, one of the club's elder statesman, was not off to a good start of the season. He hit a double and triple in the previous night's win, and that upped his batting average to a meager .214. Johnson may have turned the corner, because he came through with a groundball that went up the middle and into center, easily scoring Montañez. The Phillies led 1-0. It was the only run they'd get off Gibson, but it was the only run they'd need.

Back to work went Carlton, whose seventh inning went like this: a single to the Cards' second baseman Ted Sizemore, followed by ground-out/flyout/flyout.

It wasn't as easy for Gibson in the bottom of the seventh. He issued a leadoff walk to Denny Doyle, the first and only walk allowed by Gibby on the night. That brought up Carlton. He was hardly an automatic out as a hitter. In fact, as pitchers go, he was pretty decent with the stick. "He would put pressure on you when you pinch-hit for him," says Tommy Hutton. "He'd say to you, 'You better get a hit,' because he always thought he would." In this instance he did. Lefty drilled a base hit to left, his second hit of the night. He was getting it done with his arm, and his bat. The Phillies had something going with the first two men aboard. But after a double play and a single by McCarver, Gibson paid back Montañez, this time getting him out on strikes. The Phils touched the Cardinal right-hander for two hits, but stranded two on base.

They were the last to reach base in the game. Both pitchers were now competing with every fiber of their beings. Pupil going at mentor with everything he had; the aging star fighting him off at each turn. Two combatants reaching down to pull from within every last ounce of competitive juice he possessed. Both men retired the side in order in the eighth. On to the bottom of the ninth they went, with the Phillies' solitary run standing as if it were the Washington Monument.

This well-pitched, well-played, early-season game was not to end without a bit of controversy. Carlton got two quick outs to begin the final frame, and was one out away from his first victory at the Vet as a Phillie. Next up was the Cardinal second baseman, Ted Sizemore. Sizemore, a 15th-round draft pick out of the University of Michigan, broke into the big leagues with the Dodgers in 1969. His .271 batting average and all-around solid play in his first season earned him NL Rookie of the Year honors. Sizemore himself would later become a Phillie, and was part of the play-off teams of the late 1970s. He was also involved in one of the better trades in Phils history. At the start of spring training in 1979, Sizemore was part of a seven-player deal with the Cubs that brought Manny Trillo and Greg Gross to Philadelphia. Trillo became a stalwart at second base. Gross became the best pinch-hitter in team history. Both were important pieces in the 1980 championship team.

Now here was Sizemore, all five feet, eleven inches and 165 pounds of him, standing in front of Carlton and a victory. Representing the tying run , the right-handed-hitting Sizemore crushed a Lefty offering deep to straightaway center field. As Don Money watched from his position at third base, he felt a sinking feeling, because as soon as Sizemore made contact, Money thought the ball was gone. Back, back, back, back, back it went. Montañez, off the crack of the bat, turned and raced toward the wall, his back completely facing the infield. The Sizemore drive was going to stay in the park. The ball and the fleet Phillies center fielder reached the fence at roughly the same moment. Willie raised his glove and then made a sensational game-saving grab. Or not. No one who played in or watched the game is exactly sure.

Montañez appeared to make a juggling catch for the game's final out. At least that's how second base umpire Andy Olsen saw it and he called Sizemore out. The Cardinals claimed that third base umpire Dick Stello signaled just the opposite, that the ball had banged off the fence and was in play. Montañez described the play to reporters this way: "I caught the ball in my glove, and when the glove hit the wall, the ball bounced out and I caught it again."

The game had been televised live that night by WPHL-TV, Channel 17. Replays (still known as "instant replays" in 1972) proved that Montañez had indeed juggled the ball twice before making the catch.

"Caught it again my Ass-tro Turf" was the quote attributed to Cardinals manager Red Schoendienst. "My bullpen coach saw two feet of daylight between his glove and the wall. He trapped it," Red stated. Said Phils manager Frank Lucchesi to the Phillies beat writers, "He had it all the way, great catch."

As soon as the out was recorded, a livid Schoendienst flew out of the dugout to argue. But his displeasure at the ruling was to no avail. The game was over. The Phillies, behind Carlton, had won. The final was 1-0.

Carlton had tossed a three-hit gem, surrendering only singles. Not one Cardinal made it to second base the whole night. He only struck out five, but didn't issue a walk. Both pitchers went the distance. Gibson gave up eleven hits, walked one, and also struck out five. The effort from both pitchers was beautiful in its simplicity and its speed. Would you believe the game lasted just 93 minutes? That was it—one hour and 33 minutes. Can you imagine a game in this day and age ending in an hour and 33 minutes? As Richie Ashburn, the legendary Phillies player and broadcaster, used to say to his broadcast partner Harry Kalas, "hard to believe, Harry." That's what you got from those two starters: quick and efficient work. Phils backup Mike Ryan joked afterward that during the game he left the bench for the clubhouse to get a soft drink and missed three innings. Years later the players swore that when they left the Vet that night and scattered into the Philadelphia evening, the setting sun was still visible. They had played a nine-inning night game, and it was still light out!

Carlton, with a steady diet of sliders and curves, threw only 90 pitches. He faced two over the minimum of 27 batters. Gibson, to his credit, stranded nine Phillies on base. It was the first time in two years that the Phillies had beaten the future Hall of Famer. But for Carlton, was it a message to the Cardinals? Was he exacting a measure of revenge for their trading him less than two months earlier? His postgame comments were slightly contradictory.

This is what Carlton was quoted as saying by the *Bulletin*: "The incentive is to win. Pitching against Bob Gibson is all I need to get the juices going. He's such a competitor. Forget about the Cardinal thing, OK? Mr. Busch is a gentleman. I'm kind of sorry that he took some of the contract negotiations personally, but that's his prerogative.

"It was nothing personal, but it was the situation, me against the Cardinals for the first time. I gave them my best shot. Boy, am I tired."

So on one hand it had nothing to do with how Carlton was treated by the Cardinals. And in the next breath it was the situation, his facing the Cardinals for the first time. One thing is for sure—he indeed gave them his best shot. It's always nice to beat your old team, especially when playing against them for the first time. Most athletes like to exact a measure of revenge on their ex-clubs, make them second-guess their decision.

Hal Bodley, who was baseball editor and a columnist for *USA Today* for 25 years and is now senior correspondent for MLB.com, says Carlton had a great respect for the Cardinal organization: "He was really enamored with the Cardinals and the fact that they could be so good and win so many games." But his respect for Gibson probably ran deeper, and that's what made this victory so satisfying. "Gibby was a guy he looked up to," Bodley notes. "And to beat this guy that he admired was very important to Steve."

Two of the very best, bearing down against one another. Isn't that what the game is all about? Both pitchers competed as fiercely in the final inning as they had in the first. Carlton reached within himself and raised his game to another level, retiring the last nine Cardinals he faced.

The Phillies' new ace had made two starts, both victories. He'd pitched 17 innings, allowing seven hits and only two runs in two games. "Now I know," Bowa told reporters afterward, "how it feels to play behind a superstar pitcher."

CHAPTER 5

The One-Hitter

It was Mark Twain who once quipped that the coldest winter he ever spent was a summer in San Francisco. Major league players could relate. The wind gusts coming off the bay in summertime could turn Candlestick Park, the home of the Giants for most of their tenure in San Francisco, into a winterlike deep freeze. "Candlestick Park was no fun place to go," says Larry Bowa. "It would be freezing there at night." Everyone always complained about how it was too damn cold at Candlestick. Early in his career, Steve Carlton must've felt the same way, because he lost the first five games he pitched there. But as he evolved as a pitcher, developing a mental discipline to go with his physical gifts, he began to love pitching by the bay. "He would say he loved pitching there because everybody bitched about the weather," Bowa remarked. The way Carlton saw it, the cold weather was a distraction that too many players focused on, and that gave him a competitive advantage. While everyone is bitching about the weather, he'll be winning the game, which is what he cares about most.

Carlton's teammates usually dressed in turtlenecks and long johns under their road uniforms when playing in San Francisco, but Carlton often took the mound in short sleeves. "I'd look at him and I'd be like, you gotta be shittin' me," Bowa says with a laugh. "I don't know if he was trying to prove to everyone it wasn't cold, or trying to will it to be 80 degrees, but it was almost like he was trying to get in people's heads. He would say, 'You beat yourself; the elements can't beat you.'" Steve fashioned himself as a cool weather pitcher, but the cold, gusting, San Francisco Bay wind was a challenge to overcome.

Much of Carlton's pregame preparation was mental. He was driven by it in an oddly eccentric, almost maniacal way. Total concentration.

Extreme focus. Blocking out all distractions. Mental visualization. Those were his techniques. Before a game, Carlton would visualize himself executing his pitches. He would throw a whole game in his mind. And he would envision himself winning. By his quirky rationale, all he had to do then was carry it out physically. To have the mental and the physical working in complete concert was always his goal. It was the key, he felt, to his enormous success. Carlton would unleash the power of the mind along with the power of his physique. His was a "new age" approach to the game. It was almost mystical, as if he had been taught by a Hindu sage in an ashram in India.

"He was out there," said Greg Luzinski. The Phillies outfielder was a wide-eyed rookie in 1972, and didn't know what to make of the team's star pitcher. "Everyone liked to say that left-handers are different, and that he was a typical left-hander," Luzinski said. "But he might've been ahead of his time." Luzinski used to sit in the dugout and watch Carlton between innings. "He would sit on the bench in almost a trance. He would say, 'I knew I won the game before I pitched because I envisioned it.' His concentration level was above average."

The core ingredient for Carlton was blocking out the distractions, and that included the batter. "Tim McCarver used to say," said Tommy Hutton, "that half the time, Carlton didn't even know who the batter was. He just concentrated on making his pitches. If he made his pitches, it didn't matter who the batter was." Carlton didn't study hitters. He didn't go over their tendencies and weaknesses, didn't watch video of them in certain situations. He did his mental exercises, and carried that intense focus onto the playing field. When Carlton was on the mound, his new teammates soon found out, he was in his own little world. In a 1994 *New York Post* article about Carlton, McCarver is quoted as saying that "Lefty was the only guy I knew that could be reclusive pitching in front of 50,000 people."

Steve had won his first two starts in impressive fashion, and his earned run average was now a minuscule 1.06 as he got set to face the Giants at Candlestick on April 25th. Buoyed by their new ace, the Phillies as a team were off to a decent start, having won four of their first seven games. The pitching matchup that night was again worth the price of admission. Slated to be on the opposing mound was Giants star Juan Marichal. After beating Jenkins and Gibson in successive starts, Carlton now had to duel another future Hall of Famer. It was going to be like this all season long—Carlton matched against, not only the other guy's ace, but usually an ace whose name was destined to appear someday on a bronze plaque in the baseball museum of that upstate New York hamlet called Cooperstown. It was a challenge that Carlton welcomed.

"Again," says Joe Torre, "that came from watching Gibby. Because that was one thing Gibson never shied away from, matching himself against the other ball club's ace."

Bruce Keidan wrote in that morning's *Philadelphia Inquirer*: "You get the feeling, if Carlton knocks off Marichal, they will bring Koufax out of retirement and have him test Steve, too."

Juan Marichal was 34 years old and at the tail end of his Hall of Fame career. He had split his first two starts of the season for a Giants club that came in with a 4-5 record and was mired in a three-game losing streak. It was Marichal's job to break the skid. Carlton versus Marichal—what a buzz of excitement that would generate, one would think, even for a chilly Tuesday night in April. And yet (much like the game against Gibson in Philly that was sparsely attended), a little more than 6,000 good citizens of the City by the Bay turned out. What they were about to see, however, they were unlikely to ever forget.

This was the first West Coast trip of the year for the Phillies, an early-season swing through California. They were spending Tuesday, Wednesday, and Thursday nights in San Francisco, and then jetting to San Diego for a weekend series with the Padres that included a Sunday doubleheader. The road trip ended with three games against the Dodgers in Los Angeles before the cross-country flight back to Philly. It was going to be a grueling stretch of 10 games in nine days.

It was a cool San Francisco night, but without much wind. Candlestick Park had recently been refurbished. An upper deck had been added to the stadium, which doubled as the home of the NFL's 49ers. Carlton seemed to think that the stadium's new feature may have cut down on the wind. These windless conditions suited Carlton, although he did put on a long-sleeved, burgundy-colored undershirt beneath his powder-blue road uniform with the buttoned front jersey. (The zippered front jersey in the signature powder blue didn't come until later in the '70s.) He then headed for the bullpen to warm up.

Pitching coach Ray Rippelmeyer watched Carlton as he got loose. After the game he would tell reporters that he knew his ace was going to have a big night. While observing Carlton's warmup session, Rippelmeyer noted that the left-hander's fastball had pop, his curveball had bite, and his slider looked outstanding. With all three pitches working in top form, Lefty was ready to go.

The home plate umpire for the road trip-opening Carlton/Marichal matchup was Ken Burkhart. Burkhart himself was once a major league pitcher. A right-handed starter, he pitched for the Cardinals and Reds in the late 1940s. As a 28-year-old rookie in 1945, Burkhart posted an 18-8 record. But he never won more than six again, and was out of baseball at the end of the '49 season. Richie Ashburn, the Phillies' iconic center fielder turned broadcaster, didn't care much for Burkhart. Richie didn't care much for any umpire. Or any pitcher, for that matter. Burkhart was both of the things Ashburn disliked most: umpires and pitchers. Once Ashburn bumped into him after a game that probably didn't go the Phillies' way. The conversation was brief, with Richie doing all of the talking. "Burkhart," he said, "you were a horseshit pitcher, and now you're a horseshit umpire."

Ashburn used to tell the story of the best throw he ever made in a game. There was one out and a runner on third. Well, he *thought* there was one out. A short fly ball was then hit to Ashburn in center. Richie, assuming there was one away, fired a strike to the plate to keep the runner from tagging. One little problem—there were actually two outs. Ashburn's catch had ended the inning. Burkhart's the home plate umpire, and with the inning now over, he figures it's the appropriate time for him to come out from behind home to clean the dirt off the plate. So Burkhart steps in front of the plate, and just as he is bending over to dust it off with his brush, Richie's throw arrives. It drilled the umpire squarely in the backside. A perfect throw, if only there had been a runner.

Burkhart took his place behind home plate, ready to call the balls and strikes. Ashburn was in the Phillies broadcast booth alongside his partners, Harry Kalas and Byrum Saam. Saam was one of the giants of the industry. A veteran announcer, cut from the same vintage cloth as the Red Barbers and Mel Allens of the broadcasting game. From behind the microphone, By Saam elegantly created wonderful mental pictures. His style was so descriptive that he was referred to as "the man of a zillion words." For many years, Saam worked for both major league clubs in Philadelphia. The Athletics and the Phillies shared Shibe Park, which was later named Connie Mack Stadium. Following the departure of the A's for Kansas City in 1954, By became solely a Phillies broadcaster until his retirement in 1975. In 1990, he was honored with the Hall of Fame's Ford C. Frick Award, baseball's highest honor for a broadcaster. Kalas was similarly honored by the Hall in 2002, while Ashburn was enshrined as a player in 1995.

As a broadcaster, Ashburn provided the color commentary to Kalas' rich, baritone description of the action. In '72, the two were entering their second season together. Kalas joined the broadcast the previous year after a stint as an announcer for the Houston Astros. While at the time fans were still warming up to the young Kalas, he would one day become a Philadelphia sports institution. He and Ashburn, whom Kalas always called "Whitey," would not only become as close as brothers, but their humorous banter made them one of the most successful broadcasting tandems in the game. They worked together for 27 baseball seasons, and their close personal relationship provided for a great on-air chemistry. Their exploits off the air, and after hours, also became storied. Harry and Whitey were no strangers to the popular watering holes in each National League city. Theirs was a deep and genuine bond, and it translated through the airwaves. As a result, listeners also developed a deep bond with the two broadcasters.

Kalas, Ashburn, and Saam were calling the game on WCAU-AM, the flagship radio station of Phillies baseball. The game was not on television. Not many games were televised in those days, especially a night game from the West Coast. WPHL, Channel 17 in Philadelphia, was the TV home of the Phillies. In fact, not that many home games were televised. The Phillies' home opener, for example, was not on the tube. (WPHL offered instead a movie called *Fuzzy Pink Nightgown* starring Jane Russell!) It was more common for the road games to be on TV. The conventional wisdom was that television coverage would diminish the gate. Who would pay to attend a game in person when he could watch it for free on TV? So most of the televised games were away games. Or Sunday games. Sunday was a big promotional day and huge crowds would turn out for the giveaway item, whether a T-shirt, hat, or bat. Therefore, television wouldn't hurt the gate. It seems hard to believe by today's standards, but WPHL carried Sunday home games, many of the road games, some weeknight home games, and that was pretty much it for Phillies baseball on TV. On this night at 10 p.m., Channel 17, strangely enough, was carrying *The Johnny Bench Show*, followed at 10:30 by a rerun of the science fiction drama *One Step Beyond*. (The network affiliates were busy airing election results from the Pennsylvania Democratic Primary, won by Hubert Humphrey.)

The two managers, Frank Lucchesi of the Phillies and the Giants' Charlie Fox, met at home plate to exchange lineup cards. This was Lucchesi's lineup:

> Larry Bowa SS
> Tim McCarver C
> Willie Montañez CF
> Deron Johnson 1B
> Greg Luzinski LF
> Don Money 3B
> Mike Anderson RF
> Denny Doyle 2B
> Steve Carlton P

The Giants were facing Carlton in this order:

> Chris Speier SS
> Tito Fuentes 2B
> Bobby Bonds RF
> Dave Kingman 1B
> Ken Henderson LF
> Garry Maddox CF
> Fran Healy C
> Chris Arnold 3B
> Juan Marichal P

The legendary Willie Mays, two weeks shy of his 41st birthday, was not in the Giants' starting lineup. Playing center field instead was a 22-year-old Vietnam veteran named Garry Lee Maddox. In a couple of years, the Phillies would trade for Maddox, and he would become the defensive cornerstone of their first World Championship team. Tonight Maddox was making his major league debut.

With a shout of "Play ball!" from Burkhart, Juan Marichal took the mound to the small crowd's applause. One of the first big Latin stars, Marichal cut an imposing figure. He was known for a delivery that was punctuated by an unusually high leg kick. That delivery, imitated by sand-lot youngsters everywhere, helped yield 243 victories for Marichal in his 16 years in the big leagues. The right-hander's kick seemingly defied all laws of physiology. His left leg swung so far skyward, his foot pointing toward the clouds, that it was hard to believe his leg could stay connected to his hip. His back was arched toward second base, his right arm dangling with the baseball somewhere behind his right knee. How on earth did he keep his balance? Looking at that from the batter's box, how on earth could a hitter pick up the ball? It wasn't easy. The Phillies went three-up and three-down in the top of the first.

Now, Carlton strolled to the Candlestick mound for the first time that night. The shortstop, Chris Speier, dug in for the Giants. The right-handed hitter was 21 and a second-year pro. The Giants drafted him in the first round out of UC Santa Barbara in 1970. Known more for his glove than his bat, Speier was hardly an intimidating hitter. A three-time All-Star, he finished with a lifetime batting average of .246 in his 19-year career. In 105 career at-bats against Carlton, Speier banged out 27 hits. And one of those 27 hits was on the way.

It was Lefty's second pitch of the night, and the Giants leadoff batter sent it up the middle for a single. One man up, one man on. Not a good start for Steve. A pitcher never likes to put the leadoff man on base, regardless of the inning, and certainly not to begin the game. Next up was the switch-hitting second baseman, Tito Fuentes. The Cuban-born Fuentes, a big league veteran of seven seasons, never had much luck against Carlton. In his 13-year career, he faced the Phillies ace 53 times, and managed just nine hits.

Fuentes hit a ground ball to Don Money at third. The smart play for Money was at second. Get the lead runner, Speier, and possibly turn a double play. Money threw to Doyle, who was covering the bag. Speier was out at second, but Fuentes, a speedy runner, was too quick to allow the Phillies to get two. There was one out and a runner on first.

Bobby Bonds was the next batter. Before there was Barry Bonds, there was Bobby Bonds. He became better known later in life as the father of Barry, the controversial superstar, but Bobby was a star in his own right. One of the first members of the 30/30 club (30 home runs and 30 stolen bases in the same season), Bobby Bonds could hit, hit for power, run, throw, and catch. But with Bonds at the plate, Fuentes took off for second in an attempt to steal. McCarver bounced up out of his crouch and fired a strike to Doyle, who applied the tag. Fuentes was out. Two down, nobody on. Bonds then grounded to short, where Bowa came up throwing to Johnson at first base, and just like that, the Phils were out of the inning.

The initial two Giants hitters had reached base off Carlton, and yet he ended up facing just the minimum three batters. Imagine Kalas' voice piercing the airwaves: *"One hit, no runs, no errors, no one left on base. One inning complete here in San Francisco, and there's no score."* And now a word from our sponsor. *"Nobody bakes a cake as tasty as a Tastykake..."*

Back to live action from Candlestick Park.

The Phillies went meekly in their half of the second, Marichal again setting them down in order, and that brought Carlton back to the mound. Carlton wasn't wasting any time between pitches. That was the other thing about him that his teammates were beginning to notice. He worked quickly à la Bob Gibson. It was a characteristic that would become his trademark that season. For Carlton, it was all about repetition. Get the ball, throw the ball, establish a rhythm. No distractions. The batter is invisible. Simply focus on the target and throw the ball to the catcher's mitt.

Carlton found his groove in the second inning, and his focus and concentration were locked in. He got the first man, slugger Dave Kingman, to strike out swinging. That brought up the left fielder, Ken Henderson. Carlton struck him out, too. Next up was the rookie, Garry Maddox, in his first career at-bat. Maddox had been tearing the cover off the ball in the Pacific Coast League for the Giants' farm team in Phoenix. The graceful center fielder was batting .435, with nine homers and 22 RBI in just 11 games. Those stats earned him a call-up to the Giants just in time for this Tuesday night series opener. Now here he was, facing a 20-game winner.

He whiffed. Welcome to the big leagues, Garry.

Three Giants up, three Giants down, all strikeout victims. But Steve was just getting warmed up. In the third, the Giants went 1-2-3 again, this time with Lefty fanning only two of the three batters in the inning. Meanwhile, Marichal was matching Carlton frame for frame. No longer a power pitcher, Marichal relied on his cunning, guile, and pitch location. It was working against these Phillies. Marichal was a machine, retiring the first 11 he faced. Then, finally, Montañez broke through with a two-out single. Unfortunately for the Phillies, he was quickly wiped out at second on a fielder's choice. This game was the very definition of a pitchers' duel.

"No runs, one hit, one man left. We move to the bottom half of the fourth inning, still no score."

Carlton continued to hum along. With his mental focus and pinpoint control, the Phils starter began to economize his effort. Speier, who broke up the "no-hitter" in the first, came up for the second time to leadoff the fourth. This time it was no contest. Speier looked at a called third strike for out number one. Fuentes, the only other Giant to reach base on the night, was next. With two strikes on him, Fuentes swung and missed for strike three, and out number two. That brought up Bonds, who did the same. Carlton had struck out the side again.

In the fifth, the Phillies finally scratched out a run for him. Marichal was famous for his expert control, but he issued consecutive walks to Luzinski and Money to open the inning. Mike Anderson followed by dropping a sacrifice bunt down the third base line, advancing the runners. Doyle was up with two on and one out. Marichal got two strikes on Doyle before the second baseman lifted a fly ball to center. Maddox made the catch, but Luzinski tagged and scored. The Phillies had pushed across the game's first run without the benefit of a base hit. It was that kind of ballgame.

The Giants went quietly in their half of the fifth. Carlton struck out two more, including Maddox for a second time. From the second through the fifth innings, Carlton was dominant and dazzling. He struck out 10 of the 12 batters he faced. Only third baseman Chris Arnold (a groundout) and Kingman (foul pop-up to the catcher) made contact. It really was a masterful performance. And it wasn't over.

"To the bottom of the sixth we go, still one-nothing, Phillies."

Carlton's only hiccup came in the sixth. After Fran Healy went down on a called third strike, up to the plate once again came Arnold. He was the only Giant that Carlton had yet to strike out. Arnold, out of Arcadia, California, was an 11th-round draft pick of the Giants in 1965. He stood five feet ten and weighed just 160 pounds. Batting and throwing right-handed, he was primarily a pinch-hitter and utility infielder in a six-season career.

Arnold worked the count full. Carlton, needing a strike, delivered his slider. It was a borderline pitch on the inside corner. "Ball four," shouted Burkhart. Arnold trotted to first base. It was the only walk of the night issued by Carlton. Marichal was next and tapped one in front of the plate. McCarver made the play at first, while Arnold advanced to second, but now there were two outs. The top of the order brought Speier to the plate, and he promptly flied to center.

"Montañez is there to make the catch, and that'll do it for the Giants. We've played six complete here at Candlestick, and it's one-nothing, Phillies."

Both pitchers retired the sides in order in the seventh, Carlton notching another strikeout when he got Kingman swinging to end the inning. The Phillies were still holding a 1-0 lead in the top of the eighth. With one out and no one on base, it was Carlton who started a rally against Marichal. It had been Carlton's night on the mound, and now he would help himself with the bat. Would you believe, the tall, gangly pitcher legged out an infield hit? Carlton was aboard. Bowa then followed by smashing a double into the right-field corner, which moved Carlton to third. But Marichal countered by getting McCarver to foul-out behind the plate. Now there were two out and two on. The Giants decided to walk Montañez intentionally, loading the bases and setting up a force play at any base. That brought Deron Johnson to the plate. With Marichal on the ropes, Johnson singled to right.

"Carlton scores. Here comes Bowa, rounding third, and he'll score. It's three-nothing, Phillies!"

Carlton took that three-run cushion to the bottom of the ninth, Speier's leadoff single still the Giants' only hit. Lefty got the first batter on a groundout, and then the great Willie Mays entered the game for the first time, pinch-hitting for Marichal. The Say Hey Kid's legendary career as a Giant was nearing its end. In three short weeks the Giants would trade him to the Mets for a pitcher named Charlie Williams and $50,000 in cash. The trade returned Willie to New York, the original home of the Giants, the city where it all began for him as a rookie in 1951. Willie had gotten off to a slow start and was batting a paltry .125. He was among a handful of the very best players of all time, but tonight he was no match for Carlton. Willie struck out looking.

That brought up Speier, the guy who opened the festivities, and he was about to bring them to a close. Like Mays, he too struck out while looking.

"He struck 'eeem right on outta there, and that's the ballgame. What an amazing performance from Steve Carlton, and the Phillies win it three to nothing."

It was a breathtaking exhibition of power pitching, brilliant in its efficiency. The Phillies' newly acquired ace had shut out the defending Western Division champs on one hit. Against Carlton, the Giants could muster only a single from their opening batter. He struck out 14, and he walked just one. The solitary Giant who didn't strike out was Chris Arnold, who also drew the lone base on balls.

In the press box, Ray Kelly of the *Evening Bulletin* turned to Hal Bodley of the Wilmington *News Journal*, who was seated beside him. "Remember this one, big boy," Kelly said. "You won't see one like this very often." Kelly had covered the Philadelphia A's of Connie Mack. He'd seen just about everything in his long career as a baseball writer, a career topped with the Hall of Fame's J.G. Taylor Spink Award, the highest honor for a writer. But Kelly, who began covering the Phils in 1956, had never seen anything like this.

There was no buildup. No suspense. No white-knuckled anxiety as one waited to see just who, if anyone, could register a hit. Many one-hitters come as consolation after the pitcher has blown a no-hitter in the late innings. But Carlton was never chasing a no-hitter. "Kelly thought it was so awesome that we had been there for this game, because it was so different from a no-hitter or perfect game," Bodley recalled. Bodley covered Jim Bunning's perfect game on Father's Day, 1964. "That's something that just builds and builds. There was no buildup here. He had already given up the hit. But it really was amazing."

And it was reminiscent of a game that another Phillies pitching great once had in 1954. Robin Roberts faced the Reds on May 13th at Philadelphia's long-gone Shibe Park. It was a Thursday night, and only 6,856 were in the stands. As the visitors, the Reds naturally batted first. A third baseman named Bobby Adams was the leadoff hitter, and before a number of those 6,856 fans could find their seats, Adams proceeded to take Roberts deep to left for a home run. Roberts had a habit of giving up homers, and held the MLB record for home runs allowed in a career until 2010. Right out of the gate, Robbie and the Phils trailed 1-0. After that, one might think it was going to be a long night for him, right? Wrong. All Roberts did from there was retire the next 27 batters in a row. Think about that— he gave up a home run to the game's first batter and then was perfect the rest of the way. The Phillies won the game, 8-1, with Roberts essentially pitching a nine-inning perfect game.

Carlton's gem may not have been quite as impressive, but it was close. By comparison, Roberts had fewer strikeouts (eight) and did give up a run. Of course, Roberts was perfect from the second batter on, while Carlton issued a fielder's choice and a walk. That both Phillies aces surrendered hits to the opening batters, and after that held their opponents hitless and scoreless, is truly uncanny.

"It was our first clue that this guy was something special and that he could be the next Robin Roberts," Frank Bilovsky recalls. Afterward, in the visitors' clubhouse, the man of the hour told reporters that it was the best game he ever pitched. He may have thrown the ball harder, he thought, but never better. Carlton said this with professional satisfaction. It wasn't giddiness. He wasn't overly ecstatic, but he was self-satisfied. "He was pleased with his performance, but he wasn't jumping up and down," Bodley says. "Inside you could tell that he felt it was very, very special."

Carlton managed this feat with only 103 pitches, which is not many considering the number of strikeouts. The economy of pitches was phenomenal, an average of less than 12 an inning, and the performance feature of which he may have been most proud. Seventy-three of the 103 were thrown for strikes. Only 30 were thrown outside the strike zone.

Thirty-seven years later, Ray Rippelmeyer was still wowed by the performance. "Carlton was so dominating that night. He was like a college pitcher facing a high school team. He overmatched the hitters more than Wise did in his no-hitter. He dominated like Nolan Ryan would dominate hitters," the veteran pitching coach observed.

"For me," explained Phils pitcher Wayne Twitchell, "this stood out over any other game that Carlton pitched." Twitchell would spend 10 years in the majors, but that night he was an impressionable, 24-year-old rookie. He was totally awestruck by what he had just seen Carlton do. "It was his most overpowering outing, the most dominant pitching that I ever saw."

While Carlton shared the major league record for strikeouts in a nine-inning game with 19, he had only fanned a grand total of 10 in his prior two starts. Due to the success he was having with his breaking pitches, he had gotten away from throwing the fastball in his two season-opening wins. He even admitted to reporters that he thought he probably should've been using it more. Against the Giants he did, throwing 60 fastballs to go with 20 sliders and 23 curves; all three pitches working to perfection. From his position in center field, Willie Montañez had an unobstructed view. He mentioned to reporters that from his vantage point the Carlton curve looked unbelievable, and that he'd never in his life seen anything quite like it.

What's just as unbelievable is this: It took Carlton only one hour and 47 minutes to complete the masterpiece.

CHAPTER 6

He's Only Human

For days, everybody associated with the Phillies could not stop talking about Carlton's one-hitter against the Giants. And with good reason. A near no-hitter with 14 strikeouts is worthy of much gushing. The manager, coaching staff, players, broadcasters, and members of the media were all awestruck by Carlton's gem. Everybody was raving about the performance—except the self-effacing Carlton. By the day after his one-hitter, he was already thinking ahead to his next start. Carlton was shooting for a third consecutive shutout when he squared off against San Diego. Although the season was only two weeks old, Padres general manager Buzzie Bavasi had already made a managerial change, firing Preston Gomez after a 4-7 start and replacing him with third base coach Don Zimmer. Gomez had managed the Padres since the expansion team's inception in 1969. The Padres averaged 103 losses in their first three years under Gomez, so Bavasi, who was used to winning from his days as the Dodgers' GM and was seeing no signs of improvement, pulled the plug on Gomez. For the 41-year-old Zimmer, it was his first job as a major league manager. He lost his first game to the Mets and his second to the Phillies in the series opener, as Woodie Fryman tossed a six-hit shutout.

Young right-hander Steve Arlin, loser of his first three starts, had the task of trying to break Carlton's momentum and garner a win for his new skipper. Arlin did not enjoy a long and stellar career. He went 11-14 in his best year, and lasted just parts of six seasons. But that was OK because Arlin had a fall-back position. He had studied dentistry at Ohio State while a minor leaguer, and when his career ended at the close of the '74 season, he became an oral surgeon practicing in California for 27 years.

Watching the action closely from the Padres dugout was Arlin's road roommate, pitcher Freddie Norman. He had started against the Mets two nights earlier and would not pitch in the Phillies series. Norman had a connection with Carlton dating back to high school. Both grew up in Miami and attended public schools in the city. Norman attended Miami Jackson High School, while Carlton walked the halls of North Miami High School, starring in basketball and baseball. (He dropped basketball in his senior year to concentrate on baseball.) Carlton graduated in 1963, two years after Norman. While their schools did not play each other during the season, they participated in a tournament at Miami Stadium in 1961 when Carlton was a sophomore. Norman got a look at Carlton during the tournament, and reflecting back, likened the 16-year-old's build to that of the Phillies 2008 World Series hero, Cole Hamels. Standing six feet two and weighing about 165 pounds, Carlton was skinny in high school. When he was signed by the Cardinals in 1963—for a bonus of $5,000—Carlton had put on some pounds and weighed 178. He had also added an inch and stood at six feet three. He kept growing and filling out and by the time Norman and Carlton were Cardinals teammates for brief parts of the 1970 and '71 seasons, Steve was six feet five, broad-shouldered, and finely tuned. His weight was up to 210. Even though Carlton was early in his major league career, Norman had a feeling about Lefty. "I sensed he was a future Hall of Famer."

Physically, Norman was the antithesis of Carlton. At five feet eight and 165 pounds, he was eight to nine inches shorter and weighed 50 pounds less than his counterpart. But Norman was a crafty southpaw with a good screwball, which Milwaukee Braves great Warren Spahn taught him when he was in the minors. Norman would throw six shutouts for the Padres in 1972, finishing third in the National League. The Padres traded Norman to Cincinnati in 1973, and he became a mainstay in the Reds' starting rotation for seven years, earning two World Series rings along the way.

Norman toiled in the majors for 16 seasons, and Carlton's slider was the best he ever saw. "The batter knew it was coming and still couldn't hit it. The batter would start to commit and then the ball would drop." Norman also extolled Carlton's concentration. "He didn't look anywhere but home plate. He was so focused, so into what he was doing, so positive about where he was going to throw the pitch."

Carlton was as focused as ever in the first six innings of the game that Saturday night in beautiful San Diego, holding the Padres scoreless, and in so doing he extended his scoreless string to 24 innings. However, Arlin matched Carlton, donut for donut, through six. Finally the string ended in the seventh when backup catcher Bob Barton, a career .226 hitter, stroked a two-run single with the bases loaded and two outs. The Padres added two more in the eighth and Arlin kept mowing down the Phillies, finishing with a five-hit shutout. Zimmer held on to the lineup card as a keepsake, his first of 885 wins as a big league manager. Arlin also has fond memories of that game. "When I beat Carlton, I was on top of the world. Pitching against Carlton [and other top pitchers] was like facing a team's 3-4-5 hitters. I got up for them more, concentrated more. Whenever I faced Carlton, I felt if I didn't pitch a shutout, I wasn't going to win the game."

So it was a loss for Carlton, but he still had a 3-1 record and a gaudy 1.59 ERA when the Phillies made the two-hour bus ride to Los Angeles to complete their West Coast swing. Walter Alston, in his 19th year as manager of the Dodgers, was the dean of major league managers. He would manage the team for 23 years before giving up the reins to Tommy Lasorda late in the 1976 season. The Phils and Dodgers split the first two games of the series at Dodger Stadium, and Carlton faced Bill Singer in the deciding game. During Alston's regime, the Dodgers had turned out an array of outstanding pitchers, including Cy Young Award winner Don Newcombe, and Hall of Famers Sandy Koufax, Don Drysdale, and Don Sutton. Bill Singer wasn't in their class, but he won 20 for the Dodgers in 1969 and tossed a no-hitter against the Phillies in 1970. Frank Robinson, already a member of the exclusive 500-home run club; Willie Davis, who racked up 2,561 career hits; and promising youngster Steve Garvey were in the lineup for L.A.

Another good hitter, first baseman Wes Parker, led off for the Dodgers. Defense was Parkers strong suit—he won six Gold Gloves in a row—but he held his own at the plate, too. His .319 average was fifth in the National League in 1970, and he started the '72 season at a .321 clip. The switch-hitting Parker had batted against Carlton many times when he was a Cardinal, and after taking his cuts against Lefty that night in Los Angeles and two other games later in the season, he recognized a substantial difference. "Carlton had good stuff as a Cardinal, but he was sloppy. He didn't have as good a mix of pitches. He did not put a lot of thought into what he threw—he just threw the ball. His control was not great." But, Parker emphasized, Lefty was a completely different pitcher when he arrived in Philadelphia. "He had better stuff than Tom Seaver. His fastball was up and away; his slider was down and in. His fastball was about 94 [mph]; his slider was about 90 [mph] and broke a foot and a half. His slider broke so much, the only way to hit it was like hitting a golf ball. It was impossible to hit. He won 27 in '72 because he was that good." Parker made a good point about Carlton being a thrower and having less than optimal control with the Cardinals. In his years with St. Louis, he averaged 3.19 walks per nine innings; in 1970, he was third in the National

League in bases on balls allowed. But in '72 with the Phillies, his control vastly improved, as he averaged just 2.26 free passes every nine innings.

Parker managed a single in four at-bats against Carlton, and the rest of his teammates fared no better, as Lefty downed the Dodgers, 5-1. Even though Carlton was pitted against almost an entirely right-handed hitting lineup (Davis was the only lefty), he allowed only six hits and struck out nine. The Phillies concluded the road trip with a 7-3 record, and as the team returned home for 14 games against five teams, Lucchesi was optimistic that the winning would continue.

The home stand started with three games against the Giants. The opener appeared to be a mismatch as Champion went up against the mighty Marichal, but the Phillies somehow squeezed out a 3-2 win. The Giants came back to beat Dick Selma the next afternoon. That set up a Sunday afternoon rubber game, and for the second straight series, Carlton took the ball. It was actually Fryman's turn in the rotation, but because of the off day, Carlton had three days' rest, so Lucchesi moved Lefty up and gave him the start. Willie Mays just turned 41, and the Phillies saluted the legend with a pregame ceremony, which included the presentation of a birthday cake. Mays was not in the lineup that day and had been starting only sporadically the first three weeks of the season. Age had worn him down, and he had lost a lot of the pop in his bat and the spring in his step. Mays would make his last appearance for the Giants two days later as a pinch-hitter and two days after that, he was traded to the Mets.

Instead of Mays, Ken Henderson played center field that day against Carlton. Henderson was the Giants' starting left fielder in the three prior years, joining Mays and Bobby Bonds in the outfield. Henderson had a respectable 16-year career in the majors as he hit .257 with 122 home runs. Henderson, who hit from both sides of the plate, got his first taste of Carlton in the minors in 1966 when they were playing in the Pacific Coast League. He was impressed with Carlton's stuff then and became more impressed when he faced him in the majors. Henderson had high regard for Carlton's fastball and curve, but thought his slider made him a Hall of Fame pitcher. "It was a devastating pitch because, with the high-riding fastball that tailed away from you, he now complimented that with a slider which broke right at your knees." Henderson acknowledged, "I did not have very much success against Steve." That's putting it mildly. In his major league career, Henderson hit .091 against Carlton (3-33) and in '72, he was 0-11 with five strikeouts.

Carlton's mound opponent that day was one-year wonder Ron Bryant. The left-handed Bryant won 24 games in 1973, but only won 57 in his major league career. Lefty didn't strike out 14 Giants like he did at Candlestick Park two weeks earlier—only 13. All nine Giants in the starting lineup went down on strikes at least once. Henderson had his usual frustrating game against Carlton, 0-4 with a whiff. Carlton was touched for three runs in the eighth and ninth innings, but by then the Phillies had the game well in hand and won 8-3. Terry Harmon led the way for the Phils with the first and only four-hit game of his career. Carlton improved to 5-1, and the Phillies, who continued to buck the odds, were tied for first place with the Mets.

Another very good Dodgers pitcher, Claude Osteen, was the starter when L.A. came to Veterans Stadium the following weekend. Osteen was not good enough for Cooperstown, but he was a formidable pitcher. He won 196 games and was a 20-game winner twice for the Dodgers. When Osteen retired, he became a pitching coach, and one of the hurlers that he coached, ironically, was Carlton. Osteen was Lefty's pitching coach for the Phillies from 1982 until 1986.

Carlton's future pitching coach got the better of him at the Vet as the Dodgers beat the Phillies, 3-1. The Dodgers put up a two-spot in the third with the help of a pair of miscues by the Phillies. The rally was started with a single by 22-year-old Bobby Valentine. The man who managed the Mets to the World Series in 2000 was a two-time minor league MVP with blazing speed and a superstar in the making, or so thought the Dodgers brass. But he failed to dazzle in 1971 and '72 when he played semi-regularly for the Dodgers and was traded to the Angels after the season. Early in the 1973 season, while chasing a fly ball, he sustained a multiple compound fracture to his leg when his spikes became entangled in the outfield's chain-link fence. The fracture never healed properly, depriving him of his great speed, and effectively ending his career as a player.

That night in Philly, though, Bobby Valentine still had his excellent wheels and used them to his advantage. After Valentine singled to lead off the third, Osteen squared around to bunt in an effort to move the runner to second. In the first two pitches, Osteen took feeble pokes at the ball and fouled them off.

"Don't these guys know how to bunt?" grumbled Whitey.

"Were players better bunters in your day?" asked Harry.

"No question."

"So Whitey, who is the best bunter you have ever seen?"

Ashburn, in his trademark Nebraska drawl, replied without hesitation. "Me. I beat out 35 bunts one year." Ashburn wasn't a braggart, but since he was asked the question, he had to be honest.

Finally, Osteen got the bunt down, but it was right back to the mound. Carlton fielded it and made a rare error (he only made two in 1972) by throwing wildly to first base. Valentine raced around the bases, rounded third, and headed for the plate. Right fielder Mike Anderson fired to home, but he overthrew, and Valentine *and* Osteen scored. So Osteen circled the bases on a bunt. Even bunter extraordinaire Ashburn never did that. Osteen wasn't through at the plate, as he added an RBI single in the fourth. The Phillies plated one in the sixth on an RBI double by Luzinski, but that was it. The Phillies mounted a rally in the ninth, putting two runners on base with one out, but Jim Brewer relieved Osteen and threw a double play ball to pinch-hitter Byron Browne to end the game.

Although Claude Osteen beat Carlton that night, he had the highest praise for Lefty, especially his performance in 1972. "He was magnificent," said Osteen from his Texas home. "[His dominance was] similar to Koufax's dominance." That's a supreme compliment considering that in 1965 and '66, the two years that Osteen and Koufax pitched in the same rotation for the Dodgers, Koufax was at the top of his game, compiling records of 26-8 and 27-9 and winning the Cy Young Award unanimously both years. In Osteen's opinion, it was Carlton's slider that set him apart from the rest. Pitchers often get burned by throwing a slider (or curve) when the pitch "hangs" in the batter's wheelhouse. But as Osteen pointed out, when a hitter got a slider from Carlton, which he thought was a hanger, the bottom fell out. "The hitter would see it and then it would disappear straight down."

As a rule, right-handed hitters are able to hit a left-handed pitcher's curveball or slider more easily than left-handed hitters because the ball is breaking toward them as opposed to away from them. Carlton was an exception to the rule. "His slider gave right-handed hitters more trouble than left-handed hitters; left-handed hitters could lay off it better."

The loss to the Dodgers and Osteen left a sour taste in Carlton's mouth. That taste was about to become bitter in the coming weeks.

The Losing Skid

Since 1900, which is considered the start of baseball's modern era, only a handful of teams have been dreadful enough to lose 20 games in a row. In 1906, the Boston Americans (who would soon be renamed the Red Sox) took it on the chin 20 straight times. Cy Young himself, whose name is engraved on four of Carlton's trophies, posted 13 of his 511 career victories that year to pace the staff.

Connie Mack, who piloted the Philadelphia A's for a record 50 years, managed some powerful teams which featured all-time greats Eddie Plank, Lefty Grove, and Jimmie Foxx. Mack guided the A's to nine American League pennants and five World Championships. But he was prone to dismantling his team periodically by replacing his veterans with young players, and as a result, fielded some horrible teams. His squads in 1916 and 1943 were two of his worst, as they both strung together 20 consecutive defeats.

The standard for futility, however, was set by the Phillies in 1961. Fiercely competitive Gene Mauch, in his second of 26 years as a major league manager, endured 23 losses in a row. It wasn't Mauch's only 20-game losing streak. He was fired by the Phillies in 1968, and the Montreal Expos hired him to manage the expansion team in their inaugural year, 1969. Most first-year teams take their lumps, but Mauch's Expos were especially bad as they dropped 20 straight ballgames. Neither streak, though, stung as much as the 10-gamer which Mauch's Phillies suffered through over the last two weeks of the 1964 season. The Phils held a six-and-a-half-game lead with 12 games left, but the bottom fell out as they lost 10 in a row and were overtaken by the Cardinals.

Amid Cal Ripken's iron man streak, the Orioles opened the 1988 season abysmally, failing to win any of the first 21 games. Cal's father was dumped as manager after just six games, and his replacement, Frank Robinson, absorbed the last 15 losses.

The average record of these six wretched teams—six of the worst teams ever to don major league uniforms—was 48-107, a lowly percentage of .310.

After jumping out to a surprising 15-10 start and spending four days in first place along the way, Frank Lucchesi's 1972 Phillies came within an eyelash of joining the ignominious 20-game losing streak club. Sandwiched between a 10-game losing streak and a nine-game drought was a game in which the Phils eked out an improbable win with a run in the top of the 12th inning on an RBI groundout over the defending world champion Pirates and their star reliever, Dave Giusti. Had the Phillies not pulled that game out, Lucchesi would have joined the ranks of Mack, Mauch, and the other disgraced managers.

Loss number one was at Veterans Stadium against the Cubs and Burt Hooton, still basking in the glow of tossing his no-hitter a month earlier. This time around, the Phillies had Hooton's number as they pounded him for three hits. One of the hits, the lone highlight of the game for the Phillies, was a titanic, 450-foot home run by Greg Luzinski off the Liberty Bell in deep center field. Meanwhile Rick Monday greeted Billy Champion with a three-run homer in the top of the first, and added solo home runs in the third and fifth innings. In two games against the rookie Hooton, the Phillies were hitting .056.

It was Carlton's turn the next night. Bill Hands, trying to avenge his Opening Day loss, started for the Cubs. Through eight innings, the game was tied at two. The Phillies almost tallied another run in the bottom of the fifth inning when Carlton (a .201 lifetime hitter) stroked an opposite field single to left field, and Doyle tried to score from second but was thrown out at the plate by Billy Williams. As things turned out, that would have been a critical run.

In the top of the ninth, with Carlton still on the mound, Jim Hickman reached second base, and José Cardenal, eager to atone for his miscue that cost the Cubbies the opener, came through with a single to score Hickman. Phillies fans were not terribly optimistic for a game-tying rally in the bottom of the ninth inning when Lucchesi sent up lumbering Pete Koegel to pinch-hit for Carlton. At six feet six and 230 pounds, Koegel looked more like a tight end than a baseball player. He might have had better luck pursuing a pro football career. His lifetime average, in 86 at-bats, was .174. He played parts of the '71 and '72 seasons for the Phillies and he compiled the following key stats: Number of home runs—zero. Number of opposing managers pummeled in a bench-clearing brawl—one. More about the brawl later.

Koegel grounded out, and after Bowa singled to keep many of the fans in their seats, lefty Dan McGinn came out of the bullpen to retire Tim McCarver and Willie Montañez. It was a winnable game for the Phillies— Carlton pitched well and the Phillies left 10 men on base, but it went down in the loss column.

The Mets came to town for the weekend and promptly dealt the Phillies three losses in two nights. The Phils scored five runs in the three games; pitcher Dick Selma drove in two, and another scored on an error.

A Sunday afternoon Bat Day crowd of more than 57,000 fans packed Veterans Stadium to watch a supreme pitching matchup: Carlton versus Tom Seaver. Tom Terrific was the ace of the Mets staff and one of the game's best pitchers. Three years earlier, he had led the Miracle Mets to the World Championship and won the Cy Young Award. In addition to Seaver, several of the key players from the '69 team remained: Jerry Koosman, Tug McGraw, Tommie Agee, Clean Jones, Jerry Grote, and Bud Harrelson.

Gil Hodges managed the '69 Mets to the unexpected pennant and upset of the Orioles in the World Series. But a few weeks earlier, during the strike, Hodges died of a heart attack after playing a round of golf. He was only 47. Yogi Berra, one of the Mets' coaches, was named manager. Hodges' death seemed to inspire the Mets as they broke out to a 24-7 start and were riding a 10-game winning streak.

It was a beautiful spring day. Across from Ashburn, Kalas, and Saam, in the Mets' broadcasting booth, sat master of the malaprop Ralph Kiner, Bob Murphy and Lindsey Nelson. The trio had been together since the Mets' entry into the National League in 1962. Kiner and Murphy would remain members of the New York broadcasting team for 40 years, even longer than Ashburn and Kalas manned the microphones together for the Phillies. While some Mets fans made the drive down the New Jersey Turnpike, it was predominantly a Philly crowd, hoping that Carlton would snap the Phils' five-game losing streak.

Digging into the batters' box to lead off the game for the Mets was none other than Willie Mays. The "Say Hey Kid" had arrived in the trade with the Giants 10 days earlier. Although he was happy to return to New York, where he played the first six years of his illustrious career, he was offended that the Giants, for whom he had performed spectacularly for more that two decades, had traded him. Joan Payson, the owner of the Mets, who had been a minority shareholder of the Giants when they were in New York, was the driving force behind the trade. She had been trying to pry Mays away from the Giants for years, but San Francisco owner

Horace Stoneham refused to entertain any offers for Willie. But with Mays nearing the end of the line, Stoneham relented and dealt him to the Mets.

Payson was thrilled to have her man Mays back in New York. But Berra was not as enthralled with the deal. He had his sights set on the Mets winning the division and wasn't sure how much Mays could help. Berra told Mays that he would platoon with left-handed-hitting Ed Kranepool at first base and get some occasional starts in center field in place of Tommie Agee. Mays and Berra would endure a somewhat tense relationship during their nearly two years together. One source of tension pertained to batting practice. Berra preferred that Mays take batting practice before games with the other players. Mays, however, was afforded the privilege of devising his own schedule for batting practice in recent years with the Giants and fully expected the same leeway from Berra. Mays also did not agree with some of Berra's tactical moves. Mays rarely bunted throughout his career and was annoyed when Berra asked him to bunt twice in the same game.

Ironically, Mays' first series as a Met was against the Giants at Shea. Right-handed starters pitched the first two games for the Giants; Kranepool started at first base, and Mays sat. In the third game, though, lefty Sam McDowell was on the mound for San Francisco, so Mays got the start at first base. Batting leadoff (he usually hit third for the Giants), he was greeted with loud ovations by the New York fans each time he came to the plate. He did not disappoint them. In the bottom of the fifth inning, he snapped a 4-4 tie with a solo home run, which stood up, and the Mets won 5-4. Mays was only in the lineup twice over the next seven games, once at first base and once in center field. But his presence in the clubhouse and dugout sparked the Mets, as they ran off 10 wins in a row after the trade and tried to make it 11 straight when they faced Carlton.

Entering play that day against the Phillies, Mays held a narrow lead over Hank Aaron in career home runs among active players, 647 to 645. Had he not lost almost two years to military service during the Korean War, Mays undoubtedly would have broken Babe Ruth's historic record of 714 home runs. But because Mays was 41 and relegated to a part-time role, he had virtually no chance to hit the necessary 67 homers in order to catch the Babe. Aaron, on the other hand, was 38 and still going strong. He would hit 34 home runs in 1972 and break the coveted record two Aprils later.

Mays was one of Carlton's 14 strikeout victims in the one-hitter the month before in San Francisco, and Lefty once again got the better of Willie by freezing him with a slider for a called third strike. A lifetime .302 hitter, Mays hit a mere .177 against Carlton in his career. Carlton blew away shortstop Bud Harrelson and center fielder Tommie Agee to strike out the side. The Phillies grabbed a run off Seaver in their half on a two-out double by McCarver and an RBI single by Luzinski.

Carlton continued to mow down the Mets. Through four innings, he had allowed only two walks and struck out six. In the bottom of the fourth, Tommy Hutton, who was facing Tom Seaver for the first time that day, hit a homer. On the whole, as his career .248 average reflects, Hutton was a mediocre hitter. But he developed an uncanny knack at hitting Seaver, which started with that homer. He hit .320 against Seaver in his career—more than .400 during his six years with the Phillies—and three of his 22 career home runs were against the hard-throwing righty. Teammates would kid Hutton: "Seaver's pitching tonight; you should be good for two or three hits." In one game, when Danny Ozark was managing the Phillies, Hutton batted cleanup against Seaver. "If I hit every pitcher like I hit Seaver," joked Hutton, "I would be in the Hall of Fame with Carlton."

Carlton kept the no-hitter intact in the fifth, and with a 3-0 lead, Carlton in top form, and a raucous crowd behind them, the Phillies seemed certain to get back on the winning track. But in the top of the sixth, Mays broke up the no-hitter by smoking a double, and two batters later, Agee, known for a pair of acrobatic catches in the '69 World Series, got hold of a Carlton fastball, and trimmed the Phillies' lead to 3-2.

With the score still at 3-2, Carlton was scheduled to lead off the bottom of the seventh for the Phillies. There was no action in the Phils' bullpen, and Carlton hit for himself and rifled a single to right field. But he was erased on a force-out, and Seaver retired the next two batters.

The 10-game winning streak of Berra's Mets was in jeopardy as they were down to their last six outs. Yogi yanked Seaver in favor of a pinch-hitter, Jim Beauchamp. The journeyman wore number 24 before the trade but soon relinquished it to Mays when he joined the Mets. Now wearing number 5, Beauchamp singled to left, which brought up the top of the order and Mays. The game was on the line as the rising star squared off against the past-his-prime all-time great. Who would win the battle? Yogi didn't flash the bunt sign—Willie was swinging away. "It's a long fly ball to left field, Luzinski goes back, it is gone, goodbye!" exclaimed Ralph Kiner, using his famous phrase. The amazing Mays silenced critics who thought he should retire by delivering a two-run homer, number 648 of his career, to give the Mets a 4-3 lead. Danny Frisella came out of the bullpen and the anemic Phils offense couldn't scratch out a run in the last two innings to get Carlton off the hook. Frisella faced the minimum six batters, and Phils fans went home with a bat but not a win. It was a backbreaking loss for the Phillies and extended their losing streak to six.

The Phils dusted themselves off and headed to cozy Jarry Park, home of the Expos during their first eight years before they moved into Olympic Stadium. Originally, Jarry was a city-owned recreational park with 3,000 seats. When city officials learned in 1968 that Montreal would field a major league team in 1969, Jarry Park was expanded to seat 29,000 fans. It was bigger than the rec-park, no doubt, but it still had the smallest capacity of any park in the majors.

Expos fans, both French- and English-speaking, were enthusiastic in the team's early years, although they usually finished last or next to last in the National League East, but in the middle of the pack in attendance. Three decades later, the team's financial woes, coupled with their repeated failure to turn out a playoff team (the Expos reached the postseason once in their 36-year history), caused interest to dwindle significantly. The Expos ranked 16th and dead last in the National League in attendance seven straight years, and they were forced to relocate to Washington after the 2004 season.

With Mauch at the helm, the Expos took it to the Phillies for three straight games. Because of the doubleheader against the Mets Saturday night, Lucchesi had to reach into his bullpen for a pitcher to start the series opener. He chose Barry Lersch. Rippelmeyer did not think highly of the young righty from Denver, Colorado. "His fastball was well below average. He was never going to be a top-flight major league pitcher." Rip called that one right. Lersch won just 18 games in the big leagues and was through by his 30th birthday.

The Expos, hardly a strong-hitting team, knocked Lersch out in the fifth inning and beat the Phillies, 6-3. It was more of the same the next night as Dick Selma, who was becoming less and less effective with each start, was also sent to the showers in the fifth. The Phillies managed eight singles both nights. Ron Fairly, who played 21 years in the majors and was a broadcaster for 27 more, hit a home run in each game.

In the series finale, only a triple in the third inning by Mike Anderson stood between Expos pitcher Carl Morton and a no-hitter. It was the Phils' only extra base hit of the series. At game's end, the batting averages of two of the Phillies' starting players, Mike Anderson and Don Money, were .188 and .198, while Larry Bowa and Deron Johnson had averages just barely above the .200 "Mendoza line."

After Montreal, the Phillies paid their first visit of the season to Pittsburgh's Three Rivers Stadium. It was a carbon copy of Veterans Stadium. The teams weren't carbon copies of each other, though. Manager Danny Murtaugh, a native of Chester in the Philadelphia suburbs, led the Pirates to a seven-game World Series triumph over the Orioles in '71. Murtaugh stepped down after winning the series, and Bill Virdon, the center fielder on the 1960 Pirates World Championship team, took over as manager. Virdon inherited a lineup that was loaded with heavy hitters including Roberto Clemente, Willie Stargell, and Al Oliver.

Carlton had the formidable task of trying to shut down the Bucs' high-powered offense. His old friend from the Cardinals, Nelson Briles, started for the Pirates. Again Carlton could not find the rhythm that he had established in his dominant April starts. Clemente and fleet-footed outfielder Gene Clines, each had three hits as the Pirates banged Carlton around for ten hits and five runs. Some shaky defense didn't help; errors by Money and Johnson in the first inning opened the door for two Pirates runs.

Oliver went hitless against Carlton that night. Al Oliver was one of the best pure hitters of his time as he rattled off eleven .300 seasons, which included a batting title for the Expos in 1982. Had the owners not colluded after the 1985 season and agreed not to sign free agents, Oliver thinks that he would have been signed by a team and picked up 257 more hits to reach 3,000 and punch his ticket to the Hall of Fame. Instead, he had no choice but to retire.

Against Carlton, in more than 100 career at-bats, the man with the smooth, left-handed hitting stroke hit a meager .197. Oliver, a motivational speaker in his post-baseball days, has the utmost of respect for Carlton, both as a player and a person. "His record speaks for itself. He's a true Hall of Famer. He had great location on his pitches. He threw the ball to opposing hitters' weaknesses. He made them hit his pitch."

Oliver got to know Carlton when they were Phillies teammates in 1984, and he liked him. "He had a quiet confidence about him. He was a great guy to talk to—engaging, interesting, and entertaining. He knew the game. He carried himself well. He wasn't cocky. He never showed anybody up. I was quiet myself—I could relate to him."

Finally, in the second game of the series against the Pirates, the scuffling Phillies picked up a win. Montañez broke the team's four-game home run drought with a solo homer in the top of the sixth. It was just his third of the season and it would be his only long ball during the 1-19 skid. The Pirates evened the score in the bottom of the sixth. The game remained tied through nine innings. The Pirates threatened in the bottom of the 10th off Joe Hoerner with back-to-back singles by Al Oliver and Richie Hebner, but Manny Sanguillen grounded out to Denny Doyle.

Dave Giusti took over on the mound for the Pirates in the 12th inning. With a devastating palm ball, he was one of the premier relievers of his time. The Phillies put runners on first and third with one out, and Giusti was looking for a double play groundball to get out of the inning. He thought that he might have it when Don Money grounded to second baseman Dave Cash, who flipped to second for the force-out, but Money beat the throw to first and Tommy Hutton scored.

Lucchesi paced in the dugout as Darrell Brandon, who replaced Hoerner in the top of the 11th, tried to preserve the win. Brandon retired Cash on a ground ball, but Gene Clines doubled. Brandon induced Clemente into grounding out to Bowa. With lefty Oliver coming up and another lefty, Hebner, on deck, Lucchesi went to the bullpen and brought in Short. Oliver drew a walk, and he represented the winning run at first base. Phillies fans watching the game on television envisioned Hebner, a good line drive hitter, drilling one in the gap for a game-winning two-run double. Chris Short's curveball didn't have the snap that it did in his heyday a few years earlier. But he reached back and snuck one past Hebner for a game-ending strikeout. Short got the save, and Brandon was credited with the win.

Darrell Brandon took a rather circuitous route to the Phillies. He was signed by the Pirates as an outfielder, but made the switch to a pitcher soon after. He toiled six years in the minors, working as a milkman in the off-season to make ends meet. He broke into the majors with the Red Sox in 1966 and was part of the "Impossible Dream" Sox team in 1967. Predicted by most pundits to finish at the bottom of the American League, Boston edged out three teams down to the wire to win the pennant, and then battled the Cardinals in the World Series, losing to Bob Gibson in the seventh game. Brandon won five games for the Sox in '67, but injured his shoulder in September and missed the World Series. It would have been his only opportunity to pitch in the postseason. He spent most of the next three seasons bouncing around the minors before the Phillies acquired him prior to the 1971 season.

One of Brandon's proudest diamond-related accomplishments occurred after his playing days ended. The Phillies released him following the 1973 season, and he decided to start a baseball school in New Jersey. One of his pupils was a tall, slender righty with a strong arm who attended Cherry Hill High School East. The boy was struggling with his confidence, and his father sought Brandon's help. He gave the 16-year-old eight one-hour lessons, teaching him to throw a curveball, showing him a new grip on his fastball, and instilling confidence in him. A few years later, in 1983, Brandon flipped on the television and saw his former student pitching in a major league game. Brandon sent him a congratulatory telegram.

Brandon kept close tabs on his protégé over the next several years. In 1988, he set a major league record by throwing 59 consecutive scoreless innings and won the Cy Young Award unanimously. He topped off his season by winning the MVP of both the League Championship Series and

World Series, pitching a shutout in both. He retired in 2000 with 204 wins. In 2004, he was pitching coach for the Texas Rangers. Brandon was living in Massachusetts and working in the insurance business. The Rangers were coming to Boston to play the Red Sox, and Brandon called his man to arrange a meeting. In the clubhouse at Fenway Park, before the Rangers–Red Sox game, Orel Hershiser thanked Brandon for teaching him everything he knew about pitching.

At Three Rivers the next day, the Phils looked as if they might extend their winning streak to two when they scored a pair of runs in the top of the ninth inning to take a 5-4 lead. But it was not to be. Wayne Twitchell and Joe Hoerner couldn't get an out in the bottom of the ninth and the Pirates won 6-5. Dave Cash, the Pirates' leadoff man and sparkplug, delivered the game-tying hit. The Phillies acquired Cash from the Pirates after the 1973 season, and he spent three years as their leadoff hitter. Cash's motto, directed to his teammates and fans, was "Yes we can." In 1976, the Phillies won 101 games and the National League Eastern Division title. In Frank Bilovsky's opinion, the two players most instrumental in transforming the attitude of the Phillies from losers to winners were Steve Carlton and Dave Cash.

But in the spring of '72, the Phillies were still in a losing mode, and the losses continued to mount. Over the next four games, the Phillies were outscored 24-6. Among the four losses was Carlton's shortest outing of the season, four and a third innings, against the Mets at Shea Stadium. Carlton was tagged for eight hits and six runs. Red-headed Rusty Staub, nicknamed "Le Grande Orange" when he was with the Expos, did the most damage with three hits and four runs batted in. The Phillies hitters were no match for Jon Matlack as the rookie southpaw, who played college ball at West Chester University near Philadelphia, improved his record to 6-0 by allowing just three harmless singles.

It was June 1st, and the Phillies had lost 15 out of 16 games and were buried deep in the basement, 14 games behind the Mets. In the series at Shea, Dick Selma had another bad outing as he was given the hook in the third inning—and the hook from the starting rotation. Lucchesi replaced him with 25-year-old left-hander Ken Reynolds. It would become a season to forget for Reynolds. Tired of waiting for Mike Anderson to start hitting, the Phillies optioned him to triple-A Eugene.

Roger Freed got the start in right field the next night. Freed fit in well with the '72 Phillies, as he failed to live up to his potential. He failed miserably, in fact. Freed was the MVP of the International League in 1970 for Rochester, the Orioles' triple-A affiliate. The Orioles were loaded with good outfielders, so they dealt him to the Phillies for pitcher Grant Jackson and two players. Lucchesi gave Freed the job as right fielder in 1971 and expected plenty of production out of him, maybe 22 home runs and

109 RBI. Those turned out to be his career numbers. In '71, he hit six home runs in 348 at-bats and lost his everyday job.

Carlton's fellow Phillies learned during the team's prolonged slump that he remained upbeat and did not criticize his teammates. "He was so positive as a person, to a fault sometimes," recalled Chris Wheeler. "Anything negative to him was wrong. He never wanted to hear negatives." The broadcaster added, "He never ripped his teammates. He was a very good teammate. He was not a guy that was going to rip his teammates to people. They liked him." Larry Bowa remembered the words of wisdom that Carlton offered him on a road trip in '72. The two were sitting together on the team bus, and the topic of conversation turned to Bowa's struggles at the plate.

"Do you believe you can hit?" Carlton asked pointedly.

"The ways things have been going lately, I'm not sure," responded Bowa.

"You gotta believe you can hit. When you get in that box, you have to believe that you're going to get a hit."

With Bowa listening intently, Carlton continued with his encouragement. "That guy is not better than you. Whenever anybody steps in the box, I don't know who's hitting, but I know I can get him out. I don't care who it is, I don't care what his name is, I don't care how hot he is. I believe that I'm going to get him out." Bowa, whose average was .218 on June 1st, hit .260 the rest of the season to improve to .250.

Another time, Bowa told Carlton, "I'm no physical specimen. I'm not going to hit home runs. I'm small."

Carlton had no time for Bowa's negative thinking. "No you're not, you're not small. You can be as big as you want to be."

While he was likable and encouraging, Carlton had his quirks. One pertained to the pitching charts that Ray Rippelmeyer maintained. The pitcher who was scheduled to start the following game was responsible for charting the pitches for that game. The job involved recording each pitch—what type of pitch was thrown and whether it was a ball or strike. So if Carlton pitched, and Billy Champion was slated to pitch the next night, Champion would prepare the chart. When Carlton was finished pitching a game, he checked the chart closely to see how many fastballs, sliders, and curves he threw and what percentage he threw for strikes. Carlton, however, refused to keep the chart for his teammates. Rippelmeyer would tell him, "I'll keep the chart for a dozen golf balls." Carlton ended up owing Rippelmeyer a lot of golf balls.

Woodie Fryman was considered by Rippelmeyer the Phils' second best starter behind Carlton—a distant second. Fryman started to complain to his pitching coach that he, as well as his wife, wanted out of Philadelphia because the pitcher had grown weary of being part of a losing team. He had been with the Phillies since 1968, and the team was yet to post a winning record.

The Phils' next game illustrated why Fryman was so hell-bent on leaving. Back home at Veterans Stadium against the hard-hitting "Big Red Machine" lineup featuring Pete Rose, Joe Morgan, Johnny Bench, and Tony Perez, Fryman was dazzling as he held the Reds to just three hits and one run in nine innings. But he didn't get the win because the Phillies only scored one run through nine against Reds pitchers Ross Grimsley and Clay Carroll. The Phillies had ample opportunities to win the game in extra innings, loading the bases in the 10th and getting their first two men on base in the 12th, but the clutch hit eluded them. The Phillies finally got on the scoreboard in the 16th, but the Reds had already scored one in the top half, so the stalemate continued. In the 17th, outfielder Bobby Tolan hit an RBI single off Lersch, and Bench iced the game for the Reds with a three-run homer. Mike Ryan hit a worthless solo home run in the bottom of the 17th and the Phillies lost, 6-3. Ryan was the backup catcher, and like Brandon was a member of the American League champion Red Sox in 1967. He was a very good defensive catcher, which he had to be to stay in the majors for 11 years while hitting .193.

The 17-inning loss to the Reds was particularly frustrating for Lucchesi. If the Phillies could have pushed across a run in any inning from the ninth to the 15th, they would have had a walk-off win. But they didn't, and when they finally scored in the 16th and 17th, it wasn't enough. Lucchesi was feeling the heat and hoped the next day that his ace lefty, who had not won in nearly four weeks, could help the Phils start to turn the tide. The team flashed a rare burst of offense as Hutton socked a three-run homer in the first, and Bowa, heeding Carlton's advice, laced a two-run triple in the third. Even the potent Reds offense couldn't overcome a 5-0 deficit on the road against Carlton, could they? Maybe.

In the seventh, Bench, who always had a penchant for hitting Carlton hard, broke up the shutout with a leadoff homer. Later in the inning, infielder Julian Javier, a longtime teammate of Carlton's in St. Louis with minimal power, hit a two-run bomb to narrow the Phils' lead to 5-3. Morgan hit a double in the eighth to chase Carlton, and it was up to the bullpen to hold the lead. Perez ripped a triple off Selma to the alley in right-center to score Morgan and put the tying run at third with one out. "Oh brother, Harry," remarked a concerned Ashburn from the booth. Could the Phillies be letting another game slip away? But things looked promising when Chris Short came in and notched two key strikeouts to escape the jam. There was drama on the field as the game went to the ninth inning with Short on the mound, determined to save Carlton's sixth win.

Meanwhile, another drama was unfolding in team president Bob Carpenter's office. Earlier in the day, Carpenter had summoned Larry Shenk to his house in Delaware. This was an unusual request, and Shenk suspected that Carpenter had a bombshell announcement. Shenk's suspicions were confirmed. "We are going to make a change at general manager," Carpenter told his public relations man.

So in the ninth inning, Shenk rounded up the press corps and herded them into Carpenter's office. The writers were informed that John Quinn was "retiring," and it was "time for a change." No further details were provided. Quinn had held the job for more than 13 years; Shenk had worked closely with him for nine years. Shenk's memory of Quinn's departure is not pleasant. "That was an uncomfortable day. JQ was always nice to me. When I was hired [in 1963 at the age of 24], he was in the hospital. When he came out, he said he wanted to see me. He told me, 'You can learn a lot in this business if you keep your mouth shut and your ears open.'" Shenk recalled, "I never, ever remember him not wearing a suit." Unfortunately, Shenk never remembered Quinn watching the Phillies play in the postseason either. The collapse in 1964 when the Phils finished second was the closest he came to tasting the champagne in Philadelphia. He went out on a strong note, though. The Wise-for-Carlton trade was his last.

The players' opinions of Quinn were mixed. Denny Doyle liked the stern Irishman. "I had no problem with him. I had heard JQ had a reputation for being difficult and keeping the budget down. Many players had issues with him. He took care of me. I sustained a rotator cuff injury [in 1970], went 2-43 after the injury. JQ called me into the office at the end of the season and asked me if I could play. I said that I could. He gave me a raise, which was unexpected."

Darrell Brandon was one of the players who had issues with Quinn. "He was 'old school'—tight, didn't want to praise anybody." Brandon recalled how condescending and obstinate Quinn was during contract negotiations, especially in the 1971-72 off-season. "I was living in Houston. He called me nine at night, drunk. You could tell on the phone if he had been drinking because he would be slurring his words. He would belittle you, tell you that you're no good. He would say, 'We don't have to keep you. You can stay there if you want. You're not going to get your pension.'" Brandon stood his ground with Quinn and successfully negotiated an attendance clause in his contract. For every 100,000 fans that the Phillies drew at home in excess of a million, Brandon would receive an extra thousand dollars. Thanks largely to Steve Carlton, that meant an extra three thousand in Brandon's pocket, which was a sizable bonus considering his salary was $18,000.

Back on the field, during the impromptu press conference, the inevitable happened: Hal McRae, a late-game replacement for the Reds, homered off Chris Short in the ninth inning to tie the game at five. The Reds added a run in the 10th, and the demoralized Phillies couldn't muster a base runner off flame-throwing Reds reliever Tom Hall over the last two innings. The next afternoon, just as the game was getting under way, Shenk held another press conference and announced that farm director Paul Owens, the man with whom Quinn conferred prior to making the trade back in February, would be taking over as general manager. In the middle of Part II of the general manager saga, Johnny Bench hit a two-run double off Billy Champion and the runs stood up, as Jack Billingham and two relievers blanked the Reds 2-0. Frank Bilovsky recalled the oddity of the mid-game press conferences. "Two days in a row, we didn't see the winning run score. Only the Phillies would call press conferences during a game."

The 48-year-old Owens had been a part of the Phillies organization since 1955, when his Olean (New York) Oilers, a Class D minor league team, became a Phillies farm team. Owens was Olean's player-manager. A native of upstate New York, he served as a sergeant in World War II, and saw action in the Battle of the Bulge. A baseball star at St. Bonaventure University, he earned a degree in 1951 and had every intention of embarking on a career as a teacher. But that's when Owens, a right-handed-hitting first baseman, was offered a tryout by Olean.

On the day of his tryout, Owens figured he'd hang around to watch that night's game, so he bought a 75-cent ticket. During the game, Olean's first baseman got hurt. The manager summoned Owens out of the stands to suit up, and the future "Pope" got two hits. Age 27 at the time, he went on to bat .407 that season, earning Rookie of the Year and MVP honors in the Class D PONY League.

By 1954, Paul Owens was managing. He moved from Olean to Bakersfield, the Phillies' Class C team in the California League. Later he became a Phillies West Coast scout. In 1965, Owens was promoted to farm director, and now he was the franchise's general manager.

Owens, watching his first full game as GM, was disappointed to see the Phillies drop the series opener to the Astros, 4-3. There was a bright spot in the Houston game—the Phillies snapped their string of 24 straight scoreless innings, which extended back to the third inning of the game that Carlton started in which the Phils blew a 5-0 lead. Down 4-0 to the Astros heading into the bottom of the ninth inning, with many of the 8,237 fans already on their way home, the Phillies staged an improbable rally by scoring three runs. With Tommy Hutton on first, Lucchesi needed one of last year's big boppers, Deron Johnson or Willie Montañez, to pop one and give the Phillies a desperately needed victory. Johnson, whose thigh injury had limited him to two home runs, popped out. And Montañez, in the throes of a sophomore slump with only three homers, whiffed to end the game.

Twenty games. One win. A .209 team batting average, 2.3 runs per game, and a total of seven home runs. The seemingly interminable slump transformed the Phillies from a 15-10 record and a respectable three games out of first to a 16-29 mark and 16 games out. Carlton, who a month earlier was 5-1 with a 1.73 ERA, was now 5-6 with an ERA of 3.12. Out in St. Louis, Rick Wise was 5-5 with a 3.72 ERA. The stats of Carlton and Wise were fairly similar. Many Phillies fans still questioned whether they should have parted with their All-Star right-hander.

CHAPTER 8

The Streak Begins

The most remarkable and implausible single-season pitching streak in baseball history began on a balmy Wednesday night at Veterans Stadium on June 7, 1972. Steve Carlton strode to the mound, not thinking about starting a winning streak, but determined to end two losing streaks: his five-gamer and his club's nine-game slide. It was Ladies Night at the ballpark, one of Bill Giles' many promotions, designed to attract women to the Vet. Females were given a one-dollar discount on their tickets. A box seat cost a mere $4.25 in 1972 (nowadays that might buy a fan a hot dog at a major league ballpark), but with the dollar reduction, ladies only had to pay $3.25 for a seat near the field. Despite the promotion, less than 11,000 people were on hand for the game. Apparently, fans of both sexes were not particularly interested in watching a team which had won only once in the previous three weeks.

Carlton was facing a solid Houston lineup, which featured Jesus Alou, a tough out like his brothers Felipe and Matty; young phenom César Cedeño; power-hitting former Red Lee May; and budding star Bob Watson. Twenty-two-year-old southpaw Jerry Reuss, who pitched in the same rotation with Carlton for the Cardinals in 1970 and 1971, was on the mound for Houston. He would go on to become one of baseball's most consistent lefties of the 1970s and '80s, winning 220 games. Behind Carlton in the infield were Don Money, Larry Bowa, Terry Harmon, and Deron Johnson. Greg Luzinski, as usual, held down left field; Roger Freed, fighting for a job, played right. Willie Montañez, mired in a 1-29 slump with his average down to .209, was benched by Frank Lucchesi in favor of Byron Browne. At one time, the wiry right-handed-hitting Browne was a promising player, as he hit 16 homers for the Cubs in 1966, his rookie year. However, the strikeout was his downfall—he led the National League in Ks in '66—and he was back in the minors in 1967 where he remained for most of the next three years. The Cardinals purchased Browne's contract in 1969, and the Phillies acquired him after the season in the Flood-Allen trade. He had hit just one home run in the majors over the previous three years.

In 1970, though, Browne regained his power stroke to some extent by hitting 10 home runs in 270 at-bats for the Phils. He was on the roller coaster again in '71, shuttling between Eugene, Oregon and the Phillies; he managed just 68 at-bats for the big league club and hit three out of the park.

In the first two months of the 1972 season, Browne made 15 pinch-hitting appearances, but did not start a game. This was the first game of the season that Lucchesi had written Byron's name into the starting lineup. And the last. Although he was only 29, it would be his final start, not only of the season, but of his major league career. The Phillies optioned him back to Eugene two weeks later, and he played in the minors intermittently until 1975, finally calling it quits.

Carlton and Jerry Reuss traded five scoreless frames, each allowing two singles. Carlton struck out 10 Astros, including César Cedeño, Lee May, and Bob Watson in succession in the fourth. Carlton blanked Houston again in the sixth, and the Phillies touched up Reuss in the bottom half. Following walks to Bowa and Money, Luzinski hit an opposite field double to score both runners, and Johnson delivered an RBI single.

Could Carlton hold the 3-0 lead and salvage a victory for him and the team? The top of the seventh did not start well. Doug Rader got aboard on an infield single, advanced to second on a rare wild pitch by Carlton, and then Larry Howard walked. Jimmy Stewart, who made the first out in the ninth inning of Rick Wise's no-hitter, singled to score Rader and cut the deficit to 3-1. Carlton buckled down and struck out pinch-hitter Bobby Fenwick and then his reliable infield defense gave him a lift by turning a double play on leadoff hitter Roger Metzger. It was stretch time at the Vet, and organist Paul Richardson entertained the crowd with his rendition of "Take Me Out to the Ball Game."

With one out and the pitcher's spot up in the bottom of the seventh, Lucchesi made a questionable move by pulling his workhorse Carlton for a pinch-hitter. The skipper wanted an insurance run or two for Darrell Brandon, who was loosening up in the bullpen. Oscar Gamble, who was recalled from Eugene when the team sent down Mike Anderson a week earlier, was given the call. During his three years with the Phils from 1970 to 1972, Gamble compiled a season's worth of at-bats, 690, but his stats were mediocre: a .241 average with eight home runs. The Phillies finally gave up on Gamble and traded him to Cleveland after the '72 season. As things turned out, the Phillies threw in the towel too soon because after his departure, Gamble blossomed into a good player. He smoked 20 home runs for the Indians in '73, later hit 31 for the White Sox in a season, and had some productive years for the Yankees. All told, he hit 200 career homers. For the Phillies, surrounded by ineptitude, he never found his groove.

Gamble, with his trademark Afro, dug into the left-handed batters box. George Culver was pitching in relief of Reuss. While with the Reds in 1968, Culver threw a no-hitter against the Phillies. He retired Gamble on a fly ball to center.

Brandon kept the Astros in check in the eighth. Lucchesi pulled out all the stops to make sure that he had his best defensive players on the field in the ninth. Ron Stone, who had pinch-run for Luzinski in the eighth, took over right field. Montañez had pinch-hit for Freed and assumed his customary center-field position, replacing Browne for whom Tim McCarver had pinch-hit in the eighth. Tommy Hutton moved from first base to left field, and Pete Koegel trotted out to first. None of the three starting outfielders was still in the game.

Darrell Brandon made sure the ladies watched a victory by setting down the Astros in the ninth to preserve the 3-1 win. He was flattered when Carlton told him afterwards that he had good stuff and was glad that he had come into the game for the save. It was also a big game for Mike Ryan—it was the only win of Carlton's in which he was the starting catcher. Two streaks had ended, and though nobody knew it at the time, one long and amazing streak was under way.

Carlton made it two in a row with another 3-1 win, this time against the Braves before a Cap Day crowd at the Vet of nearly 33,000. Ron Reed was the starter for Atlanta. Reed began his pro sports career playing in the NBA *and* in the major leagues. Imagine that—you're a big league pitcher, and your off-season job is as a pro basketball player. Billy Champion worked for a cable television company, Pirate Richie Hebner dug graves, and Ron Reed banged the boards with Wilt Chamberlain and Bill Russell. Reed played two seasons with the Detroit Pistons before he gave up basketball to focus solely on baseball. Primarily a starter during his nine years in Atlanta, Reed later pitched eight seasons serving as a reliever for the Phillies. Only Tug McGraw and Joe Hoerner saved more of Carlton's 329 wins than Reed.

The Cap Day tilt followed a script similar to the Houston game four days earlier. The Phillies built a 3-0 lead through six innings, and then Carlton was touched for a run in the top of the seventh. Lucchesi let his pitcher bat in the bottom of the seventh, and he ended up going the distance, striking out nine and only walking one. In both the eighth and ninth innings, Carlton allowed a single, but then his infield turned a double play on the next batter. Don Money went around the horn in the eighth; Denny Doyle fielded a grounder, stepped on second and fired to first for the game-ender in the ninth. Both thought that the quickness with which Lefty worked kept the defense on their toes and helped them play better. "When a pitcher works slowly, the defense gets on its heels," said Money. "Steve went about his business. He got the ball, he was ready to go." Doyle: "Everybody played better behind him."

In September 1971, the Phillies were on their way to a last-place finish, 30 games behind the first-place Pirates. One day before a game, Lucchesi was at the batting cage watching his hitters practice. A team employee stood alongside, observing behind the cage. The Phillies had recently called up Luzinski and Anderson from Eugene, and they were billed as the team's hitting stars of the future.

"See these guys," beamed Lucchesi, "we're going to get better. But we've gotta make some changes around here, and the first place we have to make a change is right here," and he pointed emphatically to home plate.

The team staffer understood the manager's innuendo. "Lucchesi hated McCarver," he explained. "Timmy thought Lucchesi was a phony. They hated each other. McCarver was on to him that he was a phony. He was not a good big league manager; he was a minor league guy. He was always talking about the priests and the nuns that he visited, the people that he went to see in the hospital. He had the radio show, *The Skipper Lucchesi Show*, and he would talk about who he had seen in the hospital that day. There was never any baseball." Lucchesi's deficiencies were noticeably glaring to McCarver because he had played for top-notch manager Red Schoendienst in St. Louis for five years.

The June 15th trade deadline was approaching, and Paul Owens was eager to make some changes and shake things up on his beleaguered team. On June 14th, Lucchesi and McCarver each got his wish as Owens traded Timmy to the Expos for catcher John Bateman. On the surface, the deal appeared lopsided. Bateman was good defensively, but in his nine and a half seasons with Houston and Montreal, he was a .230 hitter. Although McCarver was only hitting .237 for the Phillies at the time of the trade, he was a .268 career hitter and two-time All-Star.

Owens was not done dealing. The next day, just under the wire, the Pope traded Joe Hoerner and minor leaguer Andre Thornton to the Braves for pitchers Jim Nash and Gary Neibauer. Owens pulled off some great trades during his 14 years as the Phillies' general manager, but this was not one of them. Hoerner was the team's only dependable reliever—his

ERA was 2.08, lower than Carlton's when the trade was made. Thornton was a local boy who graduated from Phoenixville High in the Philadelphia suburbs. Mike Piazza graduated from Phoenixville two decades after Thornton. A first baseman, he had worked his way up the Phils' minor league system; he was playing for Eugene when he received word of the deal. Owens had his doubts whether Thornton was major league material and was willing to part with him. Oops. Thornton went on to slug 253 home runs, most of which were for the Indians. One of Thornton's team-mates in 1987, his final year with the Tribe, was Steve Carlton.

Jim Nash was the key player in the deal from Owens' perspective. "Jumbo," as he was called, had a phenomenal rookie season for the Kansas City Athletics in 1966, posting a 12-1 record and a 2.06 ERA. He had won 12 or more games in a season three times since. Owens thought that Nash could bolster the Phillies' starting rotation and maybe even regain his '66 form. Suffice it to say, the Pope was wrong. Nash was utterly horrendous for the Phillies. Gary Neibauer had been a so-so reliever with Atlanta for four years. He continued in that vein for the Phils after the trade.

The Phillies' trade acquisitions met the team in Houston for the start of a three-game weekend series. With the addition of three players to the major league roster—Bateman, Nash, and Neibauer—and the subtraction of two—McCarver and Hoerner—it was necessary for the club to clear a spot. Deron Johnson, who had been battling a leg injury for weeks, was placed on the 15-day disabled list.

Lucchesi, glad that his clubhouse was rid of McCarver, warmly greeted his new charges. It was Carlton's turn to pitch, and John Bateman, a burly Texan with a weathered face and a fondness for partying, was behind the plate his first night in a Phillies uniform. Jim Nash was slated to start the following week, and Gary Neibauer joined Darrell Brandon, Barry Lersch, and the others in the bullpen.

Houston played its home games at the Astrodome, which was a trend-setting ballpark. It was the first domed stadium and the first park to use AstroTurf on the field instead of natural grass. Supremely talented right-hander Don Wilson took the hill for Houston. Wilson was 27 years old and had already thrown two no-hitters and struck out 18 batters in a game. Jimmy Wynn, who was not in the lineup when Carlton hurled against the Astros in Philadelphia, batted third and played right field. He had acquired the moniker "the Toy Cannon" for his small stature and powerful bat.

After the Phillies went down in the top of the first, Carlton went to work with his new catcher. The chemistry between a pitcher and catcher is critical to the pitcher's success. In his six and a half years in the majors, Carlton's primary catchers had been Tim McCarver and Ted Simmons, and he had excellent chemistry with them, especially McCarver. From the outset, Carlton and Bateman seemed to develop a good rhythm together. Roger Metzger hit a leadoff single, and Bateman promptly gunned him down trying to steal. César Cedeño struck out and Wynn bounced to Bowa to close out the first. Carlton breezed through three innings, then six, not allowing an Astro to reach second base. Bateman threw out a second runner, Cedeño, trying to steal in the sixth. Wilson was stingy as well, allowing five hits, including a pair of doubles to Hutton and one to Bateman, but keeping the Phillies off the scoreboard.

In the seventh, Don Wilson was lifted with one out and a man on second for Tom Griffin, who became a journeyman pitcher. Griffin got out of the inning, and the game stayed scoreless. The Astros finally got a man to second in the seventh on a single by Wynn and a walk to Doug Rader, but Bateman snared a Tommy Helms popup in front of the plate to thwart the threat. The pitchers' duel continued into the bottom of the ninth. Cedeño, who had drawn comparisons to Willie Mays for his power, speed, and glove in center field, led off with a double. Lucchesi showed Jimmy Wynn great respect by intentionally walking him to set up the double play. Carlton did not get a ground ball, but he fanned Lee May, and Bob Watson lined out to left field. A walk to Rader loaded the bases, but Helms again couldn't deliver, flying out to center.

Carlton was still out there in the 10th. Catcher Larry Howard singled, and Astros manager Harry Walker declined to pull Tom Griffin for a pinch-hitter and instead sent him up to bunt. Carlton, in a lapse of concentration, balked Howard to second. Lucchesi then utilized a unique mid-inning strategy. Because Greg Luzinski was poor defensively and Ron Stone was above average with a good arm, and Griffin as well as the next two batters were right-handed and more likely to hit the ball to left, Lucchesi flip-flopped Luzinski and Stone—Luzinski went to right field; Stone jogged past "the Bull" to left. Griffin bunted Howard over to third. Switch-hitting Roger Metzger, batting right-handed against Carlton, came to the plate with the winning run on third and one out. The Phils brought their outfield and infield in.

"It's a tough way to play baseball," Ashburn noted grimly from the booth. Ground balls move quickly on AstroTurf, and Metzger could easily slap one through the drawn-in infield. Or he could lob a fly ball over an outfielder's head. There was little margin for error. Even though it was the 10th inning, Carlton still had gas in the tank. He reared back and struck out Metzger, and then with the infield and outfield at normal depth, Cedeño grounded out.

John Bateman led off the top of the 11th with a single, his third hit of the game. Lucchesi sent out Terry Harmon as a pinch-runner. Speed was not John's forte. Fellow Expo Bob Bailey described Bateman "as slow as a treesaw." Don Money, normally not a bunter, sacrificed Harmon to second. After Bowa popped out, Lucchesi sent up Oscar Gamble to bat for Carlton.

What an exemplary performance by Lefty: 10 innings of shutout ball. He surrendered six hits, never allowing more than one in an inning. And he struck out at least one batter in every inning, finishing with 12 Ks. It looked like Carlton had regained his early-season dominance, as he had allowed two runs in 26 innings over his last three games.

Jimmy Wynn managed one hit in three at-bats against Carlton, which as he reflected back, made it a lucky night for him. "Hitting against Carlton was like hitting against Bob Gibson—you were lucky to get one hit in a game. He threw a devastating fastball, inside and out. His slider broke down and into right-handers. It broke so fast, usually out of the strike zone. You knew it was coming with two strikes. It was hard to lay off." Wynn marveled at Carlton's intensity and concentration. "He was *strictly* business. He didn't smile, even at his teammates."

Lefty didn't smile at opposing players either, although he and Wynn have exchanged some smiles and laughs in their post-playing days. In recent years, Wynn has hosted an annual golf tournament in Houston, and Carlton has been one of the Hall of Fame participants. Joe Morgan, Bob Gibson, and Fergie Jenkins have also had tee times at Jimmy's tourney. Wynn described Carlton as "down-to-earth and relaxed."

Left fielder Bob Watson, a six-time .300 hitter, took his second straight collar against Carlton and only batted .182 against him in 1972. Watson eventually figured out how to hit Lefty, batting .290 in his career against him and racking up more runs batted in versus Carlton than any other pitcher except Freddie Norman. Watson was every bit as wowed by Steve's slider as Wynn; he just had a different approach to hitting him. From the Office of the Commissioner where he holds the position of Vice-President of Rules and On-Field Operations, Watson revealed his secret. "I didn't offer at his hard slider. If you swung, you couldn't hit it fair; if you took the pitch, it was a ball. I looked for his fastball and curve [to swing at]." Watson did not swing at the slider because, unlike most hitters, he was able to recognize the pitch soon after it left Carlton's hand. Watson came up to the majors as a catcher, which trained him to watch the ball carefully while it was on its way to the plate. This, Watson said, helped him to see the spin on Carlton's slider before it broke and to resist swinging. Why couldn't other hitters do the same thing? "They weren't as smart as I was," said Watson, tongue-in-cheek. Despite his success against Carlton, he gave the left-hander his props. "When he pitched, you knew you had a good chance of going 0-4. He constantly battled you."

He certainly battled the Astros that night, and his impeccable pitching was worthy of a victory. If the Phillies were able to score Harmon from second, and the bullpen could finish the shutout, Carlton would get the win that he deserved.

Oscar Gamble did his part by stroking a single, but Terry Harmon had to stop at third. First and third, two outs, tie game, extra innings—you want your leadoff man coming up, right? Not if it's Ron Stone. Lucchesi had tried a few leadoff hitters during the season—Bowa, Doyle, and Harmon—and inexplicably went with Stone despite his .205 average. Stone completed his 0-6 night with a groundout, dropping his average to .178.

Carlton faced 38 batters and did not allow a run. Dick Selma came out of the bullpen, faced one, and the game was over. Wynn, relieved that Carlton was out of the game, greeted Selma with a no-doubt-about-it home run to left to give the Astros a 1-0 win.

The night after Carlton's masterful effort against Houston, a group of men with ties to the Republican party broke into the Democratic headquarters at the Watergate office complex in Washington, D.C. Little did anyone know it at the time, but it was the seed of what would grow into the greatest political scandal in American history. The following day, the Phillies were almost no-hit by Jerry Reuss. Larry Bowa hit a leadoff double in the ninth to spoil Reuss' no-hit bid.

Carlton was deprived of a win in Houston because the Phils couldn't muster any offense. He escaped without a loss in his next start in Atlanta because their bats came to life. Sometimes it took the '72 Phillies a week to hit two home runs. Facing Ron Reed, who was opposing Carlton for the second time in 10 days, the Phillies went deep twice in the top of the second. Montañez hit a solo shot, and Bateman followed with a two-run poke, his first of the season. Unfortunately, Carlton was off his game and the Braves scored five runs in the first five innings to take a 5-4 lead. Hank Aaron contributed to the damage, going 2-2 with two RBI. Unlike his rival Mays, Aaron always had Carlton's number, hitting .342 against him in his career with six home runs.

Lucchesi pulled Carlton in the top of the sixth for a pinch-hitter. Stone, who came through with a two-run single, upped his average to .196 and his RBI total to three. If the Phillies' bullpen could hold the 6-5 lead over the last four innings, Carlton would be credited with a win, albeit a cheap one. It didn't take long for Gary Neibauer, pitching in his second game for the Phillies and his first against the team that had traded him the week before, to squelch that possibility. After facing three Braves batters, Neibauer had allowed the tying run; he gave up the go-ahead run to the next batter for good measure before Lucchesi yanked him. Roger Freed quickly tied things up with a homer in the seventh, and the game remained

7-7 into the ninth. Submarine-throwing righty Cecil Upshaw walked the bases loaded, and light-hitting Mike Ryan delivered a two-run double. Darrell Brandon struck out future Hall of Famers Aaron and Orlando Cepeda to close out the game. It was one of Steve Carlton's only short and ineffective outings of the season. But at least he avoided a loss, thanks to the Phillies' nine-run outburst, the highest score they had posted to date in the season.

CHAPTER 9

The Brawl

He had the genius of Casey Stengel, the intensity of Billy Martin, and the iron hand of Dick Williams. Yet despite managing 26 years in the majors—nearly 4,000 games—Gene "the General" Mauch never experienced the thrill of piloting his team in a World Series.

But he came agonizingly close. Led by pitching ace Jim Bunning, rookie of the year Richie (later called Dick) Allen, and MVP candidate Johnny Callison, Mauch's Phillies in 1964 breezed through the season in first place. On September 20th, they had 12 games remaining and held a six-and-a-half-game lead over St. Louis and Cincinnati. Philadelphia's magic number to clinch the pennant was just seven. The Phillies brass was so confident that its team would win the pennant that it gave the ticket office the go-ahead to start printing World Series tickets.

But the bottom fell out for the Phillies as they lost 10 games in a row. Meanwhile the Cardinals won nine out of 10 and the Reds won nine straight to overtake the Phillies. The Cardinals ended up winning the pennant on the last day of the season. Mauch was criticized for his handling of the pitching staff during the collapse. He started his aces, Bunning and Chris Short, three times each on two days' rest, and both pitchers were ineffective. Although his Phillies let the pennant slip away, Mauch was named the National League Manager of the Year for the second time.

Gene Mauch won a third Manager of the Year award, for the Expos in 1973, but he did not win a pennant in his seven years at the helm in Montreal, nor did he during his five-year stay in Minnesota as the Twins' manager. He took over his fourth and final big league club, the California Angels, in the middle of the strike-shortened 1981 season. In 1982, Mauch pushed the right buttons and led the veteran Angels squad to the American

League Western Division title. With a lineup which included four former MVPs—Reggie Jackson, Fred Lynn, Rod Carew, and Don Baylor—the Angels jumped out to a 2-0 lead in the best-of-five League Championship Series against manager Harvey Kuenn's Milwaukee Brewers. One more win and Mauch would finally be World Series–bound for the first time. But the Brewers, nicknamed "Harvey's Wallbangers" for their powerful offense, stormed back and won three straight in Milwaukee to take the series. The Angels became the first team since divisional play began in 1969 to squander a 2-0 lead in an LCS. Mauch again drew criticism for his decision to start Tommy John and Bruce Kison in games four and five on short rest. Some of the criticism was doled out by Angel owner Gene Autry, which incensed Mauch so much that he resigned soon after the series ended.

Two years later, Mauch agreed to return as the Angels' skipper, and in his second season back, 1986, lightning struck for a third time. The League Championship Series had been extended to seven games, and the Angels led the Red Sox three games to one and took a 5-2 lead into the top of the ninth inning of game five at Anaheim Stadium. With the champagne on ice in the Angels' locker room, Boston incredibly scored four runs on two-run homers by former Angel Don Baylor and Dave Henderson to take a 6-5 lead. Henderson's blast came with two outs and two strikes. The Sox went on to win the game 7-6 in 11 innings and send the series back to Boston. The shell-shocked Angels got blown out 10-4 and 8-1 at Fenway, and Mauch had suffered his most crushing defeat. He managed one more year with the Angels and called it a career.

About his several near misses, Mauch cracked, "If it's true you learn from adversity, then I must be the smartest SOB in the world." According to Bob Boone, who played for Mauch for four years with the Angels and has been involved in several facets of the game for 40 years as player, coach, manager, and executive, Mauch was the smartest SOB in the world, at least in the world of baseball. "He was the best baseball man I have ever been around. He was way ahead of anybody in terms of running a game. All of his teams finished one or two places [in the standings] ahead of where [they should have] finished. He didn't win any championships because he didn't have championship players."

Don Zimmer, whose experience is even broader than Boone's, has the same admiration for Mauch. Zimmer's first major league coaching job was with the Expos in 1971, under Mauch. Zimmer had managed in the minors for four years and didn't think he was quite ready to manage in the majors when Montreal hired him. After a year as Mauch's third base coach and having the opportunity to observe and listen to him, Zimmer knew he was ready to manage a big league club. He got the San Diego job the following season. "I learned so much baseball from him. I was never around a guy who was on top of the game as much as he was." That's quite a compliment considering Zimmer was Joe Torre's bench coach with the Yankees for eight years. Zimmer added, "Gene was two innings ahead of the game; he knew who he was going to pinch-hit."

Mauch's brilliance extended to the rules, as he was a renowned expert of the baseball rule book. And he was not above exploiting the rules in any way he could to help his team win. In the 1960s, when Mauch was managing the Phillies, if a player entered the dugout space of the opposing team, it was fair game to interfere. The shrewd Mauch was well aware of that rule. One time when the Phillies were playing the Mets, a Phillie lifted a high popup in the direction of the Philadelphia dugout. Mets catcher Jerry Grote had a beat on the ball and extended his glove into the Phils' dugout to make the catch. Sorry, Jerry. As Grote was about to make the snag, Mauch chopped him in the forearm and prevented the catcher from making the play. Thanks to his ingenuity, it was a foul ball instead of an out, and his batter still had life.

Mauch would do anything to gain an edge on the other team. The top part of Connie Mack Stadium's right-field wall was made of corrugated metal, and balls often caromed off in crazy directions, which would allow the batter—and runners if men were on base—to get an extra base. Mauch saw a way to use the quirky wall to his advantage. The Phillies' bullpen had been located behind the left-field wall, while the visitors' bullpen was behind the right-field wall. During an off-season, Mauch had a brainstorm and the bullpens were switched, so the Phillies' pen was stationed behind the right-field wall. The following season, when the Phillies were batting, their bullpen coach would hold a white towel in his hand. If a Phillie hit a fly ball that was headed toward the right-field wall, Mauch, from the dugout on the first base side, immediately looked at his bullpen coach. If he waved the towel, that meant the ball was going to hit the top portion of the wall. Mauch would quickly flash a sign to his first and third base coaches to let them know the ball was going to clang off the metal—probably sending the right fielder on a chase—so the runners could go full steam around the bases.

Mauch's nickname of "the General" was well earned, as he did not hesitate to let his players and coaches know that he was the boss. Sometimes he would ream them out even if they didn't deserve it. Don Zimmer was on the receiving end of one of Mauch's tirades in '71. In an early season series in Chicago, Mauch suspected that the signs he was flashing from the dugout to Zimmer in the third base coaching box were being stolen by Cubs coach Peanuts Lowrey. The next time the Expos played the Cubs, Mauch held a meeting with Zimmer prior to the series to change the signs and hopefully fool Lowrey. In the first game of the series, with Boots Day on first base, Mauch wanted to hit and run but inadvertently flashed Zimmer the old hit-and-run sign, not the new one which he had given to Zimmer at the meeting. Zimmer did not relay the hit-and-run sign, and Day stayed put at first base. Mauch screamed at Zimmer from the dugout, "Wake up, goddamn it, you rock-head!" Zimmer took umbrage at being excoriated since he wasn't the one who made the mistake. When he got back to the dugout after the inning, he told Mauch to go shit in his hat. Infielder Bobby Wine, who played for Mauch for most of his career with the Phillies and Expos and was considered one of his "pets," admonished Zimmer. "You can't talk to 'the General' like that." Zimmer shot back, "Piss on you and 'the General'; you both can go to hell. I'm not taking that shit from anybody." The two patched things up after the game, and generally got along well during their year together in Montreal. But even the well-respected Zimmer could catch an earful from Mauch.

While Zimmer was brave enough to stand up to his manager, most would cower when subjected to a verbal onslaught by Mauch. Case in point: Denny Doyle, when he arrived late to spring training in 1968. He had played single-A ball for Tidewater the previous year and would head to Reading for the season to play double-A. In the off-season, Doyle returned to his alma mater in Kentucky to teach and coach basketball. Doyle was a minor leaguer, but he was on the 40-man major league roster, so he reported to Clearwater and worked out with the big league squad. In '68, he showed up five days late because he had to finish the high school basketball season back in Kentucky. Mauch was infuriated. "I took a beating," recalled Doyle. "He had the players hitting in groups and had me hitting against hard-throwing left-hander Grant Jackson. Jackson dominated me. Mauch would be yelling at me, 'How did that fuckin' basketball team do?! Maybe next year, you'll be on time.' He was trying to teach me a lesson." Doyle summed up Mauch aptly: "It was his way or the highway."

If Doyle took offense at his skipper's causticity, Mauch didn't care. Bob "Beetle" Bailey played 17 years in the majors, seven of which were for Mauch's Expos. Bailey was blunt in his assessment of Mauch: "He didn't give a shit how his players felt about him; all he wanted to do was win. Players' feelings toward Mauch ran the full spectrum from 'I really like him' to 'I really hate him.'" Bailey was at the positive end; John Bateman was at the other.

Bailey saluted Mauch's passion and acuity for the game and also recalled another quality of Gene's: his affinity for having his pitchers throw inside. "Mauch wanted Expos pitchers to be feared," noted Bailey. "They hit a lot of batters. He had two or three hatchet guys."

One of his "hatchet guys" was Ernie McAnally, and he was given the starting assignment by Mauch to pitch against Carlton on a hazy Sunday afternoon at Jarry Park. It was a cool day for late June in the mid-'60s. While 1972 was Mauch's 13th year as a major league manager, he was just 46 years old. His short black hair was flecked with gray. Some felt that Mauch's dictatorial style stemmed from having a Napoleon complex—he was just five feet ten and 165 pounds. During games, he watched intently from the dugout, arms crossed, rarely smiling.

The Expos won 52 games in 1969—a typical win total for a first-year expansion team— but they improved to 73 wins under Mauch's guidance in 1970 and won a respectable 71 in 1971. In 1972, the Expos were 27-33 going into the Sunday afternoon game and were shooting for their second straight sweep of the Phillies.

McAnally was a 25-year-old right-hander, headstrong and hard-throwing. He came up to the minors as a catcher, switched to the outfield, and then settled on being a pitcher. After an inauspicious four seasons in Montreal, he would trade in his rosin bag for a deposit bag—he returned to his home state of Texas to pursue a career in banking. McAnally freely admitted that he had the reputation of a headhunter. "There is a time and a place to flatten a batter, like if he bowls over my second baseman, or if a guy does something dirty, I'll hit him." McAnally liked Mauch's style, and in turn Mauch appreciated McAnally's willingness to drill an opposing hitter. McAnally, however, did not see eye to eye with Bateman when they were teammates. Ernie had requested that John Boccabella catch for him, which did not go over well with Bateman. McAnally carried a 1-8 record into the game. Third-string catcher Terry Humphrey was behind the plate. Boccabella played first base. Tim McCarver was on the bench.

Bateman got the start at catcher for the Phillies; it was just his third time catching for Carlton since he came over in the trade. Carlton wanted to make short work of the Expos and catch a plane with the team out of Montreal. It may have been Steve's least favorite city. "He hated Montreal," said Tommy Hutton. "He wouldn't even exchange his money." And Mauch might have been Carlton's least favorite manager. "Steve did not have a lot of feel-good for Mauch," said Doyle.

Carlton had his good stuff out of the gate as he struck out the last two batters of the first inning, Clyde Mashore and Ron Woods, and the first two batters of the second inning, Bob Bailey and Ken Singleton. He allowed just a single and a walk, both to leadoff man Ron Hunt, through three innings. McAnally also opened the game with three shutout innings, although he had to pitch out of a bases-loaded jam in the second.

The fireworks started in the top of the fourth. McAnally retired Luzinski and Montañez on groundouts. Joe Lis was up next for the Phillies.

He was yet another Phillie who starred in the minors but flopped in the majors. He slugged 36 home runs for Eugene in 1970. That was more homers than he banged out in his eight-year major league career, which also included time for the Indians, Twins, and Mariners. He hit 32 career home runs, with a season-high of nine for the Twins in 1973. In '72, with Deron Johnson battling his leg injury, Lis got some occasional starts at first base. At six feet tall, he was lean and muscular. McAnally got two quick strikes on Lis and then hit him on the forearm. Much as McAnally had a penchant for throwing inside, he insisted that it was not intentional. "I wasn't trying to hit Lis. It was a scoreless game; the count was 0-2." Carlton didn't see it that way and simmered in the dugout. "Whoever comes up first for them is going down. I'm gonna drill him," he exclaimed.

Young shortstop Tim Foli, who was acquired by Montreal the previous April in a trade with the Mets, was the unlucky batter who came to incur the wrath of Carlton. Nicknamed "Crazy Horse," Foli was a clone of Bowa's: He was high-strung, emotional, and intense. He made it to the majors in part because of his fire. He later played for the 1979 World Champion Pirates, and spent a year with Mauch's Angels. It was impeccable timing that it was Foli's turn to bat because if Carlton had to hit a batter, it might as well be somebody that he couldn't stand. Chris Wheeler was emphatic when discussing Carlton's disdain for "Crazy Horse." "He hated Foli. Everybody hated Foli. He was the perfect guy to hit. He was one of those guys on the opposition that no one liked. He was one of those annoying players."

Carlton wasted no time. His first pitch was a rocket right at Foli's head. He had no chance to get out of the way—it hit him in the ear, and he fell to the ground. In 329 innings pitched in '72, that was Carlton's only hit-by-pitch. And he hit the batter on purpose. Bowa later asked Foli if he knew that Carlton was going to hit him. "Yeah, but I didn't think he'd throw at my head."

Foli staggered to his feet and started toward the mound, spewing vitriol at Carlton. The Expos trainer hustled out of the dugout to see if Foli was all right and try to prevent him from going after Carlton. Anticipating a fight, Carlton took a couple strides toward the plate. But before Foli and Carlton had the chance to tangle, a man came flying out of the Expos dugout, made a beeline toward Carlton, took a wild swing at him and missed, and his momentum carried him to the ground. It wasn't a player, though—*it was manager Gene Mauch*. Over the years, batters have occasionally charged the mound, but a manager going after a pitcher is unheard of.

It wasn't a terribly prudent decision by Mauch. The Phillies may have been easy to beat in a game, but they were tough as nails in a fight. After

Mauch's errant punch, both benches cleared and there was a huge pileup of Phillies and Expos in front of the mound. As McAnally said, the Phillies resembled their hometown hockey team, the Flyers. Pete Koegel was six feet six and 230 pounds; Jim Nash stood six feet five and weighed 220; Greg Luzinski was six feet one and a very solid 230 pounds; John Bateman was six feet three and 215 pounds. Don Money, Roger Freed, and Joe Lis were all broad-shouldered and strong. And they all wanted a piece of the runt Mauch who used dirty tactics and had just taken a cheap shot at their pitcher. Larry Bowa recalled the chaos on the field. "Mauch must have had eight bodies on him, and they were pummeling him." The Phillies used teamwork—in the first round of the melee, Nash held Mauch so that Money could take some jabs. The umpires were finally able to restore some order and untangle the bodies. On the bottom of the pile was a badly beaten-up Mauch. His face looked like a tomato, bruised and bloody. His shirt was unbuttoned and splattered with blood. As if he were not feeling bad enough after getting the crap kicked out of him, as soon as he was able to get on his feet with the assistance of his players and coaches, home plate umpire Dick Stello broke the news to him that he had been ejected from the game.

In most major league ballparks, clubhouses are behind the dugouts, connected by a tunnel. So if a player or manager is thrown out of a game, he can make the short walk to the dugout and disappear. At Jarry Park, the clubhouses were not behind the dugouts, but all the way down the left- and right-field lines. Bowa described Mauch's deliberate hobble. "It must have taken him 10 minutes after he got ejected to walk down to their clubhouse. They were going to bring him a cart, and he said, 'Get the fuckin' cart away from me; I'm walking.' He could barely walk." Expos fans, who liked Mauch's moxie, cheered for him as he limped to the clubhouse.

With Mauch ejected and receiving treatment for his injuries, first base coach Jimmy Bragan took over managing the Expos. Foli was carried off on a stretcher, and Hector Torres pinch-ran for him. Despite throwing the beanball, Carlton was not ejected. Stello must have reasoned that it was OK for a pitcher to hit a batter in the head intentionally, but it was not OK for a manager to come out and take a swing at the pitcher. Carlton regained his composure and retired Mashore, Woods, and Bailey.

In the top of the fifth, John Bateman, who stayed in the game despite getting his arm jostled in the brawl, broke the scoreless tie by leading off the inning with a home run. Bateman didn't have much power; it was just his second home run of the season and he would hit only one more long ball in the rest of the year.

Carlton was up next. For catcher Terry Humphrey, it was time for a slow curve; for Ernie McAnally, it was time for payback. He wound up and fired a fastball at Carlton's ribs. The pitch missed its target and sailed *behind* Carlton. He shouted at McAnally and shook his bat. He had thoughts of charging the mound and had to be restrained by Bowa, who hurried over from the on-deck circle, and Ray Rippelmeyer, who wanted to make sure his star left-hander stayed in the game. McAnally felt that his beanball attempt warranted a warning, not an ejection. Dick Stello thought otherwise. Without hesitation, the umpire tossed McAnally out of the game. All these years later, McAnally has no regrets about trying to clock Carlton. "I could live with myself better throwing at him than not throwing at him. I did what I thought I was supposed to do. I didn't have to be told to do that. Some people have road rage; I had mound rage."

Reliever John Strohmayer, the winning pitcher from the night before, was summoned into the game by Coach Bragan. He had not been warming up in the bullpen, and due to McAnally's abrupt departure, he was given all the time necessary to get ready. He walked Carlton, but induced Denny Doyle to ground into a double play and struck out Bowa.

Mike Ryan replaced Bateman behind the plate in the bottom of the fifth. With two outs, Humphrey singled, and Bragan sent up Tim McCarver to pinch-hit for Strohmayer. McCarver did not like playing for Frank Lucchesi in Philadelphia, but he wasn't thrilled to be with the Expos either. He was happy when Montreal traded him back to St. Louis at the end of the season. It was unusual for him to bat against Carlton as they were teammates for many years. McCarver faced Lefty only eight times in his career and picked up two singles. This time, he hit a grounder to second, which Terry Harmon couldn't handle, and he was charged with an error. Ron Hunt flied out to end the inning.

Carlton pitched out of a second-and-third, nobody out jam in the seventh, but other than that the Expos did not mount another rally. Carlton finished with a four-hit shutout.

Bailey, who took a collar of 0-4 that day, compared Carlton to Koufax and Gibson. "When they got to the seventh inning, they brought their game to another level, which had to do with their competitive nature. They threw as hard, if not harder, in the ninth inning as they did in the first inning."

The Phillies were not able to get on the scoreboard against Strohmayer and two other Expos relievers, so Bateman's home run proved to be the difference in the 1-0 victory. It was sweet revenge for big John to hit the decisive homer to beat McAnally and Mauch.

Much like McAnally candidly acknowledged that he was gunning for Carlton, when asked later, Lefty did not deny that he was aiming for Foli. "[McAnally] threw at Joe Lis what I thought was intentionally. I retaliated by knocking down Tim Foli. I don't like to see [bench-clearing brawls].

But it's part of baseball. They will happen as long as the game is in existence."

After the game, the Phillies headed to the Montreal Airport to board a flight to Chicago. The Expos also needed to fly out of town to catch a plane to St. Louis. In those days, there were no charter flights for pro sports teams, so they flew on commercial flights. As fate would have it, the Phillies and Expos departed from gates which were next to each other. That gave the Phillies and their staff another glimpse at Mauch. It was not a pretty sight. Wheeler recalled Mauch's appearance vividly: "He looked like one of the most beat-up prizefighters you've ever seen—he had welts, a fat lip, his eyes were all swollen—he got the crap kicked out of him. He looked like he had gone 12 rounds and didn't win. And of course the joke was that his own players did it to him."

Mauch was resilient, though, and he was back in the dugout the following night to manage the Expos. Foli sat out one game and returned to the lineup Tuesday night.

A few days after the brawl, McAnally received a telegram from National League president Chub Feeney. He had been fined 50 dollars for throwing at Carlton. McAnally showed Mauch the telegram and asked him if the team would pay the fine. Mauch responded with a snarl. "Gimme that. I'll take care of it. But I should fine you for missing him."

It wasn't the last time that Ernie McAnally hit Joe Lis. In 1991, at Veterans Stadium, there was an old-timers game between the 1971 Phillies and the '71 Expos. McAnally pitched an inning, and one of the batters he faced was Lis. For old time's sake, McAnally hit Lis with a pitch. As a joke, Lis charged the mound.

CHAPTER 10

On a Roll

Although he wanted Gene Mauch, Steve Carlton never got the chance to throw a punch at "the General." Before he could swing, everyone else jumped Mauch, leaving the Phillies pitcher to spectate. It was just as well. The last thing the Phillies needed was for Carlton to get hurt in a bench-clearing brawl.

The lanky lefty was on a roll and gaining momentum as he went into his next start, a Thursday night tilt at home against the Mets on the second to last day in June. The Mets beat him twice in May during the five-game skid. Yogi Berra's team had won three in a row, including a victory over the Phillies the night before, to move into a first-place tie with the Pirates in the National League East. This was Carlton's opportunity for redemption.

It was a cloudy evening in Philadelphia. Thunder showers were in the forecast; in fact, a flash-flood watch was in effect for the Delaware Valley. Exactly what folks in the area could do without. They'd had enough flooding, thanks to Tropical Storm Agnes. Agnes ravaged Pennsylvania and much of the East Coast with flood waters a couple of weeks before. The storm left thousands homeless, and caused millions of dollars worth of property damage.

While the rains held off, the Phillies offense poured it on. They banged out a season-high 17 hits for their ace. Even Carlton got into the act with a pair of singles. His base knock in the fifth drove in two runs and sparked a four-run rally to give the Phils a 6-3 lead.

On the mound, Carlton was uncharacteristically wild. He walked five batters and threw a wild pitch in the first four innings. Was the problem that he was over-throwing? Steve felt he was trying to throw *too* hard, and as a result he wasn't throwing strikes. With the extra exertion he began to tire. But as it happened, that was a good thing. Because he was fatigued, Steve later said, it forced him not to throw as hard. Therefore, in his mind, he was able once again to find the plate. He gave up only one run from the fifth inning on.

Carlton also struck out seven Mets from the fifth inning on, including fanning the side in the eighth. He got Willie Mays for the first out of the ninth, and the last of his 13 Ks on the night. Carlton tossed a career-high 160 pitches in a 13-strikeout performance, going the distance for the 10th time. Think of it: 160 pitches. Starters today rarely throw more than 105 to 115 in a game. The calendar had yet to turn to July, and he had already thrown 10 complete games. In each of the last three seasons, Roy Halladay has led the majors with nine. No pitcher has reached double figures in complete games pitched since 1999. Carlton was now 9-6, and had won four straight.

Written in magic marker on the walls and mirrors throughout the Carltons' home in Missouri during the winter of 1972 was a small, two-digit numeral. That was it—nothing more. The scene must have looked as if it had been pulled from the pages of a psychological thriller. No words, just a simple number. And that number was 25.

On the mirror in the master bedroom: 25. On the mirror in the master bath: 25. In the hallway, living room, family room, and posted on the refrigerator—wherever a visitor would look: 25. The notes were visual reminders to the man of the house of his personal goal for the upcoming season, and that was to win 25 games.

That number was the first thing Steve Carlton saw each morning when he awoke. It was everywhere he looked in the house. He needed to visualize that goal, to fixate on that number. It was the mental gymnastics Carlton felt necessary in order to reach the goal. The 25s around the house were merely part of the process.

This was Carlton's off-season goal, the one he had set for himself after winning 20 games for the Cardinals in 1971. It was still the goal, even after the trade that brought Carlton to one of the weakest teams in baseball. At that point, for whom he pitched mattered little to Steve. The goal would remain the same. But now the mental preparation would have to be altered just a bit.

The Carltons were renting a house in suburban Philadelphia. There would be no scrawling 25 on the mirrors and walls. Steve was afraid the landlord wouldn't appreciate that too much. Still the number was constantly on his mind. It was the last thing he thought about when he closed his eyes at night. It was the first thing he thought about when he opened them in the morning. Even when Carlton shaved, he was thinking about winning 25 games. He'd take the shaving cream in his hand and not only apply it to his face, but also to the bathroom mirror, where he would write "25" in Gillette Foamy.

Never mind winning 25—just to win 20 games would be quite an accomplishment. No Phillies hurler had won 20 since Chris Short did it in 1966. And with this team behind Carlton, it would be an achievement of monumental proportions. At the end of play on July 1st, the 1972 Phillies' won-lost record was already 20 games under .500 at 24-44.

The Phils were in the midst of a whopping 14-day, 17-game home stand, their longest of the season. How times have changed—that stretch included three doubleheaders! The home team had lost four in a row as they opened a three-game series with San Francisco. It was July 3rd, the day before the City of Brotherly Love led the country in celebrating America's 196th birthday. Because of the holiday, a dazzling fireworks display was planned for both nights, the 3rd and 4th, and 43,016 fans turned out, one of the largest crowds in the Vet's short history. They turned out for the fireworks, but they were also wowed by the Phillies' left-handed starter.

The home folks didn't have long to wait to be entertained. The Phillies scored four runs on five hits before the Giants registered their first out. Giants starter Don Carrithers lasted five batters before being replaced by Frank Reberger, who promptly gave up an RBI double to Joe Lis. But Reberger and two other relievers would no-hit the Phillies the rest of the way. Those five hits and four runs, coming before the first out was recorded, were the last the Phillies mustered all night.

But it was plenty of production for Steve Carlton. He went the distance again, giving the Giants two runs on six hits and striking out seven. If it hadn't been for Dave Kingman, Carlton would've pitched a shutout. A pair of Kingman solo homers accounted for both of the Giants' runs, the second of which came with two gone in the ninth. At 10-6, Carlton was halfway to equaling Short.

Then the 43,016 fans settled in to watch the bombs burst in air as the night's sky became a canvas of exploding colors and light. Wide-eyed children watched in amazement, cotton candy stuck to their cheeks, ice cream smeared around their mouths; while adults gazed with youthful exuberance. A chorus of *oohs* and *aahs* cascaded through the stadium. It was believed to be one of the biggest fireworks shows in the country. Skyrockets raining under the stars, with Philadelphia's newest star reigning on the mound.

The slider, Carlton's money pitch, was giving him trouble. For some reason, it wasn't darting. It wasn't diving. It wasn't so daunting. For some reason, it wasn't its usual biting, baffling self. And the San Diego Padres were hitting it all over the yard. These were the same Padres that handed Carlton his first loss as a Phillie. They touched him for four runs that night back in April, and damned if he was going to let that happen again.

The great thing about Steve Carlton, anyone paying attention was quickly finding out, was that even when he didn't have his best stuff, he was still able to find a way to win—no small task when pitching for the last-place Phils. "That guy," manager Frank Lucchesi said afterward to the group of reporters in his office, "is the most competitive guy I've ever been around." He, of course, was talking about Carlton.

Of the nine hits Lefty surrendered to San Diego that night, all but one or two, he guessed, came on his bread-and-butter pitch. No worries. He had enough velocity in that rocket launcher of a left arm to keep the Padres at bay. With fastballs hissing through the warm summer air, Carlton tossed another complete game victory. He added eight strikeouts to his league-leading total of 174. The Phillies won the game, 4-2.

The team had won just three of the ten games they'd played on the current home stand. All three were won by Carlton. It was only the Phillies' seventh win in their last 26 games. Of those seven, five were won by Carlton. The other two were won in relief. The last time a Phillies starter not named Carlton won was on June 8th. No other Phillies starter had notched a victory in a month.

Carlton on phone following news of his trade to the Phillies. His son Steven looks on.
(Associated Press)

General Manager John Quinn. His final trade may have been his best.
(Temple University Libraries, Urban Archives, Philadelphia)

Rick Wise delivers pitch during his no-hitter against Cincinnati. "Two home runs and a no-hitter—it doesn't get better than that." (Associated Press)

The 1972 Philadelphia Phillies. It was about Carlton, and only Carlton. (Philadelphia Phillies)

Carlton in his first start at the Vet as a Phillie. It took him only one hour and 33 minutes to beat his ex-teammates. (Temple University Libraries, Urban Archives, Philadelphia)

Larry Bowa: "To this day, I have never seen a look like Carlton had that season." (Philadelphia Phillies)

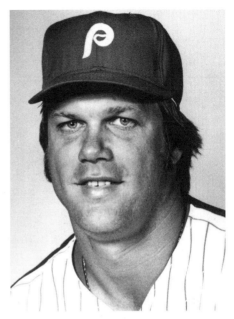

Greg "The Bull" Luzinski. His 18 home runs led the team. (Philadelphia Phillies)

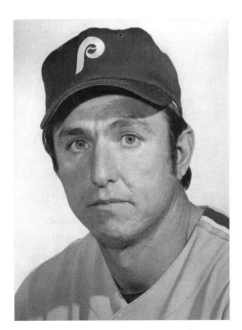

John Bateman, Lefty's battery mate for the majority of the 27 wins. (Philadelphia Phillies)

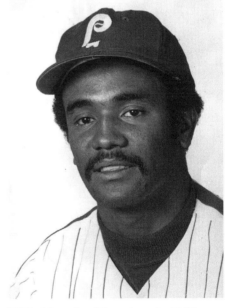

Willie Montañez. His trade to the Phillies completed the Curt Flood deal. (Philadelphia Phillies)

Don Money (left) tosses the ball to Carlton (second from right) following Steve's one-hitter in San Francisco. Tim McCarver (6) and Larry Bowa offer congratulations. (Associated Press)

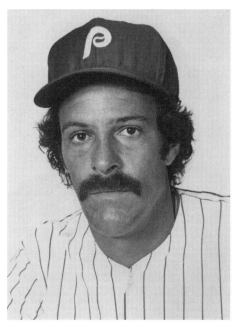

Terry Harmon. He picked the wrong year to become the player representative. (Philadelphia Phillies)

Ken Reynolds. This left-handed pitcher also had a streak in the '72 season—the wrong kind. (Philadelphia Phillies)

The always emotional "Skipper" Frank Lucchesi. (Courtesy of Rich Westcott)

Tommy Hutton. If only he could've faced Tom Seaver every night.
(Temple University Libraries, Urban Archives, Philadelphia)

Denny Doyle, one of the few players to get a raise out of J.Q. (Philadelphia Phillies)

Darrell Brandon, number 30 in your program. (Philadelphia Phillies)

Paul Owens (left) announcing that he was replacing Frank Lucchesi as manager. Lucchesi wept at the press conference.
(Temple University Libraries, Urban Archives, Philadelphia)

Carlton surrounded by reporters after a game. He was still talking to the media in those days.
(Courtesy of Rich Westcott)

Carlton waves to the crowd following his 20th victory—the 15th in a row. (Courtesy of Rich Westcott)

Super Steve gives a speech on "Steve Carlton Night" at the Vet, September 15, 1972. In the background are his wife, Beverly, and Paul Owens. (Temple University Libraries, Urban Archives, Philadelphia)

For his performance in '72, Carlton was rewarded by Owens with what was at that time the richest contract ever signed by a pitcher. (Courtesy of Rich Westcott)

CHAPTER 11

Ten in a Row
and Counting...

Greg Luzinski bounded into the Phillies clubhouse in the basement of the Vet. It was late in the morning on Monday, July 10th. Luzinski had been at a public appearance, and while it was still a few hours until that night's twilight doubleheader with the Dodgers, he decided to go straight to the ballpark. The young left fielder was the first player to arrive. He walked down the short corridor that led from the front doors to the main clubhouse area. Lining the walls to the right and left were the players' locker stalls. A small kitchen where the players ate after games was to the immediate left. The manager's office was the first door on the right, visible as soon as one turned the corner from the hallway. It was across the clubhouse from a door which led to the trainer's room and to the showers.

Luzinski headed toward the trainer's room, and as he passed the manager's office, he could hear sobbing coming from inside. "The Bull" poked his head in the office. There was manager Frank Lucchesi, seated at his desk with his head in his hands. He was crying.

"What's wrong, Skip?"

"I got fired," replied Lucchesi.

It didn't exactly come as a shock to Luzinski. The Phils' record was an abysmal 26-50, including that pathetic stretch in which they'd lost 19 of 20. On the nights that Carlton wasn't pitching they were nothing more than a glorified triple-A team. "No one likes to see that happen," Luzinski says. "But it was a reflection of what was happening on the field, and [Lucchesi] took the blame." Also receiving a pink slip was third base coach George Myatt. The next day, Myatt was seen loading a case of beer and his golf clubs into the back of his car. He and his wife decided to hit the road for a long vacation.

A press conference soon followed on that fateful morning for Lucchesi. There it was announced that newly appointed general manager Paul Owens would be replacing him. Owens would come down from the front office, put on a uniform, and manage the club's on-field fortunes. Or misfortunes, as it were. Owens was now the manager and general manager. Apparently, the idea to take over the field managing duties was his. Owens wanted to see firsthand what kind of players he had on his roster—who were the "keepers" and who were not—as he engaged in the daunting task of rebuilding the franchise.

"I was just a young guy trying to plod through my rookie season," says Tommy Hutton. "But I remember knowing the whole essence of Paul Owens taking over as manager was to assess the team." The principal was taking over the classroom and that jarring bit of reality was enough to garner the students' attention. "As soon as Owens came down," says Larry Bowa, "you knew he was evaluating. We were basically playing for our lives."

Bowa, more than anyone, had benefited from Lucchesi's tutelage. The Skipper had managed him in the minors and was one of the shortstop's biggest supporters in the organization. "Lucchesi was good with young kids," says Bowa. "But after a while he was in a tough situation. We had a good farm system, but I guess we didn't develop as fast as they thought we would."

Lucchesi cried at the press conference, too. Still he and everyone else who had been watching had to have sensed for weeks that he was a dead man walking. In fact, the previous Saturday night, a reporter from the *Inquirer* called Lucchesi and told him that the paper had learned from reliable sources that the Skipper was about to get the ax. Lucchesi didn't believe him. The next day, in a previously scheduled meeting, Lucchesi asked Owens point-blank if a change was on the way. Lucchesi claims that the GM told him that there wasn't. But 24 hours later, the Skipper was out.

At the press conference he offered no excuses to the assembled media. "I have to take some blame for this," said the fired manager. "I tried everything I possibly could with every young player that came through the farm system. Not once did I go to Bob Carpenter or John Quinn and say, 'I can't do it with these kids, you have to get me some ballplayers.' Not once."

Lucchesi survived to manage again, taking over at the helm of the Texas Rangers in 1975. In March 1977, Skipper Lucchesi was involved in as ugly an incident as there ever was between a player and a manager. Rangers second baseman Lenny Randle, upset that he had lost his starting job, attacked Lucchesi prior to a spring training game. Randle punched him in the face, and the blow was so severe that it fractured Lucchesi's cheekbone in three places. Frank spent a week in the hospital recovering. Reconstructive surgery was required to repair his cheekbone. He returned in time for the season opener, but didn't last through the year. In June, with the club 31-31, Lucchesi was fired. As for Randle, he was suspended by the Rangers for 30 days and fined $10,000. The team traded him soon after.

And so began the Paul Owens era as Phillies manager. It wouldn't be the only mid-season dugout stop that the Pope would make. In 1983, with the Phillies in first place but in his opinion underachieving, Owens fired Pat Corrales and again assumed the managerial role. That stint at the helm was much smoother. The Phillies made it to the World Series. This time they would not.

The following night, Owens scrawled "Steve Carlton, P" for the first time in the number nine slot on the lineup card. Carlton's first start with Owens in the dugout came against Don Sutton and the Dodgers, another pitching matchup of future Hall of Famers. The Phillies put four runs on the board in the second inning—a Don Money three-run double being the highlight. The four-run second was all of their offense for the evening. Carlton, in fact, chipped in with a two-out single that extended the rally. On the mound, Lefty was turning in the kind of effort that was becoming business as usual. He went the distance, scattered five hits, struck out eight and did not walk a single batter. The only Dodger run came in the eighth when Carlton uncorked a wild pitch, allowing a runner on third to score. There was no further damage in the eighth, thanks to a running, one-handed catch by Willie Montañez on a long fly ball hit by the Dodgers' Wes Parker. Instead of winning in shutout fashion, the Phillies settled for the 4-1 victory. It was Carlton's seventh straight, and his record was now 12-6. People were beginning to notice. In bold print above the box score in the next day's *Bulletin* it read, "7 in a Row for Steve."

"I'll tell you a great Lefty story," begins Terry Harmon. "We were in San Francisco that year..." It is one of those stories that cuts to the heart not only of Carlton's competitive nature, but of his sense of baseball etiquette and sportsmanship.

After completing the three-day set with the Dodgers, the Phils jetted to San Fran and another West Coast road trip. That Friday night they opened a weekend series with the Giants: Ken Reynolds facing Juan Marichal. Bobby Bonds hit leadoff for the Giants on this particular evening, followed in the order by rookie center fielder Garry Maddox. Facing starter Ken Reynolds, Bonds lined a sharply hit single to center, a routine play for a center fielder. Only Willie Montañez was a bit lackadaisical in his attempt to retrieve the ball. He didn't quite reach down far enough for it. The ball rolled through his legs! And then it rolled all the way to the wall. Meanwhile Bonds was motoring around the bases, he would touch them all. Officially, it was scored a single and a three-base error on Montañez, but the Giants had the game's first run on a blooper reel-like highlight and some speedy base running. When Bonds reached home plate, Maddox, the on-deck hitter, was waiting for him. Bonds and Maddox began celebrating, but they didn't just slap hands or high-five. They practically danced the Funky Chicken.

"They did this little showboat thing at home plate," as Harmon continues the story. "The two of them did this little dance, you know, their way of celebrating the play."

As he watched this display from the Phillies dugout, Steve Carlton began to stew. The cords of his neck stiffened. His face began to turn beet-red with anger. It was just the type of showmanship the Phillies starter considered bush league. Carlton felt it disrespectful, not only to him and his teammates, but to baseball itself. Remember, Lefty was raised in the game by the Cardinals organization. And the Cardinals always placed a heavy importance on playing the game in a professional manner. To Carlton, the Cardinals were the standard; a winning franchise that played baseball the right way—the way it was supposed to be played. To play any other way was to disrespect the game.

In the seventh inning, Bonds homered off young relief pitcher Mac Scarce. And again he celebrated with Maddox by doing their "little showboat thing." Silently, Carlton continued to fume.

"So the next night Carlton's pitching," Harmon goes on. "And once again, Bonds leads off." And once again, Bonds would touch them all. Leading off against Carlton, he smashed one out of the park. Bonds then took his home run trot around the bases, eventually reaching home plate. As was the case the night before, Garry is the next Giants hitter, and is waiting for Bobby at the plate. Same thing happens. The veteran Bonds and the rookie Maddox go into their celebratory dance thing. First they slapped hands. Then they locked thumbs. They bumped elbows. They went through an entire choreographed routine.

"They do the elbows, they do the arms, they do the wrists, the backs," Harmon recalls. "They went through about 18 different things."

As Bruce Keidan wrote in the *Inquirer*: "Maddox and Bonds…played patty-cake in a 20-second version of the Black Power salute."

Once again, Carlton stewed. But this time he was on the mound, and he intended to do something about the Giants' dancing duo. Maddox was the unfortunate recipient of Carlton's ire. "The next pitch was at his head,"

Harmon remembers. Message sent and received. Carlton then struck him out.

"Maddox says it's the most scared he's ever been," Chris Wheeler reports. "The ball was right at his ear." The intimidating Carlton stood on the mound and glared at the rookie. It was his way of saying, "You know what that was for. Go back to the dugout and tell Bonds, and don't ever do that stuff again."

And that's exactly what happened. "The next time we saw Maddox," Harmon recalls, "he said he didn't think he'd be doing that again."

Carlton achieved the desired effect with his pitch to Maddox, but that game with the Giants was one of his tougher starts of the season. He lasted only five innings, his second earliest exit of the year. He gave up four runs on five hits, struck out five and walked one. Bonds' leadoff homer, the one that touched off the incident, wasn't the only home run surrendered by Carlton. He also gave up an inside-the-park homer to Chris Speier, the man who got the only hit in Carlton's April one-hitter. Carlton left the ballgame with the Phillies trailing 4-0. But his winning streak did not end there. Remarkably, the Phillies roared back with an 11-run seventh inning—*11 runs!* In the words of Richie Ashburn, "Hard to believe, Harry." And they scored those 11 runs without benefit of a long ball. Usually in a double-digit inning one expects a grand slam to be involved. Not in this one; in fact, there wasn't even a solo home run. Giants pitchers walked in two runs. They allowed another on a wild pitch. The Phillies scored on a suicide squeeze. They hit one RBI single and two sacrifice flies. Their big blows were a two-run double and a two-run triple. The top of the seventh took 45 minutes. The Phils sent 15 batters to the plate. The Giants sent five different pitchers to the mound, tying a major league record. Luzinski walked twice in the inning, which also tied a big league record. The Phillies scored the 11 runs on six hits and won the game, 11-4. Bucky Brandon earned the win in relief, while Carlton was left with a no-decision. That, of course, is much better than a loss, and it kept his winning streak alive.

The weekend series with the Giants was the Phillies' last in San Francisco that year. And that was probably a relief to the folks who ran the team's hotel. This Phillies team was one that liked to have a good time, especially on the road. Carlton was one of the Phillies who was known to enjoy a night out, and he had been in the middle of many a night's postgame highjinks. The team hotel in San Francisco was the site of a notable night of imbibing that got a tad out of control, and Lefty was at the center of the extracurricular activity.

In addition to Carlton, John Bateman and Deron Johnson were among the usual cast of characters. In fact, Bateman and Carlton were roommates on the road, and had become fast friends since the trade that brought the catcher to the Phillies. They would go out drinking and partying on a fairly regular basis, although Carlton did not go out on the nights before he pitched. That was one rule on which he never wavered. One night in San Francisco, the party continued back at the team hotel. The boys convened at the room shared by Carlton and Bateman. Many more beers were consumed. Much carrying-on and some rough-housing followed. Maybe even a little vandalism, depending on your definition of vandalism or your definition of little. At any rate, the boys had a wild time.

The next morning the Phillies' traveling secretary, Eddie Ferenz, got a call from his contact at the hotel.

"Eddie, we have a problem."

"Oh no," said Ferenz. He knew this bunch could get crazy, and he could only imagine what the problem might be.

"What is it?" Ferenz asked.

"Well, there is some furniture in the trees outside, and it's our furniture, it's hotel furniture. We think some of your players might be involved."

Somehow the furniture from the room wound up in the tree outside the window. There was a table, a chair, and something that might once have been a lamp. It seemed the boys got a little rambunctious and tossed a few items out the window. How those items managed to land in the tree limbs and remain lodged there is still a mystery. There also may have been some damage to the room. Nothing too serious, depending on your definition of serious or your definition of nothing. The next day the players apologized and paid for the damages. No harm, no foul; the hotel management was satisfied. That was one thing about this group—crazy though they may have been, whenever their mischief caused damage, they always apologized and paid for the necessary repairs.

Like the time in Pittsburgh when Lefty did some late-night indoor golfing. After a few beers, he retires to his hotel room. Not quite ready to go to sleep, he decides it's a good time to get in some work on his short game. So Carlton goes out in the hallway with his golf clubs and a few golf balls, and starts putting balls down the carpeted corridor. After a few minutes of this, he discards the putter and picks up the wedge and begins to hit wedge shots. The target at which he's lofting these wedge shots is an opulent glass chandelier at the end of the hallway. Unfortunately for the hotel, quite a few of Lefty's pitches were right on target.

The next morning the phone rings in Eddie Ferenz's room. Poor Eddie, he was always putting out these brush fires. Eddie listened patiently as the hotel manager rattled off the list of damages. He hung up and dialed Ruly Carpenter.

"Mr. Carpenter," said Eddie, "we've got a little problem. It appears that Steve Carlton was hitting golf balls in the hallway last night and damaged a chandelier."

"Well, pay for the damages, and then we'll just take it out of his pay," Carpenter responded.

"Do you mind if I call a team meeting before tonight's game," the traveling secretary asked.

"No, go ahead, as long as you clear it with the manager first," said Carpenter.

So Ferenz called a players meeting that evening in the clubhouse. He gathered everyone around and called Steve up in front of the group. Steve had no idea what was going on, but since it was Eddie, and he loved Eddie, the pitcher obliged. Eddie handed him an envelope.

"What's this," Carlton asked Ferenz.

"Those are the greens fees from last night," Eddie replied. The other players, who had heard about what happened the night before, roared with laughter.

From San Francisco, it was on to San Diego. Following an off-day Monday, two games with the Padres were on tap. Carlton was scheduled to pitch the second game. The Phillies didn't leave their hearts in San Francisco, they left their bats. Because in the opener, they were nearly held hitless for the second time in the season. If the Phillies were the worst team in the league, San Diego was not too far behind them. Both clubs were in the basement of their respective divisions. The Phillies were 24 games out of first place in the East, while the Padres were 20 games back in the West. But in game one, Padres starter Steve Arlin pitched like an All-Star throwing for a pennant contender.

Arlin originally signed with the Phillies in 1966, but they left him unprotected in the '68 expansion draft, and the Padres selected him. The six-foot, three-inch right-hander was 26 years old in 1972, and was in his second full season in the big leagues. The season before, he totaled a league-leading 19 losses. He was headed for a 10-21 season in '72, and would once again lead the league in losses.

Steve Arlin was considered the Padres' ace. But the last thing manager Don Zimmer wanted his young club to see was Arlin get beat by Carlton. Zimmer thought it would be too demoralizing. Never mind the fact that it was Arlin who handed Steve his first loss as a Phillie way back in April. Zim moved Arlin up a day in the Padres' rotation so the young righty wouldn't have to match up with the veteran lefty. Zimmer told reporters it was because he thought Arlin had a chance to make the All-Star team, and by moving him up one day, he could be available to pitch in the

Mid-Summer Classic scheduled for the following Tuesday in Atlanta. Mind you, Arlin was 7-10 at the time.

The National League squad was announced later that day by Danny Murtaugh, who was coming out of retirement to manage the NL Stars, and Arlin's name was not on the list. Carlton, who was leading the majors in strikeouts, was named to the team. He was the Phillies' lone representative.

That night, Arlin certainly pitched like he was All-Star-worthy. He took a no-hitter into the ninth, the Padres leading 5-0. Deron Johnson pinch-hit for pitcher Wayne Twitchell to lead off for the Phillies. He lined to third for the first out. Bowa then popped out to second. Arlin was one out away. Denny Doyle was the next batter. Arlin ran the count to one and two. He was one strike away from a no-hitter. But on the next pitch, Doyle, who was batting left-handed, hit a grounder that took a big hop and bounced over third baseman Dave Roberts' head into left for a single. Bye-bye no-no.

It was Don Zimmer's fault, and he took the blame afterward. Zimmer thought Doyle was a pull-hitter, and he didn't want a swinging-bunt single to spoil the no-hit bid. So Zimmer had Roberts play in on the infield grass, despite the fact that there were two strikes on Doyle. Playing in was the last thing Roberts should have been doing in that situation. Looking back all these years later, Arlin remarked: "I jammed Doyle and he hit it straight into the ground. The ball landed right where Roberts would have been standing if he were playing in his normal position."

Arlin then lost his composure. He balked Denny Doyle to second. Tommy Hutton followed with a base hit up the middle, scoring Doyle and spoiling the shutout. The Padres still won, 5-1, but Arlin had to settle for a two-hitter—a bitter pill considering he was one pitch away from a no-hitter. After the game, his manager came up to him in the clubhouse holding a razor blade. "I'm sorry, I blew it," Zimmer said. "Cut my neck. Here's a razor blade."

The Phillies avoided the dubious distinction of being no-hit again, and now they had their ace going the next night in game two of the two-game set. Twelve days earlier, Steve had tossed a complete game win over the Padres at the Vet, evening his record against them this season to one and one. Now here he was again, and going for his eighth win in a row. The Padres were countering with Clay Kirby, whose record was a mere 6-9.

The right-handed Kirby was 24 years old and was three seasons removed from a 20-loss season. In an eight-year career, the native of Washington, D.C. compiled a record of 75-104, with a 3.84 ERA. The highlight of his career came in 1975, when he helped the Reds win the World Series, but tragically, he would live just 16 more years. In 1991, Kirby died of a heart attack at the age of 43. On this July night in 1972, he was about to lock horns with Steve Carlton in a memorable ballgame.

Both pitchers started slowly. The Phillies put a two-spot on the board off Kirby in the top of the first. Bowa and Doyle, batting one and two, both singled to give the Phillies runners on first and third. A Hutton groundout scored Bowa, and just like that it was 1-0, Phils. With two outs, Hutton stole second. Montañez then knocked him in with a base hit, giving the Phillies the second run.

The Padres got one of the runs back off Carlton in the bottom half. Like Kirby, Carlton gave up consecutive singles to the first two batters he faced. The Padres plated their first run when Nate Colbert (who would hit 38 home runs and drive in 111 that season, finishing in the top 10 in the MVP balloting) then hit into a double play. The Padres tied the game with one out in the second on an RBI triple to left center by, of all people, shortstop Enzo Hernandez.

Hernandez was a lifetime .224 hitter. The run was one of only 15 that Enzo knocked in that season in 329 at-bats. The year before, his rookie season, he had 618 plate appearances and 12 RBI! Joe Lis was in left, in place of Luzinski, and was playing him shallow. Hernandez burned him. So the game was tied at two, and it stayed that way inning after inning after inning.

Since giving up the solitary runs in each of the first two innings, Carlton was his dominant self. Kirby, after giving up the two-run first, managed to keep the Phillies at bay. Both pitchers set down the next six batters. In the fifth, the Phillies put together a mild threat. John Bateman started the frame with a single and then moved to second on a Carlton sac bunt. The lead-footed Bateman managed to make it to third on a Bowa groundout to second. But the catcher was stranded 90 feet away when Kirby also induced Doyle to ground to second, ending the threat.

Same thing in the sixth. Hutton leads off with a single, eventually makes his way to third as the Phillies this time load the bases with two outs. But again they failed to score when Kirby got Bateman to ground out.

We did mention that Carlton was his dominant self. How's this for dominant: from the third inning through the fifth inning, he retired every batter he faced. Nine in a row. In the Padres' half of the sixth, second baseman Derrel Thomas cracks a leadoff single. How does Carlton respond? He picks him off first base. Now Carlton did not have a great pick-off move. In fact, he still holds the career record for most balks. But he got Thomas at first base, and the next two Padre hitters to end the sixth.

We move to the seventh, tied at two. We move to the eighth, tied at two.

Carlton mows them down in order again, and we move to the ninth, still tied at two. Lefty was the first batter of the ninth inning and Kirby, who was still in the game, wasted no time in whiffing him. That brought up the top of the order with Bowa, who grounded out. Now Kirby has two outs, but Doyle singles and Hutton walks. Bill Robinson bats next. He entered the game in the eighth inning as a defensive replacement for Lis in left field. Robinson was 29 years old and in his fifth big league season, and he would have a long and varied career in the game. He played 16 seasons, mostly with Pittsburgh, including 1979 when the "We Are Family" Pirates won the World Series.

Robinson enjoyed his best year in '77, when he hit .304 with 26 homers and 104 RBI. The right-handed hitter had a second tour of duty with the Phillies in the early '80s, and at age 40, he was a member of the "Wheeze Kids" of 1983. He played in just 10 games that season, the last of his career. The Pennsylvania native went on to become the hitting coach for the 1986 Mets and the 2003 Marlins, both of whom won the World Series, and also spent a couple of years as an analyst for ESPN.

In 2007, Bill Robinson was working for the Dodgers as their minor league hitting coordinator. On a trip to Las Vegas to work with the club's triple-A team, he was found dead in his hotel room. While Robinson suffered from diabetes, the cause of his death remains unknown. He was 64.

With two outs and two on, Robinson stroked a single off Kirby to load the bases. The Phillies had a great chance to break the tie, with Montañez coming to the plate. But the Phils center fielder hit a fly ball to left that was caught, and Kirby escaped the jam. The Padres couldn't touch Carlton in their half, going down in order again, and the game was headed for extra innings. On to the 10th they went.

Kirby came back out, the adrenaline rush of the moment masking any fatigue. He'd face the six, seven, and eight hitters. Oscar Gamble led off and popped out to first. Don Money reached on an error, and that brought up Bateman, who flied to right. Carlton was up, but the thought of lifting him for a pinch-hitter never crossed Paul Owens' mind. He wasn't about to go to his bullpen, not the way Lefty was throwing, 10th inning or not. Carlton popped to the second baseman. Kirby was through 10, not allowing a run since the first inning.

The Padres were in a position to win; push across a run and the game would be over. But that was easier said than done against Carlton. The Phillies star quickly got the first two batters out. Padres catcher Fred Kendall then stepped to the plate. Kendall was a 12-year big leaguer and is the "padre" of Jason Kendall, who has played for five teams in a 15-year major league career. Carlton had not allowed a single Padre to reach second base since Hernandez's triple back in the second inning. That, however, changed on the next swing. Kendall roped a double.

The winning run was in scoring position. Owens instructed Carlton to intentionally walk Hernandez, who was up next, setting up a force play at each base. The pitcher was due up with two out. Wasn't this a no-brainer, "by-the-book," pinch-hit situation? And yet Zimmer let his pitcher Kirby bat. How is that possible? In today's game there is no way a manager would let the pitcher bat with the winning run on second. Even the number eight hitter probably would have been pinch-hit for. Presumably, the San Diego bullpen was rested, since it wasn't needed the night before in Arlin's near no-hitter. Much like Owens, Zimmer felt he also couldn't afford to lift his starter, given the way he was throwing. But Kirby batted with a chance to win it. By the way, he hit .068 for the year. Predictably, Kirby made the final out. On to the 11th, still tied.

The Phillies had been shut out by Clay Kirby for the past nine innings. If they were ever going to break through, now was the time. Bowa led off, lining out to center. One away. Doyle, who broke up the no-hitter the previous night, was the next hitter. Already with two hits in the game, the Phils' second baseman wasn't done. He whacked his third single of the night and was aboard as the potential go-ahead run. After a Tommy Hutton fly out to right, Bill Robinson came to bat. Two outs, runner on first, the game tied in the 11th. A righty vs. righty matchup. Robinson took the offering from Kirby and drilled it the opposite way, into the gap in right-center at spacious San Diego Stadium (later named Jack Murphy Stadium and now known as Qualcomm Stadium). Doyle flew around the bases and scored easily. There was no play at the plate. The Phillies were in front, 3-2. Said Robinson in the next day's *Evening Bulletin*, "I was just trying to get some good wood on it."

Every Phillie now expected to win the game. With Carlton at his best, there was no way they were relinquishing this precarious one-run lead. And make no mistake, Lefty was coming back to pitch the 11th. Though completely out of character for Carlton, he walked the first batter. He put the tying run on base with a leadoff walk. Unbelievable. Was he beginning to tire? It was, after all, the 11th inning, and he had pitched every single one. A sacrifice bunt put the runner on second. But the inning was now shortened by an out. Carlton got the next guy, Jerry Morales, to fly to right. Two away. The Padres best player, the always dangerous Colbert, followed. Colbert had his troubles hitting Carlton in his career, batting just .208 versus Lefty, but the Phillies did not want to tempt fate by pitching to him. Colbert was intentionally walked. First and second, two away, Phils up by a run. Up to the plate came Cito Gaston.

Gaston played 11 major league seasons, and wasn't much more than an average hitter. He batted .256 for his career, and he never hit Carlton particularly well either—just 11 for 59, lifetime. Gaston went on to be a much better manager, and as such some 21 years later, he played a role in a bitter chapter of Phillies lore. It was Gaston's '93 Blue Jays who beat the Phils in the World Series, one of the most heartbreaking losses in Philadelphia sports history—a history, incidentally, filled with more than its share of heartbreak.

But the heartbreak was on hold for the Phillies and their fans on this night. Gaston, like Morales, flied out to right. Ballgame over: 3-2 Phillies, the final in 11. Carlton had extended his winning streak to eight games, and his record was now 13 and 6. Both pitchers went the distance in an 11-inning game. Imagine that happening today. Carlton surrendered seven hits over those 11 innings, but only three in the final nine. He walked four and struck out eight. Carlton retired the side in order in the third, fourth, and fifth innings. In another stretch, beginning in the sixth and extending through the ninth, he retired 11 of 12. He did not allow a run over the final nine innings.

Kirby, whose record fell to 6-10, pitched 9 scoreless innings. He gave the Phillies two in the first and no more until the 11th—an amazing feat. It was the kind of game one would never see today: an 11-inning affair in which both teams combined to use just two pitchers. Imagine the number of moves that would be used in a game of that sort played in today's National League.

How many times would the managers summon a reliever from the bullpen? How many pitchers would be used for situational purposes, such as a lefty to pitch to a lefty? How many pinch-hitters would be used to counter those moves? There was only one pinch-hitter used in this one. The Phillies pinch-hit Oscar Gamble for right fielder Roger Freed in the eighth, and that was it. Today they'd be double-switching to death. The lineup cards for a similar game today would be undecipherable. The managers would run out of room on their cards to jot all the notations needed. This was a throwback game. The starters pitched until the game was won or lost. And here's another aspect of the game one would never see today: to play those 11 innings, it took the Phillies and Padres just two hours and 36 minutes. That's roughly a half-hour less, give or take a few minutes, than it takes to complete a nine-inning game nowadays.

Carlton's winning streak, now at eight, was becoming something of a sensation back home. It seemed almost incomprehensible to most that one pitcher on this rag-tag club could win with such regularity, while everyone else on the staff was struggling so mightily. Carlton was becoming an aberration. And how on earth was he able to win like this with such a bad group playing behind him? "At this point," remembers *Daily News* columnist Stan Hochman, "we thought that this guy was doing something remarkable with the team he had around him." Carlton was also keeping the two-man public relations staff of Larry Shenk and Chris Wheeler very busy. With the winning streak now reaching significant proportions, Shenk and Wheeler were left to determine where it ranked in Phillies history. The job wasn't exactly easy. The resources were much different in 1972 than they are today. The PR staff was forced to do it all by hand, and it was long and tedious work. Carlton had them scurrying for the club's dusty record books, looking up who might have won this many games in a row, who might have had that many games of double-digit strikeouts, who had allowed as few runs—all of the relative and pertinent minutiae. "We spent hours going through stuff," Shenk recalls. They did not have the luxury of computer data and specialized websites at their fingertips; instead they went leafing through old scorebooks and old box scores. "You know," says Wheeler, "you didn't have the stuff you have today. You had to go back into the records, and the records weren't very good and didn't go back very far, maybe to the '50s, that was it. We were stuck trying to find out what Robin Roberts had done." What they couldn't determine from club records they'd seek from the memory banks of longtime Phillies onlookers. "We'd ask some baseball historians, they were a big help," Shenk remembers.

The Hall of Famer Robin Roberts was the frame of reference. He was the franchise's greatest pitcher, and now here was Carlton, who had fast become the closest thing Philadelphia had seen to the great "Robbie." At least that's how Shenk and Wheeler felt. On one of those late nights following yet another Carlton victory that summer, as they poured through old box scores to find the last time someone had done what Carlton had done, the PR duo stopped what they were doing and just looked at one another in amazement: "I remember Larry and me looking at each other, and saying this is without a doubt the greatest pitcher this organization has seen since Robin Roberts."

Everyone in Philadelphia was getting excited, except for the man himself. Carlton did not see his string of victories as anything special, and he did not get caught up in the hoopla. Cliché though it may be, Carlton really did take things one game at a time. As Phillies author Rich Westcott explains, "I don't think he got overly excited about it. He got ready for each game as [it] came along. When one game was over, he got ready for the next one." The next one was in Los Angeles on a Sunday afternoon. It was get-away day for the All-Star Break, the final game before baseball took its three-day hiatus for the All-Star Game. Carlton's opposite number for this game was left-hander Tommy John. Yes, Tommy John is an actual, living, breathing person, and not just a surgical procedure. He may be better known these days for the elbow operation that bears his name, but John was an outstanding pitcher in the 1970s and '80s.

In 1974, John was enjoying a 13-3 season with the Dodgers when he seriously injured a ligament in his pitching elbow; the left ulnar collateral ligament to be exact. The 31-year-old John's career appeared to be finished, for it was highly unlikely that he would ever be able to throw a major league fastball again. But the Dodgers' team doctor, Dr. Frank Jobe, came up with a revolutionary idea. Jobe would replace the damaged ligament in John's left elbow with a tendon from his right forearm. It was an idea that seemed straight out of science fiction—reconstructing a ligament with a tendon. Jobe's cutting-edge surgery was successful, and John spent the entire '75 season recovering and rehabilitating. What was at first considered a career-ending injury turned out to be nothing of the sort. John was back pitching in the big leagues the following season and won 10 games. In 1977, he won 20. He was a 20-game winner twice more in a career that spanned 26 seasons. In fact, Tommy John pitched until 1989, when he was 46 years old, winning 164 games after the surgery. That happens to be one less victory than Sandy Koufax earned in his entire career. Koufax, whose own arm problems cut short his brilliant career, might have benefited greatly had the Tommy John procedure been available in his day. The surgery is so effective that it is now performed routinely, and still goes by the name of the man whose elbow was the first to be treated with that dose of medical magic.

The pre-surgery John, degenerative ulnar collateral ligament notwithstanding, tossed six shutout innings against the lowly Phils. But so, of course, did Carlton. For Lefty was reaching another realm. He was so on top of his game it was becoming scary. He was like an automaton, programmed to get batters out. Focus, visualize, block out distractions, see the target, throw to the target. Carlton's elevated game was lifting his teammates as well. Somehow when he pitched they became a different ball club. "As bad as that team was," says Frank Bilovsky, the former *Bulletin* sportswriter, "they played so much better when he was pitching." Carlton had a knack for elevating the rest of them. It may have been his will. It may have been the force of his personality. It was not a coincidence. "He almost willed us to play better defense," says shortstop Larry Bowa. "You didn't want to mess up when he was pitching. You didn't want to mess up any time, but you were really on your toes when he was pitching." Clearly, when Carlton pitched, they played harder, sharper, and with more intensity.

Some of it was the players' relief in knowing that they didn't have to score a ton of runs to have a chance to win behind Carlton. Steve wasn't going to give up many, so all they had to do was score one or two, and that would be all it might take to win. If the Phillies scored five runs for other pitchers on the staff, they might lose the game six to five. If they scored six, they might lose it seven to six. And they had a confidence in their ace that made them feel that every time he went out there, they were going to win. "We just had a different attitude," Bowa recalls.

Bowa has made a living at the game for nearly his entire adult life. He's played, he's coached and he's managed. He's seen literally thousands of games. But he has yet to see again what he saw that season from Carlton. "As a coach or manager you know your players have a different look when your ace is pitching," he says. "But to this day I have never seen a look or a feel like when Carlton pitched that year. He took it to another level, and he took people with him to another level."

Carlton's elevated level against the Dodgers extended to the batter's box. Both he and Tommy John were pitching shutouts through six innings. In the top of the seventh, Greg Luzinski stroked a single to start things off. He was then replaced by Bill Robinson, who would pinch-run and then go to left field as a defensive replacement. Willie Montañez then bunted with the intention of sacrificing Robinson to second. But the bunt was toward the mound and John, fielding it, opted to try and get the lead runner. His throw to second was not in time. Both runners were safe. That brought up Roger Freed, whom John struck out. John Bateman was next. Before the game, the catcher expected a victory. He predicted to reporters that the Phillies would score two runs, and that that would be enough for Steve. With the two potential runs now staring at the big Texan from the base paths, Bateman also struck out. The Phillies now had two men on with two out, and the pitcher coming to the plate. Much like in the San Diego game, there was no way Carlton was coming out—he was the Phillies' best chance to win, even if it meant squandering an opportunity to score two runs. But not to worry. On John's very first pitch to him, Carlton lofted a fly ball to right field. At first, it appeared as though it was a routine play for Dodger right fielder Frank Robinson. But the ball kept carrying, and Frank kept retreating. And then, all of a sudden, he ran out of room. The ball struck the fence just beyond Robinson's reach.

The Phillies' Bill Robinson scored. Willie Montañez scored. Carlton was at third base with a two-out triple. It was 2-0, Phillies. It was the only triple of the season for Carlton, who batted a respectable .197. (Respectable, that is, for a pitcher.) The two runs it knocked in represented one quarter of his RBI total for the year.

Back on the mound, Carlton fanned two of the three Dodgers he faced in the seventh, including Steve Garvey, who became his 200th strikeout victim of the season. He then surrendered nothing in the eighth, and retired the side in order to cap the ninth. The Phillies and Carlton won it 2-0, with all of the offense supplied by the winning pitcher. Bateman was right about the two runs, but as it turned out all Carlton needed was one. He was, indeed, doing it all.

The winning streak was now at nine, which tied the Phillies record held by Grover Cleveland Alexander, Ken Heintzelman, and Robin Roberts. Carlton's pitching line that day went like this: nine innings, five hits, no runs, one walk, and six strikeouts. The winning streak wasn't the only string he was putting together. Carlton had also thrown 18 consecutive scoreless innings. And he had pitched nine complete games in a row. Not a bad way to head for the All-Star Game.

It mattered not to Carlton that he had tossed nine innings two days ago; he had every intention of pitching in the Mid-Summer Classic if needed. This was Carlton's fourth All-Star Game, and it was being held at Atlanta-Fulton County Stadium, the home of the Braves. The stadium's nickname was the "Launching Pad," because home runs were a frequent occurrence in the multi-purpose venue the Braves shared with the NFL's Atlanta Falcons.

Hometown hero Hank Aaron was the only Brave to make the National League squad. "Hammerin' Hank" went into the All-Star Break with 659 career home runs, and was about 20 months removed from becoming the game's all-time home run king. Aaron would eclipse Babe Ruth's mark of 714 in Atlanta on April 8, 1974, but for now the record chase was on hold. The focus in Atlanta on this night was the All-Star Game, and the hope that Henry might give the crowd of 53,107 a thrill to remember. He did not disappoint. In the sixth inning, with Houston's César Cedeño on second, Aaron took Cleveland's Gaylord Perry deep. It was a lineshot that soared over the fence in left center for a two-run homer. It was only the second All-Star Game home run of his career, and the last, and it gave the NL a 2-1 lead. It was exactly what the fans had come to see, and they gave Aaron a standing ovation that lasted for two minutes. Afterward it was Aaron, the man whose HR record stood for 34 years, who called hitting that All-Star home run the greatest thing that ever happened to him.

A half-inning prior to the Hammer's homer, Carlton made his only appearance of the night. Facing Carlton were the Twins' Rod Carew (who that season was headed for the second of his eight batting titles), Yankee center fielder Bobby Murcer, and A's superstar Reggie Jackson. Carlton walked Carew, but then got Murcer to bounce into a 3-6-3 double play. Jackson went quietly by grounding out to Joe Morgan at second, and Carlton was done for the night. He could've been the winning pitcher, too, had the 2-1 lead held up. But former Phillie Cookie Rojas, now a Royal, put an end to that with a two-run homer in the eighth. The National League eventually won the game, 4-3, on a 10th-inning base hit by Morgan.

Steve Carlton's team had won, which in 1972 was still the objective of major leaguers. Players of that era played the All-Star Game to win, even if the only reward was bragging rights. And Steve had successfully met the challenge of three of the American League's toughest hitters.

It was a pretty enjoyable night all the way around, although Carlton admitted that his arm was "hanging" when he walked off the mound, weary from the weight of those nine innings of work in L.A. Now, after playing alongside the league's very best, for Lefty it was back to the harsh reality of rejoining the hapless Phillies.

How bad were they? The Phillies' record at the All-Star Break was 31-57, a winning percentage of .352. How great was he? Steve Carlton, at the break, had a record of 14-6. That's a .700 winning percentage. The Phillies were 16-8 in games that he started. They were 15-49 without him. The Phillies had the worst record in baseball. They trailed East-leading Pittsburgh by 24 games. There wasn't much for Phillies fans to look forward to for the rest of the season—except, that is, for Steve Carlton and his winning streak that was now at nine games.

"When I think of that season," says Frank Bilovsky, "I think of Steve Carlton, and only Steve Carlton." It was now officially the Summer of Steve, and he was the biggest thing in town. What else were Philly sports fans to focus on in the summer of '72? The Eagles? Ed Khayat's anemic team was in training camp at Albright College in Reading, and welcoming into the fold rookie quarterback John Reaves, their first-round draft pick out of Florida. Rebellious linebacker Tim Rossovich was holding out, and eventually was traded. Defensive tackle Ernie Calloway was the cause of much drama by walking out of camp twice in the same week. Things were not promising. The Eagles would go 2-11-1, costing Khayat his job. "Iggles" fever was not exactly sweeping the city. Bilovsky was right; it was Carlton, and only Carlton.

The Phillies reconvened at the Vet for the start of the season's second half, with a three-game series against the Cubs—a doubleheader on Thursday, followed by a rare Friday day game. The Phils split the double-dip, and then handed the ball to their horse for the series finale. A total of 17,349 fans passed through the turnstiles for the doubleheader, but with Carlton pitching, attendance was 24,312 for the Friday afternoon affair. It was a beautiful day for afternoon baseball, sunny and pleasant with highs in the mid-80s. Even Robin Roberts was there to see if Carlton could break the franchise's consecutive wins mark—a piece of which they both shared.

Carlton was feeling a tad bit under the weather that day, weakened from the effects of a cold. He was also lugging that tired arm from the All-Star Game. But none of the fans attending had any idea that he was at less than full strength. No one would have guessed it by watching him compete.

Carlton and the Phillies were up against Cubs righty Milt Pappas, the player rep who was on his way to a 17-7 season, the best of his 17-year career. Milt Pappas was born Miltiades Pappastediodis in Detroit. Signed out of Detroit's Cooley High School in 1957, he spent all of three games in the minors before making his major league debut that same August. In 1971, against the Phillies, he tossed a rare nine-pitch, three-strikeout inning. Two of the strikeout victims were Greg Luzinski and Don Money, both of whom were in the lineup tonight. In about six weeks time, Pappas—nicknamed "Gimpy"—would add an interesting quirk to his baseball bio.

On September 2nd, against San Diego, Pappas would find himself one strike away from a perfect game. He had a 1-2 count on the Padres' Larry Stahl, and then delivered three straight borderline strikes that were called balls by umpire Bruce Froemming (the same Bruce Froemming who called Davey Lopes safe at first in the infamous "Black Friday" playoff loss to the Dodgers in 1977). Pappas lost a perfect game by walking the 27th batter. It was the first time that that had ever happened. He got the next guy to secure the no-hitter, but he never forgave Froemming for, as far as Pappas was concerned, blowing his perfect game. "Any one of those pitches could've been called a strike," says Pappas, picking at a wound still unhealed some 38 years later.

If Carlton was elevating the talent around him, he was also apparently lifting his competition. The challenge of being pitted against him was bringing out the best in the opposing pitchers. The Clay Kirby game in San Diego is a case in point. Now Pappas was to turn in an effort every bit the equal of the streaking Carlton's. For the first eight innings, only one Phillie made it as far as third base. Tommy Hutton got there, but upon making the turn, was thrown out by Cubs left fielder Billy Williams before he could get back to the bag. Pappas allowed only three Phils to reach second. Meanwhile Lefty was a machine, mowing down the first 13 Cubs he faced. He gave up only two hits through eight innings. The game had no score at the start of the ninth.

Carlton strolled across the Vet's AstroTurf, crossed the white baseline, and calmly took the mound. He was in his element; locked-in and completely focused. Get through this inning and give the boys a chance to win it in the home half. It wasn't an entirely spotless ninth for the big left-hander. A one-out single, followed by a fielder's choice grounder and another single meant there were two Cubs on base with two away. And then Carlton bore down. He reached back for his old pal, the out-pitch slider, and unfurled it on Cubs outfielder José Cardenal. As Harry Kalas would put it, *swing and a miss, steee-ruck him right on outta there!*

Carlton did his job, but could the Phillies hitters do theirs? Push across a run against Pappas, who was back on the mound for the ninth, and the Phillies win. Tommy Hutton led off with a come-backer to the pitcher. One away. To the plate stepped Luzinski. The Bull broke his bat, but was still able to muscle the ball over shortstop for a single; just what the Phils needed—a runner aboard. Now Willie Montañez was up to bat. Montañez, who set the club's rookie home run record with 30 dingers the season before, was in a power slump in '72. He'd hit only eight coming in. Montañez kept his bat on his shoulder as Pappas threw two quick strikes by him. He fouled off the next one, then took ball one. The count was one and two. Pappas reared back. He tried to deliver a slider past Willie on the inside corner, but Willie jumped on it and crushed it. Willie stood at home plate and watched the ball travel. He started to walk toward first base. "I knew when I hit it that it was gone," Montañez told reporters. The ball landed in the right-field seats for a two-run homer. As Harry would say, *there's a loooong drive...watch that baby...it's ouuutta heeeere!*

Carlton was seated in the Phillies dugout. He jumped up out of his seat as soon as Montañez's bat struck the ball. The only question in the pitcher's mind was whether the ball was fair or foul. He, too, knew it was gone, especially when he saw Montañez standing there admiring its trajectory.

The Montañez one-out, two-run, walk-off bomb gave the Phillies a 2-0 victory. "I only needed one run, now I feel spoiled," said Carlton to the beat writers afterward. It was a four-hitter for "Super Steve," who had seven Ks. Two of the hits were grounders up the middle, Carlton getting a glove on one of them. The victory was his second straight complete game shutout, both by the final score of 2-0. The scoreless innings string was up to 27 and a third. Not bad for a guy fighting a cold and a fatigued arm. He now had 208 strikeouts on the year, tops in the majors and 60 away from Jim Bunning's club record. But more importantly, the victory was Carlton's 10th in a row. He had not lost since May 30th, a span of nearly two months. Ten in a row and counting.

CHAPTER 12

Return to St. Louis

"I need the Padre," Steve Carlton said to Betty Zeiser, "Will you get the Padre to a game?" The "Padre" that Lefty referred to was a Catholic priest friend of Betty's. Despite his self-deprecating request, Carlton hardly needed a priest. Rather it was his opponents that could've used some divine intervention against the Phillies' streaking left-hander. As the calendar turned to August 1st, he was 15-6 with an ERA of 2.37, and he was leading the league in strikeouts, all while pitching for the worst team in baseball.

Betty had gotten to know Steve through his wife, Beverly. After games, Beverly, like many of the wives, would adjourn to the nurses' station at the Vet. It was located just beyond the players' entrance to the stadium. The wives would sit and chit-chat with the nurses while waiting for their husbands to shower and dress. Betty also hung out in the first aid station with her friends Rita and Joan, who were the nurses on duty. Steve met Beverly there after games, and often would visit with the ladies before the couple headed home. "If he knew you," says Betty, "he would open up and be talkative. He would talk about everything, not just baseball. But sometimes he would say to his wife, 'come on let's go.' If he had a bad game, he wouldn't want to talk." Bad games were few and far between that season.

"You had to be there when he pitched," Betty says. "When he pitched, you went to the ballpark knowing you were going to win," she says. Not only were fans going to see a well-pitched game, and what usually was a victory for the home team, but according to Betty, there was another incentive as well. "You knew you were going to get home early!"

Carlton's fast work appealed to his teammates, who found it more conducive to playing defense, and it also appealed to the fans. It even made life more pleasurable for the Phillies staff and the stadium's employees. "On the nights he pitched," says Chris Wheeler, "you could actually make plans to do something after the game; you knew you weren't going to be there till midnight."

Of the 25 games from Opening Day through the month of July in which Steve Carlton was the Phillies' starting pitcher, the longest any one game lasted was two hours and 52 minutes, and that particular game went 10 innings. According to the Elias Sports Bureau, 2:52 was the average length of a nine-inning game in 2009. A couple of Carlton's starts went 11 and were still completed in under 2:52. Here's a list of the times of those first 25 starts (except for the June 21st game in Atlanta for which the time of game is not available):

> 2:15, 1:33, 1:47, 1:59, 2:05, 2:20, 2:27, 2:16,
> 2:02, 2:35, 2:14,   2:52, 2:09, 1:51, 2:51, 2:35,
> 2:51, 2:08, 2:14, 2:10, 2:50, 2:36, 2:00, 1:41

It was not unusual in those days for games to go just two hours. In fact, the night before, Carlton won his 10th in a row in 1:41 against the Cubs; Chicago's Fergie Jenkins and Ken Reynolds and Billy Wilson of the Phillies went 1:58 in the first game of a doubleheader. The second game saw Burt Hooton, Wayne Twitchell and four other pitchers go 2:27 in a game the Phillies won in the bottom of the ninth. Games were generally played faster in 1972 than they are today. But in an era of briskly played ball, Carlton's games seemed to move with even greater alacrity than most.

The Phillies were in desperate need of a quickly played game on the night of August 1st. It was the second game of a Tuesday night doubleheader between the Phillies and Mets at Shea Stadium. The country was buzzing that night from the news that Vice Presidential candidate Thomas F. Eagleton had resigned from the Democratic ticket. Eagleton was George McGovern's original running mate in the 1972 Presidential race against Richard Nixon and Spiro Agnew. Eagleton was forced to step down when it became public that he had been treated for mental health problems and had received shock therapy. These were stunning developments in the summer of '72, even as Nixon and the Republican machine appeared unbeatable. As unbeatable as Steve Carlton appeared that summer.

Carlton was scheduled to pitch against the Mets' veteran left-hander Jerry Koosman, one of the heroes of the '69 "Miracle Mets." Game two was certainly the highlight of the twin bill, and no doubt the 31,846 fans were there to see the nightcap more than anything else, especially given that Carlton was now in search of his 11th win in a row. But this double-header was more like a triple header. The opening game went 18 innings!

The marathon matched a pair of youngsters on the mound: 24-year-old righty Wayne Twitchell of the Phils versus 22-year-old lefty Jon Matlack of the Mets. Not only did Matlack attend college at West Chester, outside Philadelphia, he grew up in that Pennsylvania town watching the Phillies. This was the third time he was facing his hometown team.

Matlack beat them twice during the Phillies' horrid stretch of 19 losses in 20 games, including a three-hitter two months earlier. The lefty from West Chester was in his first full season in the big leagues, and by the time it was over, he would win 15 games and the National League Rookie of the Year award. This would not be one of those 15.

Matlack took a 2-1 lead into the bottom of the ninth—a Cleon Jones solo homer off Twitchell in the Mets' eighth providing the one-run cushion. Matlack was three outs away from victory. But the first Phillie he pitched to in the ninth, Don Money, blasted a game-tying homer. Matlack was relieved by Tug McGraw with two gone in the ninth, and while the future Phillies icon was pitching to outfielder Bill Robinson, the Mets nailed Tommy Hutton trying to steal. The inning was over, but the Phils and Mets were headed for another full-game's worth of extra innings.

McGraw was instrumental in the Mets' pennant victory the following season, but he will forever hold a place in the hearts of Phillies fans. His strikeout of Kansas City's Willie Wilson for the final out of the 1980 World Series is the enduring image from the franchise's first World Championship, and a moment etched in time for a generation of Philadelphians. McGraw became one of the most beloved sports figures in Philly history, as much for his impish sense of humor and bubbly personality as for his athletic prowess. Ever ready with a snappy one-liner, McGraw called the fastball that fanned Wilson the slowest fastball in history, because it took 97 years (the age, at the time, of the Phillies franchise) to get there. Once, when asked which he thought was better, AstroTurf or grass, Tug replied, "I don't know, I've never smoked AstroTurf." Upon signing a new contract, he was asked by reporters what he intended to do with the money he was about to make. Tug replied, "Ninety percent of it I'll spend on women and Irish whiskey. The other ten percent I'll probably waste." No one was fuller of life than Tugger. Sadly, his life ended in 2004 due to complications from a brain tumor. He was 59.

In the epic game one of that doubleheader, Tug, in the prime of his youth, pitched six and a third scoreless innings, allowing the Phillies just three hits while keeping the Mets in the game. McGraw gave way to Ray

Sadecki in the 16th. Meanwhile the Phils bullpen was turning in some surprisingly strong relief work. Billy Wilson, Dick Selma, and Mac Scarce shut out the Mets from the ninth inning through the 15th. Scarce, the lefty in his first season with the big league club, was tall and used a sidearm delivery. He was projected to become the Phillies' top left-hander out of the bullpen. In the 15th inning, the callow rookie impressed his manager with an eye-opening stint.

The winning run was on second base when Scarce came on to replace Selma with one away. That's when the Mets summoned Willie Mays to pinch-hit. Mays was greeted with a rousing ovation from the Shea Stadium crowd. What could be better than seeing the fabled star end things in storybook fashion by driving in the game-winner? But the ovation, the presence of Mays, and the game situation hardly rattled young Mac. He whiffed the great Mays on a 1-2 slider. Paul Owens, looking on from the dugout, and still in the process of evaluating the talent assembled around him, could not have been more impressed. Scarce wasn't done, though; he struck out the next batter, outfielder Dave Schneck, keeping the Phillies and the ballgame alive.

Scarce gave way to Darrell Brandon (number 30 in the program), and he tossed two perfect innings. The endless game moved to the 18th inning. The Phillies had the go-ahead run on third and one out. But Ray Sadecki got Terry Harmon and Larry Bowa in succession, ending the threat. Brandon wasn't as fortunate in the bottom of the 18th. He loaded the bases with one out, and then served up a game-winning base hit to Cleon Jones, who came through in the clutch for the second time that night: Mets 3, Phillies 2...in 18 innings.

Brandon tried to keep the ball down against Jones, but it didn't go where he wanted it to. Instead the pitch was up in the strike zone, and the Mets left fielder hit it over Roger Freed's head in right center. As Brandon left the mound in disgust, he flung his glove in the direction of the Phillies dugout. That toss was also a little too high. The glove sailed over the dugout and into the front row of seats, where two boys grappled for it. Bucky had to sheepishly ask the boys to give it back.

After four hours and 28 minutes, the seemingly never-ending opener had come to a close. It was a good thing the Phillies had the fast-working Carlton on the mound in the nightcap. There was still a significant wait for the second game to begin. It was Banner Night at Shea, and that meant a one-hour delay between games for the Banner Night festivities. Had it not been for that lengthy delay, Carlton could have had the chance to earn two wins in one day. Owens and Rippelmeyer thought about bringing him out of the bullpen in game one. "We kidded about it in the dugout in the 18th," Owens said to reporters. "I told Rip, 'We've gone about as far as we can go, let's bring Carlton in.' If it wasn't for the delay between games, I might've used him and then let him come back for the second game." Carlton said he would've done it, too.

Finally, the second game was under way—Carlton versus Koosman. The two pitchers became good friends after their retirements. In fact, they were Phillies teammates in 1984 and '85. But at this point in their careers they were rivals. "When I faced Carlton," says Koosman, I felt I had to pitch a shutout just to get a tie. He intimidated all the Mets hitters." Koosman lost the shutout in this game in the third inning. The Phillies put a run on the board as Harmon knocked in Hutton. It was Harmon's only hit in 12 at-bats that day. Carlton retired nine of the first 10 he faced, issuing only a second-inning walk. The Mets evened the score in the fourth. Mays singled and went to second on a passed ball by Phillies catcher John Bateman. This was atypical of Bateman, who was a very good catcher and someone with whom Carlton had developed a rapport, both on and off the field. Bateman, who joined the club after Carlton did, had earned the pitcher's trust and respect as a player. Sportswriter Frank Bilovsky remembers asking Carlton, in '72, who was the best catcher he'd ever thrown to. Steve replied, "Right now I'd have to say John Bateman." Bilovsky added, "Obviously Bateman knew what to call; of course, you only had to put down slider all the time."

Bateman wasn't afraid to call the two-strike slider in the dirt either. Carlton trusted he'd block it, and the majority of the time he did. However, this was not one of those times. With Mays on second base, Cleon Jones, whose hot night continued in game two, singled him home. The unearned run tied the score at 1. Jones had knocked in every one of the Mets' four runs on the day. While it was now becoming a long day's journey into night, the night appeared far from over. More extra innings seemed likely as the 1-1 deadlock progressed to the top of the ninth. The teams had already played 26 full innings—how many more did they need? The Phillies probably decided it was in everyone's best interests if they ended the thing right there. So, with two out, Don Money got things going with a single. Before that, Jerry Koosman had retired 16 in a row, but now things began to slip away from him. Greg Luzinski followed with a single, and Deron Johnson walked to load the bases. Bill Robinson then cleared them with a double. All three runners scored. It was 4-1, Phillies. Carlton went back to the mound, three outs away from his 11th win in a row. He was perfect. Lefty induced groundouts from Mays, Jones, and Jim Fregosi (the same Jim Fregosi who managed the pennant-winning '93 Phillies), in that order. The final score was 4-1, Phillies. Time of game: one hour and 45 minutes! It was another victory, and another complete game for Carlton, whose record now stood at 16-6. The streak was at 11 straight.

Lo and behold, Carlton's latest victory sparked a four-game winning streak. The feeble Phils magically began to play good baseball, taking three out of four from the Mets. Riding the new found string of good fortune, the Phillies traveled to St. Louis for a weekend series and took the first game with reliever Billy Wilson earning the win. It had not been a particularly good year for the Cardinals. They found themselves two games under .500, and in fourth place in the NL East. Now they were facing their old teammate in the second game of the series. It was the first time they'd seen him since the first week of the season. More interestingly for Carlton, this was his first start in St. Louis since the blockbuster off-season trade.

Surprisingly, there was little fanfare for Carlton's return to St. Louis. All of the newspapers handled it with their standard coverage. In this day and age it would be a media circus, especially considering the winning streak. Attention was certainly building with each of Carlton's starts, and so the spotlight was not as much on his return, but rather his streak. And even with the streak now taking on a life of its own, the media didn't give it the all-out coverage that it would surely garner today. "The Phillies were so bad," recalls Stan Hochman, veteran columnist of the *Philadelphia Daily News*, "that we didn't send a guy on the Carlton beat, despite the fact that no one had done what Lefty was doing."

As the streak progressed, Carlton remained unflappable. He knew how many games he'd won in a row, but the consecutive victories were, for him, simply a by-product of the much larger goal that he had set for himself, the goal of finishing the season with 25 wins. "I've won 11 in a row," Carlton told Hochman in a column that appeared in the *Daily News* prior to the start in St. Louis. "I don't go around thinking that nobody can win 12 in a row in this league, but I just approach the next game as the next game. I have only one objective, winning 25 games."

It was a muggy night in St. Louis, the kind of night that saps your energy and soaks your shirt with perspiration—typical August weather for the city hard by the Mississippi River. Carlton still maintained a home there, but this was a business trip; he'd never allow himself to think of this game as being bigger or more important than any other. It might be the first time he'd pitched in St. Louis since the trade, but for Steve it was the next game, and it was the Phillies, not him, versus the Cardinals. Much like in his first start against them at the Vet in April, he gave no hint of any lingering rancor for having been dealt. To quote a line from *The Godfather*, the movie that won the best picture Oscar in 1972, it was business, not personal.

Many felt, inwardly at least, that his return to St. Louis provided added incentive for Carlton. The game back in April was against Bob

Gibson, and that alone stoked the competitive flame. But this time it was Steve, back in front of the St. Louis fan base again. Despite what Carlton might be saying, observers felt it was not just "the next game" for him. Knowing how highly competitive he was, how could it have been? He might not have been pitching like it, but he was, after all, only human. "I'm assuming he came into St. Louis without any hesitation at all," says his former Cardinal teammate, Joe Torre. Joe would be at third base in this one, and batting cleanup in Red Schoendienst's lineup. "Probably, he had a little anger in him, too, because of the way he felt he was treated," Torre added. "I'm sure it helped. A different pitcher might have become a little tentative, but Lefty attacked all the way. Because that was the only way he knew how to play."

As he took the Busch Stadium mound, Lefty received a warm ovation from the crowd of 25,505. He was already working with the lead, as the Phillies had staked him to a 1-0 advantage in the top of the first. Three straight singles off Cardinals starter Reggie Cleveland, the last from Tommy Hutton, knocked in the game's first run. Now it was Carlton's turn. He gave up successive singles to Donn Clendenon, who was playing first base for the Cards, and to Torre, with two away. But he induced Ted Simmons to fly to center, ending the St. Louis threat. It was the last time a Cardinal would reach second base until the ninth inning.

Revenge may have been the furthest thing from Carlton's mind on this night, but he was making the Cardinals brass acutely aware that the trade was a mistake. At the time the trade was made, Gussie Busch may have considered Carlton to be a malcontent who wanted more money than Busch thought he was worth. The left-hander was now proving to Busch, and everyone else, that he was most certainly worth every penny. Carlton was the winningest pitcher in the league, had won 11 straight, and was doing it for a club that had a team batting average of .238. And Mr. Busch watched helplessly as his beloved Cardinals could do nothing against the pitcher he had traded away.

Carlton retired 18 in a row in one stretch. Three up, three down, from the second inning through the eighth. In between, the Phillies got a pair of two-run homers from Bill Robinson and Greg Luzinski. The Bull had spent the previous two games on the bench, exiled there by manager Paul Owens. He bounced back with a 387-foot shot to left center that made the score 5-0, Phillies, in the fifth. The five runs of support represented one of the bigger offensive outbursts that Carlton had received all season. On only four previous occasions was he backed by as many runs as he enjoyed in this game.

But by the seventh inning, Carlton began to tire. He had thrown a steady stream of sliders throughout the first half of the ballgame, and he felt that the pitch was taking a lot out of him. With the humid conditions a factor, Carlton was battling fatigue as well as the Cardinals. He decided to scrap the slider and threw few, if any, from the fifth inning on. He didn't appear to need the slider. His fastball was dominant and his curve ball evasive.

In the top of the ninth, Lou Brock led off with a double, thus becoming the first Cardinal to make it to second since the first inning. Brock got no closer to home plate than where he stood, 180 feet away. That's because Carlton then got Ted Sizemore and Donn Clendenon on back-to-back groundouts. His old friend, Joe Torre, now came between Carlton and his sixth shutout of the season (and second against St. Louis). Torre, a nine-time All-Star, was never afraid to face Carlton. Some hitters were. The way he'd bury that slider down and in on a batter, and the fact that he wouldn't hesitate to put that fastball under the batter's chin, could be scary. And as mentioned earlier, Carlton had his way of intimidating. But none of that ever fazed Joe, who hit a respectable .271 against him in 68 plate appearances. Having been a friend of Lefty's may have helped. "Probably the guy who never met him would have a tougher time against him," says Torre. "He stood out there and let the hitter know in no uncertain terms that he was out there. Lefty and I were fairly close, so I was a little more comfortable against him, I didn't fear hitting against him. It was no easy day, but the fact that I knew him personally made it easier for me." Torre might have been comfortable, but he couldn't come through with a base hit in this instance.

Torre lifted a fly ball to center field that Willie Montañez hauled in for the game's final out. The final score was 5-0, Phillies; time of game: one hour, 48 minutes. The Fightin' Phils had won five in a row, their longest winning streak in two years. It was another shutout and another complete game for Carlton. His six shutouts in the season tied Curt Simmons' team record for shutouts by a left-hander. He had not surrendered an earned run in 45 innings. With seven strikeouts on the night, his league-leading total now stood at 220. The effort lowered his ERA to 2.18. His record was now 17-9, and he had won 12 in a row. The numbers were ridiculous, but so were these numbers: 39-62. That was the Phillies' record. How much longer could his winning streak go on?

CHAPTER 13

Win Day

Carlton strolled into the visitors' clubhouse at Three Rivers Stadium in Pittsburgh, and headed toward his locker. Many of his teammates were in various stages of undress. Others were idling the pregame time by playing cards. Carlton announced his presence.

"It's win day, boys," he said out loud to no one in particular, but everyone in general.

"Today is win day." And that was all he said.

Carlton's pronouncement that it was "win day" had become part of the routine on the days that he pitched. It was part of the pregame ritual, and it had been going on now for a good portion of the season. Carlton's turn in the rotation came up every fourth day. Before every start, he entered the clubhouse and proclaimed it to be "win day." That meant that no matter what had happened in the previous three days, this was his day to pitch—the fourth day—and on the fourth day the Phillies would win. Not only did his teammates believe him, they looked forward to the games Carlton pitched. As Tommy Hutton put it, "We knew with him out there we had a chance to win that day. And then it would be the Ken Reynoldses and the Billy Champions the other days." It was another example of how he elevated everyone's game.

After announcing it "win day," no one dared approach Carlton. That was also part of the routine. The other Phillies had learned to stay away from Lefty on the days he pitched. He wouldn't engage in conversation. He wouldn't get drawn into practical jokes and other forms of tomfoolery. It was "win day." There was no time for screwing around. His game face went on soon after he entered the clubhouse, and he was all business. "He was in a different universe when he pitched," Luzinski remembers. "He would get in his pitching state of mind." That included his pregame mental preparation—the mental visualization, the playing out of the pitch sequences in his mind. "I have never seen a guy more focused before a game," Hutton says. "He would sit in front of his locker, facing the wall, and he would go through all this neck gyration stuff, flexibility stuff." And when he was doing that, it was as if he was wearing a "do not disturb" sign around his neck. "Forget about talking to him," adds Hutton. "It was like the simmering of the volcano on the days he pitched."

Rookie right-hander Wayne Twitchell was afraid to talk to Carlton. "He would go into a shell. He was not friendly. He was in his own world on days he pitched. The next day, he went back to being Steve. He was a fun guy to be around, except the days he pitched."

The fans were probably thinking that this is where the streak would end, here in Pittsburgh, against the defending World Champions. It was Wednesday, August 9th, his next start following the win in St. Louis the previous Saturday. Since then the Phillies had lost the getaway game to the Cardinals, and then after an off-day Monday in Pittsburgh, dropped the opener of the series with the Pirates. Would Lefty break the two-game slide and extend his winning streak to 13?

Carlton's opposite number that night was righty Steve Blass. The 30-year-old Blass was one of the heroes of the Bucs' world championship, having pitched two complete game victories in the '71 series. He brought a 12-5 record into the contest with the Phils, and by season's end, he would be 19-8 with a 2.49 ERA. It was perhaps the best season of his 10-year career. Had it not been for Carlton, the Pirates star would have won the Cy Young Award. He finished as the runner-up in the voting—a distant runner-up, but a runner-up nonetheless. And then a funny thing happened to Steve Blass. He contracted Steve Blass Disease. That's how it's referred to nowadays. When a player seemingly forgets how to throw a baseball accurately, they say he's got Steve Blass Disease. Because that's what happened to Steve Blass. The following season he suddenly, strangely, mysteriously, inexplicably could no longer throw strikes. In 1973, Blass walked 84 batters in 89 innings. He hit 12 batters, the most in the league. His ERA ballooned to 9.81. Blass had also walked 84 the previous season, but that was in 250 innings. He pitched in one game in '74, giving up eight runs, seven walks, and five hits in five innings of work, spending most of the season in the minors. He tried once again to regain his old form in the spring of '75, but it was no use. The Pirates released him and Blass retired.

The curious case of Steve Blass' "disease" was a development that still lay in the future. Tonight he was a first-rate pitcher, and he was locked in a duel with the game's hottest hurler. "I was proud to be in the same league as Steve, and to compete against him," Blass recalled. "It was a rush to pitch against him. He was obsessed to find out how good he could be. You can't teach that." Matching up with the league's best was apparently a rush for the Pirates hitters as well. "When we knew we were going to be facing him," noted outfielder Gene Clines, "we got extra fired up."

The defending champs welcomed the challenge of facing Carlton, and they hoped to be the team that finally broke his winning streak. After all, with a 65-38 record, the Pirates were running away with the NL East, sitting nine and a half games in front of the second-place Mets. Five of the players in their lineup brought .300 averages into the ballgame, and as a team they were hitting at a .292 clip. "We were a very confident team," stated Al Oliver, looking back over the years.

With the extra rush of adrenaline, the Pirates took to the artificial turf of Three Rivers Stadium. Things began well enough for Blass and company. Steve issued a two-out walk to Tommy Hutton, then promptly picked him off first base, and the Phillies were gone in the opening half-inning of the game. In the bottom of the first, the Pirates quickly learned that they were seeing Carlton at his finest. "He was intense from the moment he hit that mound until the moment he left," Gene Clines remembers. "You knew it was going to be a war." And it was. Clines, the Bucs' lead-off batter, whiffed to start the home half. Oliver, playing center, stared at a called third strike to end it. Al knew this was going to be one of those nights when Carlton had pinpoint control of all of his pitches. "That's what made him so tough," says the seven-time All-Star, "He threw the fastball up and in to keep me honest and threw the slider away."

The Phils put a run on the board against Blass in the second. After Willie Montañez opened with a single, Greg Luzinski dropped a broken-bat single of his own into right field. Clines, starting there in place of Roberto Clemente, mishandled it, allowing Montañez to score. It was an unearned run off Blass, but it put the Phillies in front, 1-0. Although it was early in the game, it looked like it might be the only run Carlton would require. He got them out 1-2-3 in the Pirates' half of the second, striking out first baseman Bob Robertson to end the inning. Says Robertson, "Carlton could make a perfectly good day miserable."

This day was headed toward misery for the Pirates. Carlton was the first Phillie to bat in the third. If Blass was stoked to pitch *against* him, after this at-bat he probably wasn't too thrilled to pitch *to* him. With the count one and two, Blass hung a curveball, and Carlton crushed it. He hit it deep to right field for a solo home run. It was his only homer of the season, and the fourth of Carlton's career. He would hit nine more before moving to the American League in 1986, and then calling it quits in '88. The solo shot made it 2-0, Phillies. "He was so locked in, he probably didn't know what the score was," says Steve Blass.

Carlton now had the luxury of working with a two-run lead, and that was more than enough. He struck out shortstop Jackie Hernandez and pitcher Blass in the bottom of the third. He struck out Al Oliver and future Hall of Famer Willie Stargell in the bottom of the fourth. He struck out Robertson, Richie Hebner, and Hernandez again in the bottom of the fifth. He struck out Blass again and Clines one more time in the bottom of the sixth. Carlton didn't strike out any more batters after that; he already had 12 for the game. He retired the next six in a row, anyway. Lefty took the 2-0 lead, and his 12 Ks, to the ninth. He had allowed just two hits to this point.

That's when the great Roberto Clemente entered the game. He came on to pinch-hit for Blass, to lead off the Pirate ninth. Within five months, Clemente would be dead. On New Year's Eve, 1972, while on a humanitarian mission to earthquake-ravaged Managua, Nicaragua, the small plane Clemente had chartered, loaded down with supplies and relief aid for the victims of the quake, crashed into the ocean shortly after takeoff from San Juan, Puerto Rico. His body was never recovered. Clemente was 38 years old. He was inducted into the Hall of Fame in 1973, the only player for which the mandatory five-year waiting period was waived.

Clemente had been beset by injuries in what turned out to be his final season. He played in just 102 games in 1972, but still managed to bat .312. His 118 hits that season gave him exactly 3,000 for his career. He would reach the coveted 3,000-hit plateau on September 30th, with a double off the Mets' Jon Matlack. On this night, the pride of all of Latin America toted a .309 average to the plate. In his career, Clemente batted 20 for 60 against Carlton. He never homered off Lefty, but hit four doubles and a triple. He also walked four times. This was going to be one of those times. Clemente worked the count to three and two, and then fouled off about a half-dozen pitches. As Carlton said to reporters afterward, "that's the type of hitter he is. He'll keep fouling them until he gets something he likes. He worried me more than anyone tonight." Clemente never got one he liked, and was aboard with a leadoff walk.

The Pirates decided to use a pinch-runner for Roberto, and brought on pitcher Dock Ellis, the winner of the previous night's game, to run for him. Up next was Gene Clines, who was 0 for 3 with two strikeouts to that point. "You could go 0 for 4 against Carlton with no strikeouts and feel like you had a good game," Clines claimed. His game was about to get a lot better. Carlton also ran the count full against Clines, who then laced a single to center. It was only the Pirates' third hit of the night and the first since a Rennie Stennett double in the fourth. The tying runs were aboard, there were no outs, and Stennett was up. Batting from the right side, the native of Panama was known as a pretty good contact hitter. He's probably best known for getting seven hits in a nine-inning game in 1975, the first player in the modern era ever to do that. In this at-bat against Carlton, Stennett got the bunt sign. He squared around, but popped the bunt attempt into the air. Carlton alertly sprinted off the mound, made a shoestring grab just before the ball hit the turf, and fired to second base. He nailed Ellis to complete a double play.

But it wasn't over yet. Al Oliver was up next, and Carlton threw him a 2-2 fastball. Oliver swung with all of his might, the barrel of his bat meeting the ball flush with a loud, cracking sound. As the ball flew high into the air, Carlton craned his neck to check its arc. He didn't like what he was seeing. "Oh no," he thought as he looked away. He looked a second time as the ball traveled toward the fence in right center. Right fielder Roger Freed went back…back…back. With his shoulders squarely against the wall, Freed hauled in the Oliver drive. Carlton breathed a sigh of relief. The game was over.

The final score was Phillies 2, Pirates 0. It was one of Carlton's finest outings of the season—a season increasingly full of fine outings. "Hitting him tonight," said Stargell, "was like trying to drink coffee with a fork."

Carlton had pitched a three-hitter, walking just one. He finished with 12 strikeouts, all coming in the first six innings. His major league-leading total was at 232. For the fourth time in five games, he'd thrown a shutout, his seventh of the season, breaking Curt Simmons' team record for a left-hander. It had been 54 innings since he'd allowed an earned run. He hadn't given up a home run in 79 innings. In every way that one crunched the numbers, it was more and more ridiculous. Carlton's ERA continued to plummet, now down to 2.09. His record was at 18-8, the streak now at 13. Would he ever lose again?

The Sunday doubleheaders at the Vet always produced decent crowds, even for an awful ballclub like the '72 Phillies. The concrete bowl was alive with a double-dip of baseball, hot dogs, peanuts and Cracker Jacks. A lot of that had to do with the promotions. There always seemed to be a promotion on a Sunday. But a lot of that also had to do with Steve Carlton. The crowds were bigger when he pitched. A total of 30,207 fans clicked the Vet's turnstiles for his next start, the first game of a Sunday doubleheader with Montreal, with Lefty looking for win number 14 in a row. As if that wasn't big enough, the fans on this Sunday were also going to be treated to a performance from the Great Wallenda. As the Philadelphia press put it the next morning, it was the Great Carlton and the Great Wallenda.

Karl Wallenda was a 67-year-old tightrope artist and the patriarch of the "Flying Wallendas," the high-wire troupe made up of Karl's family members. Between games of the doubleheader, he would attempt to walk 640 feet across the top of Veterans Stadium, 140 feet in the air, on a steel wire less than an inch wide, and without a safety net. It was a death-defying act, and one of Bill Giles' most memorable promotions. Wallenda had crossed the 1,000-foot-deep Tallulah Gorge in Georgia, but this was his first crack at a stadium. That may have been enough to lure some fans to the event, but the vast majority of them were there to see Carlton—Wallenda was a bonus. As all professional franchises eventually learn, winning is always the best promotion.

In the period from July 11th through August 21st, Carlton made five starts at the Vet. The Phillies' average attendance for those home games was 33,510. For the 12 home dates on which he did not pitch during that time span, the average attendance was 18,700. Attendance jumped by 14,800 for Carlton's games. "Every time he pitched," recalls Giles, "we drew an extra 15 thousand."

"It was more of an event when he pitched," says Larry Shenk, the longtime Phillies executive.

"Very few players put people in the seats, but he was one of them." There was a buzz surrounding Carlton's starts, an excitement that filled the air, especially during the streak. His games couldn't be missed. And that presented the Phillies staff with unusual but welcomed problems. As Shenk remembers, "We needed more game-day employees on the nights that he pitched."

They needed more of just about everything when he pitched, and so Phillies team executives would hold special staff meetings on the days leading up to a Carlton home start. Because larger than normal crowds were expected, special arrangements were needed. "Everything changed when his starts were coming up," Chris Wheeler notes. "We had to have more of this, more of that. We had to have more vendors, more security people. We had to have more concession stands open. We had to have more ticket windows open, because the walk up for tickets would be greater. We had to have more hot dogs. We had to plan differently when he pitched, and the next night we'd be back to normal." Armed with the additional vendors, security guards, ticket-takers, and hot dogs, the Phillies geared up for the Sunday doubleheader with the Expos, Carlton's first start at home in over two weeks.

Betty Zeiser was among the 30,000-plus fans on hand to see if Super Steve could make it 14 straight (not to see if the Great Wallenda could successfully traverse the Vet). She was always on hand. "Even when he didn't pitch, we went anyway," says the 80-year-old retired insurance company manager. "We'd say, 'Well, Carlton's pitching tomorrow, we'll win tomorrow.'" The Phillies have been a big part of Betty's life for as long as she can remember. Growing up in North Philly, she would go to the games at Connie Mack Stadium with her dad and her older sister

Anne. They'd take the 56 trolley to the end of the line, and then grab a bus to Lehigh Avenue and Connie Mack Stadium.

In 1952, Betty made her first trip to spring training. She and Anne made it an annual tradition. For 53 straight years they made the trip. Decade after decade, the Zeiser sisters were fixtures at the Carpenter Complex. They were fixtures before there was a Carpenter Complex. From Richie Ashburn and Robin Roberts to Johnny Callison and Dick Allen, to Lefty and Schmidty and The Bull, to Dutch and Kruker and Schill, to Rolen and Burrell and Rollins and Utley and Howard—the sisters were there, cheering them on and chatting them up. In the early days, they became as close as siblings to them. As the years passed, they became like surrogate aunts to the younger generations of players.

The 53-spring streak ended in 2005. That was the year Betty lost Anne to cancer. Betty didn't feel much like making the trip after that. For a couple of years, the rite of spring would have to go on without her. She'd wait until April, when the team came north, to catch up with her boys.

With time the pain subsided, and she was ready to make the pilgrimage again. Betty was so looking forward to being in Clearwater for spring training 2009 that she scheduled knee replacement surgery for the previous fall, despite the fact that it meant she'd be unable to attend the playoffs and the World Series. No matter, Betty watched on television as the Phils captured their first title in 28 years. It was still sweet, even if she didn't see it in person.

But Betty didn't make it to Clearwater that February. Over the winter, she slipped getting into a car and fell, reinjuring her surgically replaced knee. Months of painful rehab followed. She now walks with the aid of a cane, but that hasn't kept her from Citizens Bank Park. One can find her at almost all of the Phillies home games, seated in section 117, row 33. "The first two years of the new ballpark, my seat was in the 16th row," Betty explains. "But there are no railings, and it was hard to make it down all those steps, so I moved." Most nights she's there seated beside her friend Josie, whom Betty has known for decades. She and Anne met Josie years ago at Connie Mack Stadium and they hit it off immediately. "Josie was an A's fan at first," Betty recalls, "but then the A's moved and she became a Phillies fan."

As Carlton's victories began to mount, it didn't take long for Betty and other fans to forget about Rick Wise. "His first couple of wins, I thought, 'beginner's luck,' but then I became a Carlton fan," she says. And she wouldn't miss a Carlton start. While at the height of the winning streak Carlton's games saw attendance spikes, there were still tickets available. "You could always get tickets," according to Betty. "They might be upstairs, but you'd work your way down. We'd get seats wherever we could get one."

As the baseball gods would have it, this was Carlton's first start against the Expos since the infamous brawl on June 25th. And, wouldn't you know, Ernie McAnally, the Expos' starter in the "Brawl Game," was on the mound again. Some bad blood still remained from the melee in Montreal, and the Phillies would be ready to rumble if things again got out of control. The *Philadelphia Inquirer* quoted Carlton this way three days before the game: "That wasn't the first time I've been involved with the Expos, but I can't say I'm ever the aggressor in that situation," said Steve. "I won't be thinking about it when I go out and pitch Sunday. I don't know what Mauch's thoughts are, but if it happens again [an Expos pitcher throwing at a Phillies batter], I'll be glad to oblige him."

While Carlton was putting together a dominant streak, Ernie McAnally had been struggling. He brought just a 1-12 record, in 18 starts, to the Vet that day. But McAnally pitched well, giving up only two earned runs on five hits in seven innings of work. The Phillies got both of those runs in the first inning, and with two outs. Willie Montañez scorched an RBI double, and then came home on a single by Luzinski. That was it for the Phils offensively all night. McAnally may have pitched well, but not well enough to beat Carlton. In keeping with the theme of many of Lefty's starts, extensive run support wasn't needed. In fact, since taking over in the Phillies dugout, Paul Owens always played for an early run in Carlton's games. His rationale was that, with Carlton on the mound, an early run usually meant an early win. Scant run support never bothered Carlton. He figured if his team didn't hit, he'd just keep the other team from scoring.

Carlton retired 10 of the first 11 Expos before Bob Bailey stepped to the plate. Bailey knew it wasn't going to be a day at the beach facing Carlton—it never was. "I thought he was the best left-hander of that time," Bailey freely admitted. The Expos' third baseman expected Philadelphia to play with an extra measure of intensity, especially with Carlton on this roll. "The Phillies thought they were going to win every time that he pitched," he added. With one away in the fourth, Bailey connected against the man whom he considered to be the best lefty then in baseball, and sent a fly ball to left. It carried just far enough to make it over the fence. It was a rare home run ball from Carlton, and the first earned run he'd surrendered in 57 and a third innings. The Bailey homer was the Expos' first hit of the game, and it cut the deficit in half.

It was as close as the Expos would get. Carlton surrendered just two more hits, leaving the potential tying run stranded at second to end the game as the Phillies hung on to win it, 2-1. It was another three-hitter for Lefty, who struck out eight and walked three. His sixth K of the evening, his 238th of the season, broke Chris Short's team record for strikeouts by a left-hander. Carlton's ERA was now down to a paltry 2.05, while during this winning streak—which now hit 14 games—it was a microscopic 0.93. As Richie Ashburn would say, "hard to believe, Harry."

Also hard to believe, and in keeping with the other theme of Carlton's starts, the time of game was a blistering one hour and 48 minutes. For the fifth straight game, Carlton had completed his work in under an hour and 50 minutes. The last time he pitched a game that lasted two whole hours was the 2-0 shutout of the Dodgers on July 23rd in Los Angeles, and that one went exactly 120 minutes. The big left-hander seemed to be working more rapidly and with greater efficiency than ever. He explained it this way to Bill Conlin of the *Philadelphia Daily News*: "I haven't been behind too many hitters. I haven't given up many hits or walked many batters. The length of a game is definitely related to how many men are on base. The tempo naturally has to slow down."

"Working fast feels very comfortable for me," Carlton added. "There's nothing to do on the mound but get the ball and pitch."

From one great performance to another—it was time for the Great Wallenda. The narrow, braided steel cable hung across the top of the stadium. The little man appeared above the right-field line, clutching a pole he used to balance himself atop his high-wire, to a standing ovation from the more than 30,000 spectators below. Twenty members of the Phillies' grounds crew, usually employed to roll out tarps and line the playing field, had been given the task of rigging Wallenda's tightrope. They used over two dozen guy wires and pulleys in the hope of maintaining the line's required tension.

Wallenda's manager was not impressed with the job, to say the least. He was very concerned, feeling that the wire was poorly rigged and hardly tight enough. He even remarked to reporters that it might be the most dangerous wire Karl had ever performed upon. Wallenda himself agreed. He felt he had never walked on a rope this loose in his career. It was going to be an even riskier proposition than usual. Wallenda's daughters, who watched from the platform above right field, pleaded with their father to call it off. The Great Wallenda wouldn't hear of it. The show must go on.

The crowd hushed as he inched across the cable. The players in both dugouts watched, mesmerized. At one point, Wallenda stopped and gestured to the ushers below, who were holding the wire. He wanted them to make the cable more taut. "I wasn't sure if it was really a problem, or whether he was putting on an act, and I'm still not sure to this day," says Bill Giles.

Wallenda continued his walk, and when he reached the area around second base, some 140 feet above the infield, the veteran circus performer stopped. There, teetering atop the tiny, bowing wire, the Great Wallenda stood on his head!

"I was in a state of shock. I was looking and looking, and hoping and praying that he wouldn't fall," Giles remembers.

Finally, some 17 minutes after he began, and to the amazement and relief of the fans, Karl reached the left-field roof. Once there, he turned and waved triumphantly to the crowd. He called the walk across the Vet the toughest he ever made. Then the Great Wallenda went to the press dining room and downed two martinis.

The Phillies couldn't top that in the second game. As Chris Wheeler commented, after Carlton, everything went back to normal. Which meant Billy Champion was lit up by the Expos. Champion gave up four runs in the fourth inning en route to his 10th consecutive loss. Following the Expos' 8-3 victory, Champion was immediately demoted to the bullpen. Owens replaced him in the rotation with Darrell Brandon.

CHAPTER 14

Taking 20 Bows

It was nice to have something to anticipate. That was Chris Wheeler's thought. The PR assistant was referring to Steve Carlton's starts: "His starts were all we had to look forward to. Even if he won 30 games, we were still going to finish last." It also made Wheeler's job of putting together the pregame notes and statistics much more pleasurable. When Lefty pitched, at least there was something good to talk about. That wasn't always the case on the other three days. "It was fun, because now you got to spend time researching positives, instead of 'this guy is one for his last 22.' We were so bad, but everything with Lefty was so positive," he added.

Knowing that Steve was their only promotable player, the Phillies' marketing department never wasted an opportunity to pitch their ace hurler to the public. For two nights at the ballpark they hyped Carlton's next appearance. Every couple of innings or so, the electronic scoreboard in right field flashed the reminder that "Super Steve goes for win number 20 and 15 straight Thursday night." As if the fans needed reminding.

The NL West–leading Reds, now in town, had won the first two of a three-game series. Having also lost the nightcap to Montreal on Sunday, the Phillies were in the midst of a three-game losing streak. It was, indeed, "win day" with Carlton on the mound for the series finale with the Reds. He never had much luck with the Reds, though. His lifetime record against them was just 1-6. They were the only team in the league that he hadn't yet beaten. Maybe it was because with so many talented right-handed hitters in their lineup—including Johnny Bench, Tony Perez, and George Foster—the Reds were simply murder on lefties.

Bench, in particular, had a tendency to wear out Carlton. Johnny batted .298, with 12 homers and 30 RBI against him in 124 career at-bats. "What I loved about Carlton was his attitude,"recalls the Hall of Fame catcher. "Here's the pitch, try and hit it. If you did, he just got the next guy out."

One night, a couple of years later, Bench was coming out of the famous Bern's Steak House in Tampa, Florida. Suddenly a strange woman approached him. She stopped Johnny and said,"Why don't you lay off my husband?" It was Steve's wife, Beverly.

Carlton did not lay awake the night before worrying about facing the Reds with his 20th victory on the line. In fact, he slept until one in the afternoon. John Bateman picked Steve up at his home and the two batterymates drove to the stadium together. Steve couldn't have been more relaxed. He even fit in a nap during his pregame routine.

There used to be a pitcher's mound in front of the home dugout at the two-year-old Vet. Sixty feet, six inches away from that mound was a home plate. This was a characteristic of the new stadium borrowed from the Phillies' old ballpark, Connie Mack Stadium. There was a mound in front of the dugout at Connie Mack, too. It was where Phillies pitchers warmed up back then. In the more modern days of Veterans Stadium, most pitchers warmed up in the bullpen before a start. Not Steve Carlton.

Before every home start—after he announced in the clubhouse that it was "win day," gave his teammates the silent treatment, went through his mental paces, and did his stretching—Carlton threw his warmup tosses on the mound in front of the Phils' dugout. It was part of the routine.

Another part of that routine was to throw to a batter. While Carlton warmed up, he did so with one of his teammates standing in and feigning an at-bat. Since win number three of the Carlton winning streak, it had become Bill Robinson's job to stand at the plate. So, prior to the night's game with the Reds, for the 11th straight time, Robinson stood at the plate while Carlton warmed up. The previous Sunday, before beating the Expos, win number 14 in the streak, Joe Lis tried to stand at the plate. Carlton, all business, told Lis to get out of there.

He was reluctant to call it a silly superstition. When asked about it by the media, Carlton said, "It adds to my peace of mind. It could be that I unconsciously associate all the good things that have happened during the streak with his [Robinson's] being there."

As was usually the case, a large group of fans congregated behind the home dugout, watching as Carlton warmed up, with Robinson acting as phantom batter. When he had thrown the final warmup toss, Carlton turned to the stands and searched the crowd for a young fan. This had also become part of the pregame ritual when pitching at home during the streak. When he was done warming up, Carlton would throw a ball into the stands to a young fan that he would pick out of the crowd. When he located his target, he held the ball up above his ear, and flipped it toward a young boy, making the kid's night.

Now it was time to win number 20.

Three bus loads of youngsters from the Souderton (Pa.) Little League made their way east on Route 76, better known as the Schuylkill Express-way, the main highway artery that runs through the City of Brotherly Love. When they passed the Sunoco refinery and saw the round oil tanks painted to look like baseballs, they knew they were close to the stadium. That was every kid's landmark on the trip from the suburbs to the Vet—when you saw the baseball oil tanks, you knew the ride wouldn't be much longer.

Young Brad Nau was among the 100 or so boys from the Souderton Little League. These days he's Executive Producer for Special Projects at Comcast SportsNet, Philadelphia's regional TV sports network. He couldn't have been more excited to be going to this game. By the luck of the draw, the league's annual bus trip to see the Phillies just happened to fall on this night, the night Carlton went for his 20th win, and his 15th in a row. "It was riveting all summer. Every time he pitched, you thought it was going to be an automatic win," recalls Nau. "To be there to see him go for his 20th, and the 15th in a row, was a thrill I'll never forget. I still have the ticket stub somewhere."

The Little Leaguers from Souderton were among the 53,377 that packed the Vet. More hot dogs, vendors, and security people were certainly needed for this one. The Phils drew only 17,106 the night before for a 3-0 win by the Reds. The stadium was crackling with excitement; the electricity in the air was the type normally felt during the postseason. "I was psyched," said shortstop Larry Bowa. "I felt like I was playing in a World Series."

The fans, and his Phillies teammates, were all pulling for Lefty. Deron Johnson admitted he was also extra keyed up. He didn't want Carlton to lose. In the second inning, Johnson belted a two-run homer, giving his pitcher a pair of quick runs with which to work.

Carlton gave those runs right back in the third. The troublesome Reds, aptly referred to as "The Big Red Machine," weren't easy to keep down. Dave Concepción led off with a single and scored on a Bill Plummer double. Pete Rose then singled home Plummer. Rose stole second, and scored on a Joe Morgan RBI double. Suddenly the Phillies trailed, 3-2. It could've been worse, but with two outs and a runner on, Steve froze Bench with a called third strike. Bench had been on a tear coming in, too. He had enjoyed a five-RBI game in Atlanta four days earlier, and had 26 homers and 85 RBI for the year. Bench was on his way to becoming the National League's MVP.

If anyone in the house thought Carlton would wilt after giving up a three-run third, they were greatly mistaken. A lesser pitcher may have hung his head and never recovered. But the ultra-intense, hyper-focused Carlton simply shrugged it off and bore down.

The hottest pitcher in baseball did not have his best stuff. This was a struggle for Carlton. He couldn't keep his curveball down, and he was leaving his fastball up in the strike zone. But warrior that he was, Carlton battled and battled. After the third inning, he stopped throwing the curve, and relied more on that one-of-a-kind slider. Meanwhile, surprise of surprises, the Phillies hit. They drove in runs. In fact, they furnished their ace with the most runs he'd seen since scoring nine in the 9-4 win over the Mets on June 29th.

The Phillies came back with three runs in the fifth. The highlight of the inning was a two-run bomb to right from Willie Montañez, which chased the Reds' starting pitcher, Ross Grimsley. While Grimsley doesn't remember the details of a game played so many years ago, he does remember what it was like to pitch against Steve Carlton.

"He was in a class all his own," recalls Grimsley, now a minor league pitching coach in the Giants organization. "He had the best slider I ever saw from a left-hander. I would've paid to watch Carlton pitch."

The Phillies placed a crooked number on the scoreboard in the second, fifth, sixth, and seventh innings, and carried a 9-3 lead into the top of the eighth. Bench, Carlton's nemesis, was 0-2 in the game when he batted with one away in the eighth. He wasn't about to finish with such a collar. With Bobby Tolan on second base, Bench laced a single to left. Tolan scored, but it was a meaningless run.

Carlton pitched a scoreless ninth. He got Rose to bounce out to Bowa at short, 6-3 for those scoring at home, and the ballgame was over. "Phillies 9, Reds 4" read the giant electronic scoreboard in right field. Carlton had done it. He had won his 20th, and 15th straight.

Steve was mobbed by his teammates as soon as the final out was recorded. The Vet's 53,000-plus crowd gave a thunderous ovation. As the night's hero disappeared into the Phillies dugout, a spontaneous cheer rose through the stadium. "We want Steve, we want Steve, we want Steve," the crowd roared. Just then their hero appeared, tipped his cap, and waved. The Carlton curtain call spontaneously morphed into a kind of victory lap with Steve shaking the hands of fans seated in the field level boxes. He even signed some autographs. After about 15 minutes, he retired to the clubhouse. The on-field celebration was over.

Young Brad Nau and his Little League teammates had watched the game from the nosebleed section in right field. They didn't care that they were way up in the 700 level. Their only disappointment of the night was that, from their vantage point, they couldn't see the modern, state of the art, electronic scoreboard. That was a real drag. The scoreboard was one of the coolest features of the stadium. But it was positioned in the lower level of right field, just above the fence. It couldn't be seen from where the Souderton Little League group was seated. So, on the way out, soon after the game had ended, Brad made a mad dash down the exit ramp. He got to a lower level on the right-field line, and sprinted across the concourse to where he could see the playing field. He *had* to get a look at that scoreboard. In super-sized bright lights it flashed:

SUPER STEVE

It was quite a night in South Philly, and quite a night for the Carlton family. Not only did Steve continue the streak and win his 20th game of the year, he did so on Beverly's birthday. It was exactly the gift she had hoped for. Three weeks earlier, when Steve's win total was at 15, Bev realized that he'd be pitching on the 17th, her birthday. She told her husband that a 20th victory was the birthday present she wanted. Super Steve, pitcher of the year, and, now apparently, also husband of the year, delivered.

The next morning, the *Philadelphia Daily News* trumpeted the news of Carlton's latest achievement with this headline:

"Hey, Super Steve, Take 20 Bows"

Carlton-mania was reaching a crescendo. He was 20-6. It had been six years since a Phillies pitcher had won 20 games. He had a 15-game winning streak going, and was undoubtedly headed for the Cy Young Award. Phillies pitchers don't win Cy Young Awards. None ever had. But the award had become Carlton's to lose.

CHAPTER 15

The Niekro Game

Larry Bowa knew it was going to be a tough night for him and his Phillies teammates. That was because Phil Niekro was pitching. The Atlanta Braves were in town and they were sending Niekro, the master of the knuckle ball, to the mound to face the Phillies. Bowa remembers, "Every time Niekro pitched against us, he gave us fits." It was that damn knuckle ball of his.

It's right there, coming at you in slow motion. But when you take a mighty cut at the ball, somehow the ball has disappeared. You're left swinging at nothing but air. Niekro's knuckler was one of the best in baseball history. It is the reason he's in the Hall of Fame.

"I threw 75 to 80 percent knuckle balls," says Niekro, now in his 70s. "One game I pitched against Cincinnati, I threw 108 pitches—105 were knuckle balls. I used to mix in a fastball more for surprise."

Everybody hated to hit against Niekro. Even with Carlton and his dazzling slider going for the Phils, it had the potential to be a long night. Niekro's father taught him and his brother Joe how to throw the knuckler in the backyard of their Ohio home when Phil was just a boy. Joe also grew up to be a major league pitcher. Together the Niekro boys became the winningest brother combination in baseball history. Phil accounted for 318 of their 539 wins, in a career that spanned 24 seasons. Phil played until he was 48 years old, and held the record as the oldest pitcher to toss a shutout when he threw one at age 46. That record stood until May 2010, when 47-year-old Jamie Moyer of the Phillies duplicated the feat.

It was the knuckle ball that provided Niekro with such longevity. Once mastered, it can be thrown forever. Unlike other pitches, it produces very little wear and tear on a pitcher's arm. Niekro was so adept at throwing the knuckle ball that everyone in baseball began calling him "Knucksie." The nickname has stuck ever since.

It was Knucksie versus Lefty at the Vet. A crowd of 41,212 converged at the corner of Broad Street and Pattison Avenue to see this latest Carlton "event." That was the only way to see it, because it was not being televised. On Channel 17 that night, unlucky Phillies fans were served the western series *High Chaparral*, followed by *Dr. Who*. The description in the TV listings for the *Dr. Who* episode read, "Investigating irregularities at the site of an atomic research station, Dr. Who is attacked by a prehistoric monster." High drama, indeed. If Philadelphians wanted to watch real drama unfold, they needed to be at the Vet.

Ruly Carpenter, the Phillies' future president and team chairman, took a seat in the front row, directly behind home plate. Carpenter loved to sit close to the action at the ballpark: "That year I used to always go down behind the Plexiglas window with the grounds crew when Carlton pitched. You really got a feel for the action on the field at that level, because you roughly have the same view as the home plate umpire. I loved being that close and watching him throw his slider. He would make the best hitters in the game look helpless."

All eyes were on Lefty, and from all vantage points in Veterans Stadium that night. Could he extend "The Streak" to 16 in a row? No pitcher had won that many consecutive games since former Phillie Jack Sanford won 16 straight for the Giants in 1962. Lefty hadn't lost in two months. It's doubtful anyone in the crowd on this Monday night even considered the possibility that Carlton might actually *lose*.

It was a fair but warm evening. Highs that day had reached the upper 80s. The Republican National Convention commenced that afternoon in Miami. The GOP gathered to nominate Richard Nixon to run for a second term as President. In less than three months, Nixon would win in a landslide over Senator George McGovern.

Phil Niekro exited the visitors' dugout, which was on the third-base side of the field, to warm up. As he did so, he heard a huge roar from the crowd. "I thought maybe it was for me," he recalled. Just then he realized he was mistaken. Across the diamond, Carlton appeared for the first time from the Phillies dugout. "The cheering was for him," Niekro said with a chuckle. "I knew Carlton had the streak going. He was on a roll."

Super Steve warmed up on the first-base sideline (with Bill Robinson in the faux batter's box). When he was finished, he picked out a youngster in the crowd behind the home dugout and tossed him the ball. The pregame ritual was complete. It was time to go to work.

Carlton's teammates were pumped, even though they knew facing Niekro wouldn't be easy. It was another big crowd...it was Lefty on the hill...it was win day again. "It seemed like every time he pitched, second half of the season, he won," Larry Bowa noted. "We liked playing in front of the crowds he drew. We had more bounce, we knew we had a chance to win."

It was a scoreless game as they entered the third inning. Carlton opened the frame by easily fanning his counterpart, Niekro. He then got the Braves' leadoff man, the "Roadrunner" Ralph Garr, on a called third strike. Two quick strikeouts to start the third, but that's when things got a little dicey for the streaking lefty. Braves second baseman Felix Millan was the next batter. Felix the Cat was a Gold Glove fielder who had a decent bat—a lifetime .279 hitter. Millan roped a two-out double to center field.

That brought up Hammerin' Hank Aaron. Aaron came in batting .260, sub-par for the all-time great. He'd finish the year with 34 homers, but just a .265 batting average, the lowest of his illustrious career to that point. With the count two and two, Carlton tried to beat him with a curveball. But Henry rapped a grounder into left field for a single. Millan scored. It was 1-0, Braves.

Carlton settled into a groove from there. Over the next six innings he would allow only two Braves to reach base. He walked a man in the fourth, but stranded the runner. In the fifth, he was tagged for an extra base hit. It was Millan again—this time he doubled to left. In his 12-year career, the little second baseman from Puerto Rico faced Carlton more than any other pitcher: 106 plate appearances. And in those 106 plate appearances he hit seven doubles. Two of those doubles came on this night.

But the Braves left Millan stranded on second base when Carlton struck out Aaron, and induced center fielder Dusty Baker into an inning-ending groundout. It would be another six innings before the Braves threatened again. Yes, this was going to be a long night, and it was far from over. That's because Niekro was every bit as effective on the mound. His patented knuckle ball was fluttering like a Monarch butterfly, and the Phillies were without an adequate net to corral it. The ball danced. It dipped. It floated. And it totally flummoxed the Phillies.

They swung and swatted and swiped at the ball, but they couldn't hit it. For the first seven innings, the Phillies failed to get a runner past second base against Niekro and his daunting knuckler. That slow-moving target was in constant motion and it dropped the Phils batters to their knees. "He made us look so bad that night," Chris Wheeler recalls. "It was like they were swatting flies. And the guys really wanted to win for Carlton."

Then, in the eighth inning, trailing 1-0, the home team finally broke through. Willie Montañez, known for his flair for the dramatic, led off the inning by sending a shot down the line in right. Willie chugged into second with a standup double. Next up to the plate stepped that young slugger known as "The Bull."

Greg Luzinski's rookie year had begun with high expectations from the fans and media alike. At six feet one and 230 pounds, the thickly muscled 21-year-old had the strength and size of a bull. Blond with boyish good looks, he was tapped as the franchise's next superstar—a power hitter to follow in the footsteps of past Phillies stars like Richie Allen, Johnny Callison, and Del Ennis. Mike Schmidt was still a minor leaguer honing his game. At this stage, it was not Schmidt that was expected to be the slugging future of the Phillies—the young star around whom the lineup was to be built. That honor belonged to Luzinski.

On the other hand, the fans and media had grown critical of the rookie outfielder. A home run–hitting slugger? It was late August, and The Bull had just a dozen homers. A heart of the order run-producer? He came into the Niekro game with an RBI total of 49. That Luzinski was playing the outfield at all was a stretch. A first baseman in the Pacific Coast League at Eugene, Luzinski expected to be the heir apparent to Deron Johnson. One day during the previous off-season, Luzinski was in the Phillies offices when he learned that the club had traded for a triple-A prospect named Tommy Hutton. The Bull was familiar with Hutton from their PCL days, when Tommy had led the league in hitting. He also knew that Hutton played first base.

"What did we get him for?" Luzinski wondered out loud.

The Bull didn't know it, but he was about to become a left fielder. "I basically learned to play the outfield at spring training that year. It wasn't easy, but it was a chance for me to play in the big leagues."

Luzinski came up with the tying run on second in the person of Montañez. Niekro, dealing from the stretch, delivered (what else?) a knuckler. However, this knuckle ball didn't have quite enough flutter to it. The butterfly didn't dance, and The Bull crushed it. As if shot out of a cannon, the ball rose toward right center. Dusty Baker went back, back, back.

"I thought I hit it out," Luzinski remembers. But it just barely stayed in the park. The ball hit the wall on a fly and caromed back onto the Vet's AstroTurf surface. Montañez scored easily. Luzinski was on second with a double of his own. Back-to-back doubles to start the inning, and now the game was tied at one. The Phillies had something going here in the eighth. The next batter was Tommy Hutton. He had pinch-run for Deron Johnson in the sixth, and stayed in the game at first base. Now he was up for the first time that night, and with the go-ahead run standing on second base.

"I never hit Niekro well," Hutton admits. "Someone once sent me a statistic of every pitcher I ever faced, and I was like one for 18 or something against him, something terrible." He was exactly one for 18 versus Niekro in his career. The one hit happened to be an RBI single. It did not come in this at-bat. Tommy struck out. One away.

It is funny how certain things stay with us throughout our lives. Some 37 years later, Hutton sits in a hotel coffee shop in Philadelphia and reflects on that at-bat. He's currently the TV analyst for the Florida Marlins, who are in town to play the Phillies on this, the final weekend of the 2009 regular season. "I was up with a man on, and I didn't get the run in. I remember that, I do remember that," he says, all these many years later. "I was just so upset that I didn't get that run in." (Interestingly, while Hutton, a .248 hitter for his career, batted just .056 against Niekro, he hit a ton against three of the best pitchers of his era. Not only did Hutton bat .320 vs. Tom Seaver, but he also hit .321 vs. Fergie Jenkins, and .323 vs. Bob Gibson. Go figure.)

The Phillies had more chances to get the tying run home. With men on first and third and one out, Bill Robinson flied out to right. Now there were two away and the number eight hitter, John Bateman, was up. The Braves didn't hesitate to walk him intentionally. Carlton was the next batter, and he was going to bat. There was no way Paul Owens was going to lift him for a pinch-hitter. Not with The Streak on the line. Not with the way Lefty was pitching. Besides, who did they have to bring out of the bullpen? The only way they were going to win this game was with Carlton on the mound. So there was Carlton at the plate facing Niekro with the bases loaded in the eighth inning of a tie ballgame. Carlton popped-up to shortstop, and the inning was over. On to the ninth.

One-two-three went the Braves in the top half against Carlton; one-two-three went the Phillies in the bottom half against Niekro. After nine innings, the score was still 1-1. The game was headed to extra innings.

Shock of shocks, the '72 Phillies were not particularly good in extra-inning games. They were just five and ten on the year when playing extras. The '72 Phillies were also not particularly good—surprise, surprise—in one-run games. They won 20 and lost 29 games which were decided by a single run. As has been documented in these pages, the '72 Phillies were not particularly good, period.

The Braves could do no damage in the 10th. Carlton got out of the inning unscathed, thanks in part to his own defensive play. The leadoff batter, shortstop Marty Perez, reached on an error. Niekro tried to bunt him over, but with two strikes, he fouled one off for strike three. With one away, Ralph Garr hit one back up the middle that Carlton snared. The gangly left-hander turned and fired to Bowa, who was covering second base. Bowa threw to Hutton at first to get the fleet-footed Roadrunner. A 1-6-3 double play, and the Braves were gone in the 10th.

The Phils now had a chance to walk off with a win. But Niekro was as tough as he had been all night. The crafty veteran set the Phillies down in order, freezing both Greg Luzinski and Don Money with called third strikes. That was it for the home nine in their half of the 10th. Then it was on to the 11th, with both starting pitchers going strong. As Chris Wheeler notes, "11th inning and they were still out there. Think about that. That doesn't happen now."

Carlton started strongly by getting two quick outs. In fact, he got the second by fanning Hammerin' Hank. Dusty Baker was up next, and Lefty didn't have the same luck with the Braves center fielder. He blasted a double. There might've been two away, but now the Braves had the go-ahead run in scoring position. The next batter was Braves catcher Earl Williams, whom the Phillies intentionally walked. That brought up Mike Lum.

Lum entered the game in the seventh inning as a defensive replacement for Rico Carty. The Braves were trying to preserve their slim lead and manager Eddie Mathews, the former slugger who belted over 500 homers in a Hall of Fame career, moved Ralph Garr to left and had Lum take over in right. Lum was at the plate with two out, and with the chance to be a hero.

Michael Ken-Wai Lum was born in Honolulu. The outfielder and first baseman had a modest 15-season career. He also has the distinction of having hit more home runs (90) than any other Hawaiian-born player. Lum was one of broadcaster Harry Kalas' favorite big leaguers. Kalas' own career took off as the play-by-play voice of the triple-A Hawaii Islanders, and the young midwesterner fell in love with the islands and their culture. So the Hawaii connection surely struck a chord. In addition, Harry loved to say Lum's name. It was never just Mike Lum, it was *Mike Ken-Wai Lum*. Harry loved to elongate his pronunciation. He would stretch out every consonant and vowel, so it became *Miiike Kennn-Whyyy Luuummm* in that distinctive, resonant, Harry Kalas signature cadence. Only Harry could make a monosyllabic name sound orchestral. Kalas wound up saying that name more often than he probably hoped he would.

Lum dug into the batter's box. Carlton kicked and dealt. Lum swung. The meeting of wood on horsehide cracked Lum's bat, but he got enough wood on the ball to drop it into center for a base hit. Baker rounded third and scored with ease. Said Carlton to the *Philadelphia Inquirer*: "It was a hell of a pitch, low and away; it broke his bat, but he just stayed with it."

Miiike Kennn-Whyyy Luuummm had delivered a two-out, broken-bat single in the 11th inning to give the Braves a 2-1 advantage. It was the first hit, and first run, allowed by Carlton since way back in the third inning. Now the Phillies had to score two in the bottom of the 11th to give Carlton another win, and to keep his remarkable winning streak alive.

Bill Robinson led off for the Phils in their half of the 11th. Niekro had him struck out, as Robbie swung and missed at yet another knuckler. But the catcher, Earl Williams, had trouble securing the floating pitch. Catching a knuckle ball is almost as difficult as hitting a knuckle ball. The passed ball on the third strike allowed Robinson to reach first base. The potential tying run was aboard.

John Bateman was next, and he tried to bunt Robinson into scoring position. But his bunt attempt was fielded by Niekro, who threw to second, nailing Robinson. That erased the lead runner and put the slow-footed Bateman on first with one out. Carlton was due to hit next, but Paul Owens sent Terry Harmon to the plate instead. His ace, his horse, the pitcher who could magically turn the sad-sack Phillies into a team that did a startling impersonation of a contender, was done for the night. If the Phils tied the game here, someone other than Steve Carlton would be entrusted with the responsibility of finally winning it.

Lefty's night was over, but his consecutive games winning streak was not necessarily finished. He was still the pitcher of record should his teammates come through with a pair of runs for a walkoff victory. Terry Harmon was not a home run hitter. In fact, the 28-year-old Ohioan was in his fourth full season and had yet to touch all bases. Was there enough magic in the South Philadelphia moonlight to enable Harmon to bang a game-winner, the first HR of his career? No, there wasn't. Harmon grounded out to third. Denny Doyle was the Phillies' last hope in extending the Carlton Streak. It didn't happen. Doyle bounced to second and that was it. The ballgame was over, and so was The Streak.

Everyone seemed stunned. "We couldn't believe he lost, because he had pitched so well in that game," Chris Wheeler recalled. In 11 innings, Carlton had held the Braves to two earned runs on seven hits, and struck out 10. Niekro was just a tad better. He gave the Phils the lone run on nine hits, and also struck out 10. Both guys went the distance and put up double digits in strikeouts. What a ballgame, and what a tough way for The Streak to come to an end. "You get that far," said Carlton in an interview for the club's end-of-year highlight film, "you hate to see it terminated in a game like that, 11 innings, 2-1. It was a bad feeling because we could've won the game so many times. But you have to accept the fact that Niekro was better than me that night. He pitched a super ballgame."

For Niekro, it was just his 10th win of the season against a dozen losses. "I thought it was the best knuckle ball I've had all season," he told the *Inquirer* afterward. "I must've thrown it 95 percent of the time. The last two or three innings I had a better knuckler than I had the whole year."

It was Carlton's first loss since May 20th. In winning those 15 straight games, he had pitched 135 innings, and 14 of the 15 wins were complete games. Five were shutouts. Lefty had given up only 84 hits, 19 runs (17 earned) and three home runs. He struck out 119 and walked 33. His ERA was a sparkling 1.13. He hit one batter, and he did that on purpose.

Shortly after the final out was registered and the game had ended, reporters filed into the Phillies clubhouse. It was a somber room, as the players quietly showered and dressed. Carlton's was the last locker stall along the wall on the left side of the clubhouse. The press corps congregated there, as they did following each of Lefty's starts. Carlton was gracious in defeat, giving credit to Niekro and the way he had pitched.

Across the room, reporters were also getting Larry Bowa's thoughts on the tough loss. One cub reporter, apparently new to the baseball beat, asked Bowa what had happened to the Phillies out there. The bespectacled young writer quickly displayed a lack of baseball knowledge.

"What was wrong with you guys tonight?" he asked. "Niekro was throwing so slowly and you guys couldn't hit it. It looked like a beer league softball game." Evidently, he did not know what he was watching. Bowa erupted as only Bowa could.

"What the hell kind of question is that?" he shouted. "Get the fuck out of here, you four-eyed motherfucker, asking me a question like that!"

It was a reaction clearly resulting from the heat of the battle. Soon after, Bowa had completely forgotten about it. About a month later, and totally out of the blue, the Phillies shortstop received a note in the mail. It was a letter of apology from a reporter. The person wrote how sorry he was for being ill-informed during an interview, and for asking an upsetting question.

At the bottom, the note was signed, "The four-eyed motherfucker."

CHAPTER 16

Playing Out the String

The Streak was over, but the winning wasn't. Not for Carlton. For the Phillies as a team, the winning was usually over when his turn in the rotation passed. The only question that remained for Phillies fans was how many more would Carlton put in the win column? He already had 20. His preseason goal was 25, one he had set for himself back when he thought he'd be working for the Cardinals this season. But that goal had not wavered even after the trade—after the realization that reaching that goal just got significantly more difficult. Carlton forged on, and was having a season for the ages. Why stop at 25? Maybe 30 was doable. After all, there were enough starts left on the schedule.

The streak-ending loss to Phil Niekro and the Braves was part of a five-game losing streak for the Phillies. Lefty now set his sights on starting a new winning streak. His next start was the following Saturday, August 26th, against the always tough, West-leading Reds in Cincinnati.

Meanwhile, across the Atlantic Ocean, more than 7,000 athletes from 121 nations gathered in Munich for the opening ceremonies of the XX Olympiad. The games of swimmer Mark Spitz and his seven gold medals, and of diminutive Soviet gymnast Olga Korbut, a balance beam ballerina, were officially under way.

While the Reds were a team that historically gave Carlton trouble (remember that his win over Cincinnati nine days earlier was his second against the Reds in 14 tries), Lefty managed to help his cause this time with the bat. In the sixth inning, with the Phillies in front 1-0, Carlton came to the plate to face Reds starter Jim McGlothlin with the bases loaded and one away. Carlton drilled a single off the 28-year-old right-hander, scoring Greg Luzinski from third, and giving the Phillies a 2-0 lead. Don Money followed with a sacrifice fly to make it 3-0 after the sixth.

McGlothlin pitched for nine seasons in the big leagues, mostly with the California Angels and Cincinnati. He had a couple of good years. His best was 1967, when at age 23, he went 12-8 for the Angels with a 2.96 ERA, led the league in shutouts, and made the All-Star team. The 1973 season was his last. Two years later, and just two days before Christmas, McGlothlin succumbed to leukemia. He was 32.

It wasn't the low-hit, high-strikeout effort that fans had come to expect from Carlton, but he was certainly effective. Lefty fanned only five, but kept the high-octane Reds off balance, stranding runners with ground-ball outs, pop-outs, and fly-ball outs. A glance at the Riverfront Stadium scoreboard showed nothing but zeroes for the home team through the seventh inning. Carlton had pitched seven scoreless innings.

With one out in the bottom of the eighth, Carlton got touched for a double by Bobby Tolan. Johnny Bench was up next, and Carlton, trying to pitch carefully to the Reds slugger with a runner in scoring position, uncorked a wild pitch. Tolan moved to third base. Bench grounded out to short, but it was enough to get Tolan home, ending the shutout bid. Carlton wasn't out of trouble, however, because Tony Perez then blasted a two-out, solo homer to straightaway center field. The home run was Perez's 18th of the season, and cut the deficit to a lone run.

Fortunately for the Phillies, Tommy Hutton got a run back in the ninth inning with an RBI double to left off Reds reliever Clay Carroll, who had replaced McGlothlin in the eighth. The run was crucial, for it provided some much-needed insurance. That's because Carlton hit the wall in the bottom of the ninth. He faced three batters and they each got hits. The last was an RBI single from pinch-hitter Julian Javier. It made the score 4-3, and chased Carlton from the game.

Enter Mac Scarce. The Phillies' young reliever pitched out of that ninth-inning jam. With the potential tying and winning runs in scoring position, Scarce struck out Joe Morgan and Bobby Tolan to end the game. The Phils hung on 4-3, giving Carlton win number 21. Nine more and he'd reach 30 for the season.

But, alas, it was only a one-game winning streak. In fact, it was the Phillies' only win in a 10-game stretch. From Cincinnati, it was on to Houston for three games with the Astros. Carlton started the middle game of the series opposite the Astros' Jerry Reuss.

In front of a meager crowd of about 10,000 at the Astrodome, Carlton kept the home team hitless through the first four innings. Terry Harmon gave him a run in the top of the fifth. The HR-challenged Harmon hit just four round-trippers in his 10-year career, and was still searching for his first in the big leagues. Harmon sent a line drive to right that began to sink just as right fielder Jimmy Wynn charged. Wynn tried to make a shoe-string catch. He missed. The ball rolled along the Astrodome turf and bounced off the fence. Before anyone could get to the ball, Harmon was around third base and heading for home. He could've made it safely even if he had crawled. He slid across the plate anyway, just to be sure. It was an inside-the-park home run, the first HR of his career.

Carlton took his no-no into the bottom of the fifth, and after issuing a one-out walk, Tommy Helms singled for the Astros' first hit. A double and a bases-loaded groundout later, and Carlton trailed 2-1.

A mistake proved costly for the last-place Phillies in the seventh, and it turned out to be the difference in the game. With Houston leading 3-1, fleet-footed outfielder César Cedeño attempted to steal second. John Bateman made a terrific throw. It would have nailed Cedeño, except for one important detail. No one was covering the base. Denny Doyle failed to cover, and Bateman's great throw sailed instead into center. Two runs scored, and that was pretty much the ballgame.

Carlton lasted just six innings. He gave up three earned runs on only three hits, but walked four. It was indeed a quality start by today's standards, but not by the dominant left-hander's. The Phillies lost 5-3: a rare "L" for Super Steve. But he continued with his usual, single-minded focus—and that was to win the next game.

That steel-trap mental focus was on display in Atlanta on September 3rd. Carlton, bolstered by an eight-run third inning, went the distance on a five-hit shutout. The Phillies sent 12 men to the plate in the marathon frame. Carlton, Doyle, and Bowa each batted twice. It was Carlton himself who started the rally with a leadoff single. Joe Lis and Greg Luzinski highlighted the eight-run third with back-to-back homers. The Phillies didn't score another run the rest of the night, and won it by a final score of 8-0.

Strangely, every one of the five hits Lefty allowed—one double and four singles—was delivered by the first three Braves in the batting order. The top of the order got all the hits! And we're not talking about three of the game's immortals, but just one of them. As it happens, Oscar Lee Brown, brother of "Downtown" Ollie Brown, had two hits, including the double. Rod Gilbreath, batting second and playing second, had a single. The number-three hitter, Hank Aaron, went two for three with a walk. Aaron one can understand. But Oscar Brown played 160 games in a five-season career, registering only 77 major league hits. Gilbreath was a 19-year-old rookie who was four for 17 prior to the game, and would finish the year nine for 38. "Hard to believe, Harry."

With the victory, Steve had improved to 22-8. The victories kept on coming, while for the rest of the Phillies staff, the losses kept on mounting. The ace had now won 22, for a club that was presently 47-81. Carlton had nearly half of the wins.

Two days later, on Tuesday, September 5th, the world was shaken by events unfolding in the predawn hours in Munich. Eight members of a Palestinian terrorist organization had stormed into apartments housing the Israeli Olympic team. Two Israelis were murdered; nine others were taken hostage. Chilling images of machine gun–toting men in ski masks, standing on a balcony in the Olympic Village, were beamed around the globe. The terrorists, members of a group known as Black September, demanded the release of 234 Palestinians imprisoned in Israel.

Hal Bodley was in Munich covering the Olympiad for the Wilmington *News Journal.* "I really hated to leave the Phillies to go to Munich, the way that Carlton was going," he recalled. On the morning of September 5th, instead of reporting the details of competition, he quickly found himself knee-deep in events of more obvious importance. "Early that morning I was at a press conference for Mark Spitz," Bodley continued. Spitz was the undeniable star of the 1972 Summer Games, and had won another of his then-record seven gold medals. It was at the Spitz presser that Bodley and the other reporters present first heard the awful news:

"We left Mark Spitz and went over to the Olympic Village to see what was going on. We didn't sleep for the next 20 hours or so. We covered it around the clock."

September 5th was an off-day for the Phillies, who had just returned home after having been swept in a two-game series in Pittsburgh. The Phils were about to entertain St. Louis the next night, the opening game in an 11-game home stand. Like most Americans, the players spent the day off riveted to the horrible news that was breaking at the Olympic Games. Carlton, however, had to pull himself away from such real-world grimness, for it was "Steve Carlton Night" at Brandywine Raceway, a local harness racing venue. The Delaware Valley's newest hero was on hand to greet the fans, and he did so graciously. The featured race that night was the Steve Carlton Trot.

Meanwhile in Munich, competition had been suspended for the day, as the hostage standoff continued into the night. By 10 p.m., the drama moved to a nearby airbase where German authorities attempted a rescue plan. A gun battle erupted there between the Black September members and German snipers. The snipers managed to kill five of the eight terrorists. But during the blaze of gunfire, the Arab terrorists murdered all nine of the Israeli athletes. "They're all gone," ABC's Jim McKay famously announced to the world.

The following Thursday it was time again for Paul Owens to hand the ball to Carlton. He was once again facing his old team, the Cardinals. And Carlton was closing in on a Phillies milestone: Jim Bunning's team record for strikeouts in a season. Another record was within reach in this record-setting season of Super Steve. Bunning whiffed 268 in 1965; Steve came into the game with 263, a mere five strikeouts shy of the mark. Many had the sneaking suspicion that the record would fall this night.

That feeling was reinforced with a quick glance at the lineup Cardinals manager Red Schoendienst rolled out. It was full of rookies and September callups. The Cardinals, 21 games out of first place, were officially in a rebuilding mode and apparently wanted to get an eyeful of what the future may, or may not, hold. This was Red's starting eight, charged with the task of facing the best pitcher in the game:

> Bill Stein, LF
> Mike Tyson, 2B
> Luis Melendez, RF
> Skip Jutze, C
> Ted Simmons, 1B
> Ken Reitz, 3B
> Jorge Roque, CF
> Mick Kelleher, SS

No Lou Brock, no Joe Torre, no Matty Alou. On the mound was Al Santorini, a 24-year-old righty who would be out of the league the next year after making 70 career starts.

Bill Stein was a 25-year-old rookie playing in the second game of his career. Mike Tyson (not *that* Mike Tyson) was 22, had made his big league debut two nights earlier, and would have a solid nine-year career. Luis Melendez was also 22. Skip Jutze had been in the majors for a week. The 21-year-old Ken Reitz was playing the third game of what would become an 11-year career. Jorge Roque was 22 and had played in 21 big league games. Mick Kelleher, 24, had also been called up a week earlier. Only Ted Simmons was a regular. Just 22, "Simba" played 152 games that season, the second full season of his 21-year career. The '27 Yankees this was not.

Carlton struck out the second batter of the game, Mike Tyson, who would later have the dubious distinction of sharing his name with the controversial boxer. Carlton added another K in the second frame. He then fanned two of the three Cardinals he faced in the third inning. A third of the game was in the books, and Carlton was one strikeout away from Bunning's mark.

The 12,151 fans at the Vet were counting them down; the total was four after three innings, 267 on the season. Lefty was two strikeouts away from besting Bunning's club record. The fourth inning came and went without a whiff. Then in the fifth, with two on and two out, he got Stein swinging—the tying K, number 268. Carlton needed one more to break the club record.

It was a certainty that the faithful would get what they came to see, but would they see any runs? It was a 0-0 game after four and a half innings. That quickly changed in the home half of the fifth, thanks to a two-out triple off Larry Bowa's bat. The pesky shortstop broke the scoreless deadlock when Tommy Hutton followed by poking a triple of his own to center. The consecutive triples gave Carlton a 1-0 cushion. An inning later, Greg Luzinski belted a solo homer. Now it was 2-0, Phillies.

All that was left was the business of Bunning's record. The rookie-laden Cardinal lineup actually presented a challenge for the regimented Carlton. Though thought of as the man who always had a plan, Steve had no idea at first how to pitch to these guys. He managed, however, to figure it out. In the seventh, with one on and nobody out, he faced young Jorge Roque. It was just the 40th plate appearance of the 22-year-old's career. At zero for two on the night, he was no match for Carlton. The ace got him swinging for strike three. Home plate umpire (and Philadelphia native) Shag Crawford rang up Roque, and the Phillies franchise record for strikeouts in a season belonged to Carlton. The Cardinals scratched out a run against him later in the inning, and now the focus in the stadium was on whether Carlton could hang on for another victory.

Super Steve was back out there in the ninth inning. Protecting a one-run lead, he retired the Cardinals in order, registering another strikeout for the final out of the game. He finished with nine on the night, and now had 272 on the year. The 2-1 victory was his 23rd against eight losses and was, incidentally, his 100th major league win. It was yet another complete game for the dazzling left-hander, who now had 24 on the season, and 16 in his last 19 starts. The 23 wins were the most ever by a Phillies lefty in a single season. The records and milestones, like the wins and strikeouts, continued to pile up. And 30 victories—that Holy Grail of a number—was within his reach. It would mean pitching on two days' rest in the final week of the season, but Carlton was open to the possibility. That left him with seven starts remaining. Of course, he had to win them all. But wasn't that always his intent—to win every game he pitched?

Carlton's next start was on September 11th. (No one could have known at the time what emotional significance that date would one day hold.) The Mets were in town with their own lefty, Jerry Koosman, on the mound. Koosman came in struggling, a loser in six of his previous seven decisions.

Closing ceremonies for the tragedy-marred Munich games took place the day before. It would soon be back to the baseball beat for reporters like Hal Bodley, an abrupt and not so smooth transition: "I remember watching a game and saying to myself, 'this is so unimportant' after covering the Israeli massacre and all the things I had to cover at the Munich Olympics."

Unimportant, yes, in the grand scheme of things, but it seemed relatively crushing to Phillies fans when Carlton squandered a 2-0 lead in the fourth inning. For some reason, he just couldn't throw strikes. This was a complete anomaly for the hurler who had taken on something of a superhero-like persona. What baffled Carlton was that he felt great. He should've been pitching much better. He couldn't understand it.

Lefty issued consecutive walks to open the fourth inning. *Consecutive walks*? He hadn't walked two batters in a row since May 30th. Steve was having problems locating his fastball. "It must be a flaw in my mechanics," he thought. The fastball just didn't have its usual movement. Carlton was frustrated that he couldn't get it to run back inside and paint the corner for a strike. Normally, he owned the inside corner of the plate. Not tonight.

The bases were loaded for Mets catcher Duffy Dyer, and he laced a grounder deep in the hole at short. Larry Bowa, ranging to his right, made a splendid play—fielding the ball, and then making a difficult throw to gain a force out at second base. Bowa's athletic play allowed only one run to score, and kept the damage in check. Things could've been far worse for Carlton, especially given what happened next with Mets first baseman Jim Beauchamp at the plate. Carlton came inside and jammed him with a curve. But the right-handed-swinging Beauchamp managed to fist a looping line drive over the first-base bag. It rolled down the line for an RBI double, tying the game, 2-2.

It was one of those nights for Carlton, one he rarely experienced in this super-season. In the sixth inning, Duffy Dyer punished a disobedient Carlton fastball. The pitch stayed up and flowed right down the middle of the plate, which was hardly where Lefty wanted it. It landed in the Mets bullpen for a home run.

In the eighth inning, Cleon Jones hit a ground ball to Joe Lis at first base. But on his follow-through, Steve landed off balance. As a result, he was late in covering the base and Jones had an infield single. Carlton paid for the miscue two batters later as Dyer again inflicted the damage. The Duffer hit a Carlton offering sky-high and off the top of the right center-field fence for a triple.

Trailing 4-2 in the bottom of the ninth, Paul Owens lifted his starting pitcher for a pinch-hitter. Rookie catcher Bob Boone, who only the day before had made his major league debut, went to the batter's box in place of Carlton. Boone would go on to play 10 of his 19 seasons with the Phillies, becoming one of the best catchers in franchise history, and a veteran leader of the 1980 World Series champs. But in this, his third big league at-bat, he struck out.

Boone played in 16 games that September, after catching 138 out of 148 games in the Pacific Coast League before his call-up to the Phillies. From September 12th on, he was behind the plate every single day with one exception: "I caught every day, except when Steve pitched." John Bateman continued do to the honors on those nights. The only time Boone ever caught Carlton that season was during spring training, while Boone was in the big league camp. It was quite an awakening for the young catcher: "I thought, this is what it's supposed to be like. It was as if I had been driving a Volkswagen, and then someone loaned me their Mercedes."

Owens offered no explanation to Boone as to why he didn't catch Carlton. No explanation was really necessary. "I put two and two together," Boone recalls. "He and Bateman had something working." The seven-time Gold Glove winner understood completely. "When I teach catching, I emphasize that it's about the relationship between the catcher and the pitcher. It's about two guys being on the same page. It's like a certain jockey riding a certain horse." Only Bateman was allowed in the saddle of the Phillies' own Secretariat.

The big horse failed to reach the winner's circle against the Mets that night. The Phillies lost, 4-2, dropping Carlton to 23-9. For the 25th time in the season he pitched a complete game. But he gave up eight hits and walked four. Each of the four runs was earned. Steve threw 150 pitches, going deep in the count time and time again. When he got two strikes on a hitter, he just couldn't seem to finish them off.

When the game ended, Ralph Bernstein, the veteran beat writer for the Associated Press, headed for the Phillies' clubhouse. Bernstein always liked to be among the first reporters to show up for postgame interviews. After descending in the Vet's press box elevator to the basement floor, Bernstein walked briskly through the bowels of the stadium toward the clubhouse. He beat everyone else down, and was the first member of the press contingent to enter. The grizzled scribe made his way over to Steve Carlton's stall, at the end of the row of lockers on the left side of the room. Carlton was seated facing the wall. He had removed his jersey, and was stripped to his undershirt and uniform pants. Steve's red spikes, adorned with the trademark three stripes of the Adidas brand, were tossed in the bottom of the locker. He was just sitting there in his stocking feet with his head down, wearing a rather dejected expression.

"What's wrong, big guy?" Bernstein asked. "You really look down."

"I now know," said Carlton, "that I cannot win 30."

Surely he was disappointed at the loss, and at an effort that was sub-par by his supernal standards. But the atypical dejection Carlton displayed was due more to the realization that 30 wins was now a complete impossibility.

The quote attributed to Carlton in the next day's *Philadelphia Daily News* was this: "I was confident I could win 30 as long as it was mathematically possible." It was no longer.

The following evening, September 12th, a skinny youngster with two bad knees from Dayton, Ohio, played seven innings at third base for the Phillies in what would be a 4-3 loss to the Mets. The rookie singled in his second at-bat, driving a sharp ground ball through the hole between shortstop and third. He finished the night 1-3, walking once and striking out twice. And thus began the Hall of Fame career of Michael Jack Schmidt, one of the greatest third basemen of all time.

Three days later, on a warm, mid-September night, the Phillies honored their star pitcher with "Steve Carlton Night." They showered him with presents—a new Chrysler Imperial, a color TV, a pair of rifles, bicycles for his two boys, golf clubs, and a set of luggage.

Steve's parents, Joe and Anne Carlton, made the trip from Miami for their son's special night. Joe was an airline maintenance man; Anne was a homemaker. They raised Steve and his two sisters, Christina and Joanne, in a small house in North Miami. Steve grew up there much like a modern-day Huck Finn, tearing around the Everglades with his buddies. They hunted for small animals and fished for snapper, using live shrimp as bait. The boyhood Steve became skilled at knocking birds from trees with rocks. It was a skill that extended quite well to the baseball diamond, allowing for pinpoint accuracy with his fastball.

Carlton was a high school standout in both baseball and basketball, giving up the latter after his junior season to concentrate on baseball. That same year, in the ballpark used by the Baltimore Orioles' triple-A club, Steve tossed a no-hitter—a feat that eluded him as a major league star.

One day, after graduating in 1963, Steve and a friend went to a local field to throw for a scout from the St. Louis Cardinals. By the afternoon's end, the scout signed Carlton to the contract for $5,000. Now here he was some nine years later, a big league sensation feted with his own "Night."

It would have been a huge letdown for the 20,000 fans at the Vet for "Steve Carlton Night" had Steve then gone out and lost the ballgame. The Phils were hosting Montreal. "I felt a special obligation to win," said the Phillies starter afterward. It was 1-1 in the third inning when the going got a bit sticky for Carlton. He surrendered successive singles to open the inning, one of them to Expos pitcher Mike Torrez. Then, in attempting to pick Torrez off second base, Lefty threw wildly. The ball sailed into center field. Don Money booted a ground ball one batter later, and the bases were loaded. The Expos brought home two with a pair of sacrifice flies; Carlton and the Phillies were down 3-1.

Lefty wasn't happy with his fastball. He felt it was lacking. Normally he could count on it exploding into the catcher's mitt as if shot out of a rifle. Not tonight, and oddly, a TV talk show host may have been to blame.

By this point in the season, Carlton's disdain for throwing between starts was well-known. Many pitchers throw side sessions between starts, but Steve never touched a baseball. He did his own brand of exercises, like squeezing a pair of small, stainless-steel balls. "He got them from a company out of Chicago," as Greg Luzinski remembers. "He'd constantly move them around in his hand to strengthen his forearms and hands. He always had them in his hands. In the airport, in the dugout, you'd go out to dinner and he'd have them."

Two days before the "Steve Carlton Night" game with the Expos, the Phillies star was a guest on *The Mike Douglas Show*. The nationally syndicated afternoon talk show featured interviews with actors, musicians, and the occasional sports star. In fact, the world got its first look at golf superstar Tiger Woods as a three-year-old interviewed by Mike Douglas. (The appearance lives on in a now-famous piece of archival footage.) For years, the show's home base was Philadelphia, at the studios of KYW-TV on Independence Mall, a short distance from where the Founding Fathers signed the Declaration.

For Carlton's appearance, the producers dreamed up a bit where the best pitcher in baseball would toss balls at a dunking machine in order to drop Douglas' co-host, Ron Carey, into a water tank. Ever the perfectionist, Carlton warmed-up to get his arm loose. He threw more balls at the target to get a feel for the bit. He then rehearsed the act, throwing even more pitches. Finally, with the studio cameras rolling during the actual show, Carlton tossed the baseballs at the dunk tank to the satisfaction and delight of Douglas and the show's producers. But as far as Carlton was concerned, the entire schtick was the equivalent of a bullpen session. He was afraid it may have taken a small toll on his arm, leaving him at less than full strength for his upcoming date with Montreal.

Carlton was down 3-1 to the Expos in the third inning of that game when Willie Montañez came up. The Phillies' center fielder, batting cleanup, came through with a two-run single that tied the game. Then in the sixth, it was The Bull to the rescue. With the count at 0-1, Mike Torrez tried to fool him with a breaking ball. Instead, Luzinski hit it deep to center and gone. No one was more elated by the "Bull Blast" than the starting pitcher. "Bull's home run really pumped me up," said Carlton in the next day's *Daily News*.

The Phillies went on to win the game, 5-3. Steve was a little upset that he gave up three runs, but he was content to notch his 24th win of the season. It was another complete game—his 26th—a new franchise record for a left-handed pitcher. With his next victory, he would reach his pre-season goal of 25.

The following evening, that youngster with the bad knees from Dayton played in his third big league game. In the seventh inning, with the Phillies down 1-0 to Expos left-hander Balor Moore, the rookie stepped to the plate. There were two men on and two men out. The Expos intentionally walked Roger Freed, the number-five hitter, to get to the rookie who was batting next. But the tactical move backfired. The rookie sent a Moore offering on a long drive. That ball was *outta here*! It was a three-run homer to give the Phillies a 3-1 victory. And thus was struck the very first of 548 home runs hit by Michael Jack Schmidt, one of the greatest home run hitters of all time.

As the Baseball Gods would have it, Carlton's next start was against Rick Wise—yes, the same Rick Wise for whom he was traded some seven months earlier. The game was in St. Louis against the Cardinals, but only 5,569 fans showed up for the showdown between Carlton and Wise. It was the second smallest crowd of the season at Busch Stadium. Too much time had passed since the blockbuster deal, knocking the luster off the Carlton-Wise matchup. Two weeks earlier, when Lefty last faced them, the Cards were out of the race and going with a youth movement, although Lou Brock and Joe Torre were both in the starting lineup for this one. Because the Phillies were the worst team in the league, there wasn't much interest in a late-September contest such as this.

Both teams were playing out the string. There were only two weeks left in the season, and there were few questions still unanswered. But chief among those few was this: How many victories would Carlton get by season's end? The quest for 25 was a done deal. Even he knew it.

"I still wrote '25' on my mirror with shaving cream before I shaved every morning," Carlton told reporters. "I try never to lose sight of a goal, but I've known for some time that I was going to reach that goal."

Reach it he did, and against the pitcher whom Phillies fans wished to keep back in February, instead of exchanging him for Carlton, now baseball's winningest hurler. This had been a hard-luck season for Rick Wise. He entered the game with a record of 15-15. Of the losses, 11 were by one run. In fact, 17 of his 31 starts had been decided by a single digit. Six of Wise's losses were 3-2 finals, and two of them were by 2-1 scores. He lost two games, 4-3, and he lost another game, 1-0. "He could've won 20 by now, easy," said his manager, Red Schoendienst.

Both clubs put a run on the board in the first inning. Denny Doyle opened the game with a double off Wise. He scored on a single by Tommy Hutton. In the home half, Lou Brock also led off with a double. Then Brock, the man who would retire as baseball's leader in stolen bases, promptly made a theft of third. He scored on a single by the very next batter, Ted Sizemore. But that was all for the Cardinals against Carlton. It was 1-1 after one inning, and it stayed that way for the next five. In the sixth inning, the Phillies moved out in front. Bill Robinson's fielder's choice grounder scored Hutton from third base to make it 2-1, Phils. That was it for the offense on this night.

Wise was lifted for a pinch-hitter after going seven innings. He gave up two runs on six hits. Carlton went the distance. He surrendered a run just two batters into the game, and then pitched shutout ball the rest of the way. He faced 34 batters; only one scored—the first batter he faced in the game. And for the fourth time since June, Robinson had the game-winning RBI. All four came in games won by Carlton.

Carlton was now 25-9. He'd reached 25 wins, but as it turned out, that wasn't the peak of his emotional accomplishment. As Lefty admitted afterward, the emotional highlight of the season was the 15-game winning streak. Through the subsequent years, that would remain near the top of his very long list of career accomplishments. Meanwhile, it was another one-run loss for Wise, who dropped to 15-16 on the year. In case anyone was scoring at home, Carlton had gone 4-0 versus his former team.

The season of Steve was headed for three more starts, three more chances for baseball fans to watch him pitch, and three more chances to add to the victory total. The first of the remaining three was a marquee matchup: another showdown with Tom Seaver.

It was the first time the two stars had squared off since the May 21st game before a packed house at the Vet. Seaver and the Mets won that one. This was the fifth and final time that Carlton would be facing Yogi Berra's team, which had faded in the NL East race. It was currently in third place, 16 and a half games back. So meaningless was this Phillies end-of-the-schedule run that the *Philadelphia Inquirer* didn't bother to send a reporter to Shea Stadium to cover the game.

It didn't begin well for Lefty. The first batter he faced, Tommie Agee, took him deep. The second batter, second baseman Lute Barnes, doubled. But Carlton roared back by fanning the three Mets that followed to end the frame. He didn't allow another run until the eighth inning, when a Barnes sacrifice fly plated Ted Martinez, who had advanced to third on a throwing error by John Bateman.

An inning earlier, Bill Robinson had tied it with a solo homer off Seaver, but that was all the Phillies could muster against Tom Terrific. Trailing 2-1 in the top of the ninth, the Phillies went down in order. Seaver got the first out of the inning, then exited for Tug McGraw, who struck out both batters he faced to nail it down. For only the 10th time in 1972, Steve Carlton had lost.

And Steve had lost again to Seaver in another duel between the future Hall of Famers. It had been another typically brief day at the office for Lefty, as the game was completed in a swift one hour and 53 minutes. Carlton had gone eight innings, allowed two runs (one earned) on seven hits, whiffed nine, and didn't walk a batter. Seaver went eight and a third, scattered five hits, gave up one run and struck out six. They each surrendered a homer. Basically, an error cost Carlton the ballgame. The margin between victory and defeat is often that slim.

It was that slim in his next start, the penultimate of his season. The final was again 2-1, but this time Carlton was on the right side. He beat the Pirates back at the Vet in front of a Thursday night crowd of 12,216, a surprisingly sparse attendance figure given that it was Lefty's last start at home and the final Phillies home game of the year. The only run Carlton relinquished on this night came on a second-inning sac fly. He even sparked a two-run, fifth-inning Phillies rally with an RBI double.

Pirates great Roberto Clemente led off the fourth inning with a single. It was the 2,999th hit of his glorious career. As fate would later have it, Clemente added just one more.

In the sixth inning, Super Steve reached yet another milestone. To this point he had struck out seven Pirates. That brought him to a grand total of 299 for the year. One more and he'd notch the magical total of 300. No Phillies pitcher—not Ol' Pete Alexander or even Robin Roberts—had ever struck out 300 batters in a season. The Pirates sent Bob Robertson to pinch-hit for Clemente with two away. Carlton got him swinging. *Swing and a miss, struck 'eem out*! Robertson was his 300th strikeout victim of the season. It was only the second time in National League history that a pitcher struck out 300 batters in a season.

Lefty never fashioned himself as a power pitcher, and he wasn't known as someone who put up massive strikeout totals, the 19-strikeout game in '69 notwithstanding. In fact, he never struck out more than the 210 he K'd that season. But Carlton never before had as many starts as he had this year, he had never been part of a four-man rotation, and never before had he been a staff ace. "Pitching in a four-man rotation, I think, is the secret to my success this year," Steve said in an interview for the club's season-ending highlight film. "It's allowed me to be very consistent."

Leading 2-1 in the seventh, the Phillies got a game-saving relay play. Tommy Hutton, in right field, hit Denny Doyle, who threw a strike to John Bateman, to nail Rennie Stennett at the plate. It was another complete game win for Carlton, who pitched a six-hitter. He finished with 11 strikeouts, getting Willie Stargell three times. Once again, Willie was "drinking coffee with a fork."

The Fightin' Phillies, with their pitiful record of 56-94, hit the road for the final week of their strike-delayed, loss-filled season. Only Steve Carlton had rescued the season from being a complete and utter disaster. He was the lone bright spot, or rather, a shining beam in the shrouded fog. In closing out the string, the Phils played three in Montreal, losing two, and three in Chicago, where they won two.

One of those two, as one would imagine, was Lefty's final start. It is a bit surprising that Carlton even made this start. Each of the Phillies' final six games was the very definition of meaningless. Would anyone have objected if Paul Owens had skipped Carlton's turn in the rotation on this, the second-to-last day of the season, and instead given the ball to a young prospect? Owens, of course, was still "auditioning" his team to determine its future makeup. The Phils brass had long concluded that Carlton was the stud pitcher around which the rest of the team would be built. Suppose he suffered a serious injury? It's likely that no one would have objected to shutting down Carlton. No one, that is, except Carlton. If it was his turn, he was taking the ball; in his mind no game was meaningless. So there he was, 26-10, on the mound on Tuesday afternoon, October 3rd, in front of an intimate gathering of 2,264 baseball fans in the friendly confines of Wrigley Field.

The Cubs were in second place in the East, but a whopping 10 games back. The Pirates had long since clinched the division. The Cubs weren't playing for anything, and their lineup reflected it. Billy Williams, Ron Santo, Rick Monday, and José Cardenal all had the day off. Glenn Beckert, Don Kessinger, and Randy Hundley merely pinch-hit. Facing Carlton were Bill North, Gene Hiser, Jim Tyrone, Carmen Fanzone, Pat Bourque, Ken Rudolph, Al Montreuil, and Dave Rosello. On the mound for the Cubs was a lefty named Dan McGinn. He was 0-4, and was making what turned out to be the final start of his five-season major league career.

Carlton, as could probably be guessed, had little trouble. Neither did the Phillies offense. They gave their ace, in his final start of the year, his greatest amount of run support. The Phillies scored 11 times—the most runs they scored in a game in which Carlton earned a decision. He only needed two runs, and he got those in the second inning on a two-out, two-run homer from Bill Robinson. He got four more in the third, highlighted by back-to-back homers from Don Money and Greg Luzinski. In the fifth inning, Money and Luzinski went back-to-back again. The same guys back-to-back twice in the same game! It gave Luzinski a team-leading 18 on the season.

"I remember that game," Luzinski says as he sits in an outdoor booth at Bull's BBQ, his food stand at Citizens Bank Park in Philadelphia. It is roughly an hour before game time on a drizzly, midweek evening in June. "I remember it because I ended up hitting two out," he adds.

Bull is dressed in a green pullover emblazoned with a Phillies Spring Training logo on the breast. His blond hair is now flecked with gray. He wears it slicked back above his tanned face. The ex-slugger smiles as he greets patrons, signing autographs and shaking hands. These days Greg carries a bit more than his playing weight from 1972, but he still looks as if he could crush a baseball 400 feet.

The Chicago native loved playing at Wrigley, and going home was always special for him. But that October game in '72, Carlton's 27th win, was particularly gratifying. "I had been ripped by the sportswriters who expected more power from me," said Luzinski. "But I was in a learning curve. I was getting my feet wet. And we didn't exactly have a dynamic lineup. But I remember the two homers, and Lefty winning his 27th."

The Phillies hit six home runs that day. Even Terry Harmon, for just the second time in his career, went deep. Carlton tossed seven scoreless innings before giving up a run on two hits in the eighth. That was the only thing that separated him from his ninth shutout. The final score was 11-1. Carlton's line went like this: nine innings, nine hits, one run (earned), one walk, and seven strikeouts. He had lowered his ERA to 1.97, the best in the league. The seven strikeouts gave him a league-leading 310. And the victory gave Carlton a 27-10 record for the season. He had won the pitching Triple Crown in the National League: most wins, most strikeouts, and lowest ERA. The feat would not be matched for another 13 years, and since then it has been equaled only twice in the National League.

The following day the Phillies closed out the year on a winning note. Barry Lersch pitched a four-hitter to lead the Phils past the Cubs, 2-1. Mercifully, the Phillies' 1972 campaign was over. The team's final record was a dismal 59-97. They played 156 games, having lost the first week to the players' strike. The '72 Phillies finished dead last in the NL East, 37 and a half games behind the division champion Pirates.

Steve Carlton, however, was able to rise above the ineptitude in a manner that had never been seen in the annals of the game. In 1972, Carlton earned 27 victories for a 59-win club. Take a moment to digest that. Roll the figures around in your head. Repeat after me: 27 of 59! Now do the math. To win 27 of 59 means that Carlton accounted for 45.8 percent of the team's total victories. It rounds up to 46 percent: *46 percent* of the games were won by Carlton! It remains the largest percentage of a team's victories won by a single pitcher. No one has ever come close.

CHAPTER 17

The Rest
of the Squad

Larry Bowa still marvels when he thinks back to Steve Carlton's magical 1972 season. "Every time he won, a couple guys would say in jest, 'Okay, we're good for four days.' Because we were bad, and it was like, we got that out of the way. Now we'll go back to being horseshit."

They were horseshit, for sure, in between Carlton's starts. Complete, unadulterated horseshit. The difference between how the Phillies fared in the last two-thirds of the season when Carlton took the mound and when he did not is absolutely astounding. From June 7th, when Carlton began his 15-game roll, until the end of the season, the Phillies were 24-5 in games that he started; his record was 22-4 and he had three no-decisions. Conversely, during the same time frame, in games that Lefty watched from the dugout, the Phillies posted a 19-63 record. No other pitcher won more than three games. The disparity was particularly striking from June 10th until July 27th, when Carlton went 8-0 to extend his winning streak to nine, while the Phillies were 2-27 in "non-Lefty" starts. Remarkable. Over nearly a seven-week period, about a quarter of the season, the Phillies won *two* games without Steve Carlton. Soon after, there was a three-and-a-half-week stretch in August, during which the Phils dropped 15 of 16 games, when Lefty did not get the ball. Meanwhile, he was extending his winning streak to 15. As Jayson Stark noted, "For [the Phillies] to win when Carlton didn't pitch, it took a miracle."

Denny Doyle, using the car analogy like Bob Boone, explained the Carlton phenomenon in '72. "We didn't try any harder when Lefty pitched—but you feel different when you're driving a Porsche versus a Chevy Nova. Other teams knew we were better when he pitched. He gave us confidence which was contagious. We knew we were special when Lefty pitched. He gave us an edge. Every game was like a World Series game."

No doubt, in one out of four games, the '72 Phillies played like a World Series team. But in the other three games, they played like the '62 Mets. That infamous team posted a 40-120 record and is the benchmark whenever the subject of bad baseball teams is broached. When the Mets' season was over, manager Casey Stengel, who maintained his legendary sense of humor despite all the losses, cracked, "No one man could have done all this." Likewise, no one man could have been responsible for the '72 Phillies' abominable record in games not started by Carlton. Several pitchers on Ray Rippelmeyer's staff contributed to the carnage.

Dick Selma was in the middle of a five-game losing streak when he was ousted from the starting four in early June. Selma lost two more in relief to extend the streak to seven and finished the season with a 2-9 record. He was released by the Phillies the following May.

Ken Reynolds replaced Selma in the rotation and was a regular Phillies starter for the remainder of the season. Reynolds was born in the Philadelphia suburb of Trevose, grew up and went to high school outside of Boston, and attended college in New Mexico. The lefty won a respectable 124 games in his professional baseball career. Unfortunately, 117 of his wins were in the minors.

Reynolds' first start in '72 was on June 9th. It was not until September 1st—his 17th start—that Reynolds finally chalked one up in the win column. Before he broke through with a victory on Labor Day weekend, Reynolds lost 12 straight games to tie a National League record for most consecutive losses by a pitcher at the start of a season. Reynolds was not entirely to blame. His 4.26 ERA for the season was on the high side but not atrocious. In the last 10 losses of his losing streak, the mighty Phillies offense generated a total of nine runs and was shut out four times. Could Reynolds, with an 0-12 record in late August, have developed an inferiority complex sitting next to Carlton on the bench after he had just gone on a 15-0 binge? Reynolds closed out his forgettable year with a 2-15 record and was traded to Milwaukee in the off-season.

In June and July, Woodie Fryman stayed in the rotation with Carlton, Reynolds, and Billy Champion. The season had started well for Woodie, as he was 2-1 in mid-May with a pair of shutouts. Six weeks later, he woke up with a 2-9 record. As the losses piled up, both for him and the team, Fryman continued to grumble about how disenchanted he was with pitching in Philadelphia. "If I don't get traded, I'm quitting," he fumed to Rippelmeyer. Paul Owens wasn't able to swing a trade for Fryman, but on August 2nd, the Phillies put him out of his misery by placing him on waivers. Detroit, in the thick of a tight race in the American League East, grabbed him. All Fryman did for Billy Martin's Tigers in the last two months of the season was to go 10-3 with a 2.06 ERA, and to win the division clincher against the Red Sox on the last weekend of the season.

Like Fryman, Billy Champion broke out of the gate strong, winning his first three decisions. The fourth-year righty was optimistic that he was on his way to a breakthrough season. A 1-13 drought, with an 11-game losing streak on the back end, curbed Champion's enthusiasm. Owens dropped him from the rotation in mid-August, and he was shipped to Milwaukee as part of the off-season housecleaning.

Jim Nash, who came over in the June trade with the Braves, was the biggest bust of the bunch. Nash lost his first four starts for the Phillies, went on the disabled list with a sore shoulder for a few weeks, was activated in September, and lost four more games. His final stats for the Phillies: an 0-8 record with a 6.27 ERA. He didn't make it past the fifth inning in six of his eight starts. Nash's lone contribution to the Phillies was holding Gene Mauch down so Don Money could slug him in the brawl at Montreal. The Phillies released him at the end of spring training in 1973.

Steve Carlton had the same defense behind him as the other pitchers, and the same offense supporting him. But look at the final records and longest streaks of Carlton and several of the other starters:

Pitcher	Record	Streak
Carlton	27-10	15 (winning)
Champion	4-14	11 (losing)
Fryman	4-10	8 (losing)
Reynolds	2-15	12 (losing)
Selma	2-9	7 (losing)
Nash	0-8	8 (losing)

Why did Carlton shine so brilliantly while his fellow pitchers struggled so profoundly? He debated this issue with Ray Rippelmeyer over dinner in late August, right after Lefty's winning streak was snapped by Phil Niekro and the Braves. The Phillies arrived in Cincinnati the day before the start of a three-game series, and Carlton and Rippelmeyer, along with their wives Beverly and Glenda, dined at a restaurant on the riverfront. As the wives chatted about their children, Carlton and Rip pondered the woes of the young Phillies pitchers. Carlton, whose mental approach to the game was vital to his success, offered this offbeat opinion:

"The other pitchers could throw the ball harder if they *thought* they could." Rippelmeyer was bewildered and let Steve know it. "That's the dumbest statement I've ever heard an intelligent man make." Rip acknowledged that for a pitcher to thrive, it's important that he maintain a positive attitude and a high level of confidence. But, Ray insisted, a pitcher also needs the God-given talent to throw hard, which Carlton was blessed with and the other pitchers were not. According to Rip, a pitcher can't be taught to throw harder, nor can he throw harder simply by thinking that he can. Either the pitcher has the arm to throw hard or he doesn't.

Rookie Wayne Twitchell, who replaced Woodie Fryman in the rotation, had one of the better arms on the staff. It's hard to say if he had good velocity because he was born with a strong arm or because he thought he could throw hard. While growing up in Portland, Oregon, Twitchell's idol was Robin Roberts, and he aspired to make the majors and pitch for the Phillies. He had a cup of coffee with the Brewers in 1970 and then was traded to the Phillies in the following year. He pitched well as a late-season call-up for the Phillies in '71 and made the club's Opening Day roster in '72.

Lanky and six-feet-six, Twitchell didn't light the world on fire, but his 5-9 record wasn't so bad when compared to Champion, Reynolds, and some of the other pitchers. He tossed a shutout against the Astros in August and won back-to-back games in September, which was only the second time since May that a Phillies hurler other than Carlton won two straight starts.

Back in his hometown of Portland, Twitchell recalled the thrill of pitching in the same rotation as Carlton for part of the '72 season. "He had wonderful stuff, wonderful control. He became tougher when the game was on the line." Twitchell didn't consider Carlton a mentor but still learned a lot from him. "He helped me because I was able to observe the level of intensity which he took to the mound. It was eye-opening. I would watch the sequence of his pitches and try to incorporate them into my game. He led by example; he was not a rah-rah guy."

Steve Carlton's presence helped turn Wayne Twitchell into a winner. Twitch won 13 games in 1973 and ironically he, not Carlton, was the team's lone representative at the All-Star Game. He sustained a knee injury in 1974, which slowed him down, but he pitched for the Phillies, as both a starter and reliever, until 1977. Of all the playees on the Phillies at the start of the 1972 season, only Carlton, Luzinski, and Bowa remained with the team longer than Twitchell.

In chronicling Steve Carlton's amazing season of 1972, we have discussed a few Phillies players—including Chris Short, Byron Browne, Ron Stone, Jim Nash, and John Bateman—whose major league journeys ended that year. Add to the list one of the September call-ups, 20-year-old right-hander Dave Downs. The brevity of his major league career is incredible.

As soon as Downs arrived from double-A Reading, Paul Owens pressed him into service, naming him as the starter in the second game of a doubleheader against the Braves in Atlanta on September 2nd. Downs responded by doing what few pitchers in history have done: He threw a complete game shutout in his first major league appearance. Downs admitted afterward that he was stunned by his accomplishment. Owens thought he may have found a pitcher to complement Carlton in the rotation. Things didn't quite pan out, though, as Downs *never won another major league game*. He started three more games in September without a win and was sent home to Utah with a sore arm stemming from tendonitis. His arm problems kept him on the shelf for the entire 1973 season. Downs tried to come back in 1974, returning to the minors, but his arm was still bothering him and he was hit hard. He missed the 1975 season but gave it another shot in 1976 with Spartanburg, one of the Phillies' single-A affiliates. For Spartanburg, Downs had a 9.39 ERA in 10 starts and he never pitched again.

A stroke of coincidence: Fourteen years after Dave Downs' spectacular major league debut, his younger brother Kelly was called up in mid-season from the minors by San Francisco. He made his first start at Dodger Stadium and pitched respectably, allowing two runs in five innings, but the Giants lost to L.A. and Fernando Valenzuela, 2-1. Carlton watched Dave's first game from the Phillies' dugout in '72 and Kelly's first game from the Giants' dugout in '86. The Giants had claimed Carlton off waivers on July 4th, and Kelly made his debut on July 29th. Nine days later, Carlton announced his retirement; he had just struck out his 4,000th batter. He reconsidered, and the following week the White Sox signed him. (The Giants would have released Carlton even if he didn't "retire.") Kelly Downs went on to win 57 games for the Giants and A's in an eight-year major league career.

Much as we have maligned the Phillies' pitchers, we would be remiss if we failed to spend some time disparaging the hitters. After all, their shortcomings played a critical role in that 59-97 record. The Phillies' team average of .236 ranked ninth in the 12 National League clubs. Terry Harmon hit .284 to lead the team, but he only played in 73 games and had 218 at-bats. Of the hitters who played in at least 100 games, Greg Luzinski was the leader at .281; only he and Tommy Hutton (.260) batted higher than .250. To provide a frame of reference, the Pirates hit .274 as a team, and Billy Williams won the batting title with a .333 average. The Phils hit 98 home runs as a team—tied for ninth in the National League; Luzinski paced the squad with 18. The Bull also led the team in runs batted in with 68. Larry Bowa's 67 runs were first on the Phils. Those are not very impressive run production numbers considering that Johnny Bench totaled 40 home runs and 125 RBI, and Joe Morgan scored 122 runs. The Phillies weren't terrors on the base paths either. César Cedeño led the National League with 55 stolen bases. The Phillies' *entire team* stole 42 bags.

Based on these dismal numbers, it's no surprise that the Phillies had an inordinate number of low-scoring games. They were shut out 13 times, scored a single run in 31 games, and plated two in 22 games. So in 42 percent of their games, they scored two or fewer runs. They were no-hit by Burt Hooton, and almost no-hit by Carl Morton (Mike Anderson's triple in the third inning was the Phillies' lone hit), Jerry Reuss (Bowa broke up a no-hitter in the ninth), Steve Arlin (Denny Doyle did the same, also in the ninth), and Fergie Jenkins (Willie Montañez's fourth-inning double was the Phils' only hit).

Tepid as the Phillies' offense was, they stepped it up a notch when their ace was pitching. They averaged 3.76 runs a game in Carlton's 41 starts, compared to a 3.02 average in all other games. Steve Carlton, in the greatest season of his Hall of Fame career, inspired his teammates to bear down and deliver the clutch hits.

CHAPTER 18

The Case for Carlton

"How many guys pitching in last place ever had the kind of year Carlton's had," Red Schoendienst wondered out loud after watching his former starter blank his own Cardinals. The answer would be, quite simply, none. In the entire modern era of baseball, no pitcher except Steve Carlton has ever won as many as 27 games for a last-place squad. Not before, and certainly not since.

In fact, just one other pitcher besides Carlton has ever won 20 in the modern era for an NL team that finished last. His name is Frank "Noodles" Hahn, and in 1901 he went 22-19 for the last-place Cincinnati Reds. That's it. Only Lefty and Noodles have ever won 20 or more for an NL cellar-dweller. Carlton became the sixth hurler since 1900 to achieve the feat. Four American League pitchers, all right-handers, also did it, each winning 20 games.

By any standard, Carlton's final numbers for 1972 were mind-boggling. For a last-place team they were otherworldly. His record of 27-10 was phenomenal. He made 41 starts and completed a staggering 30 games. He pitched eight shutouts. His earned run average of 1.97 was exceptional. His innings total was a massive 346 and a third. He surrendered just 84 total runs; 76 were earned. Carlton allowed 257 hits; 17 were home runs. He walked 87 and struck out 310. His walks and hits per innings pitched computed to .993—less than one base runner an inning.

As noted previously, Carlton won the Triple Crown for pitchers in 1972, leading the league in wins, ERA and strikeouts. It would be 13 years before another National League pitcher did likewise (Dwight Gooden in 1985), and another 25 years before it was again done in the American League. (Roger Clemens, in 1997, was the first to win the Triple Crown in the AL since Hal Newhouser in 1945.) Carlton's number of starts, complete games, and innings pitched also led the league. And he did all of this while pitching for a ballclub that won a mere 59 games. "He was just awesome," says Phillies chairman Bill Giles. "I've never seen a pitcher dominate like he did that year."

As expected, Carlton dominated the Cy Young balloting. The Phillies star received every single first-place vote. He finished with 120 points to win in a landslide over the Pirates' Steve Blass, who was a distant second with 35. It was the first time in history that the award was won by a pitcher from a last-place club. And Carlton held that distinction for another 37 years, until Zack Greinke won it for the last-place Kansas City Royals in 2009.

The numbers posted by the Royals' righty in his Cy Young season pale in contrast to Carlton's. Greinke went 16-8 with a 2.16, made 33 starts but pitched only six complete games. He struck out 242 and walked 51. Greinke worked 229 and a third innings. He tossed three shutouts.

Zack Greinke had two fewer losses than Carlton, for a Royals team that won 65 games. As amazing as it was that Greinke was able to win 16 for those Royals, the '72 Phils were worse, and astonishingly, Carlton was able to win 27. Their ERAs were fairly comparable. Greinke allowed fewer earned runs, home runs, and walks. But the Royals ace had 11 fewer wins and 68 fewer strikeouts; he pitched 117 fewer innings and faced 915 batters to Carlton's 1,351. He had a higher WHIP (walks and hits per innings pitched): 1.073. Carlton pitched more shutouts (eight) than Greinke had complete games.

Things are different today. Starting pitchers are only expected to get to the seventh inning and then let the bullpen take over. But one must still give the edge to Carlton, who had nearly as many complete games as Greinke made starts. "Whenever people talk about a pitcher rising above the deficiencies of his team—such as happened with Zack Greinke and the 2009 Royals—Carlton's 1972 season forever will be the standard," adds Tom Verducci of *Sports Illustrated*.

"Thirty complete games? For some guys that's a career," Larry Bowa has said. "You talk about a horse, Carlton was a horse."

In November 2009, Bowa watched the TV sports shows as the results of the Cy Young Award voting were announced. It was no surprise to anyone that Greinke, a pitcher from a last-place team, had won in a runaway. There was no question that he was deserving, having had a tremendous season for a terrible Royals team. Bowa expected him to win, but in his opinion, it wasn't close to the performance the former Phillie witnessed firsthand 37 years earlier. Bowa watched as the TV analysts gushed with effusiveness about Greinke. "I'm going, what's the big deal? They won 60-some games, he won 16. Look at what Carlton did."

No one seemed to make reference to what Carlton did on a team that failed to win even 60 games. Bowa couldn't believe that so little mention was made of Carlton during the 2009 Cy Young news cycle, something that made the old shortstop stew. "I don't think people realize how few games we won. They know we were bad, but I don't think they know we didn't win 60 games. I'm telling you, he was unbelievable," said Bowa of his old friend in reminiscing about their first season as teammates.

In 2010, another American League hurler rose above the "deficiencies" surrounding him to garner the Cy Young. Seattle's Felix Hernandez, despite a 13-12 record, was the top in votes. The voters were impressed with his major league–leading ERA of 2.27 and his AL best-innings-pitched total of 249 and two-thirds, all for a squad that finished 61-101, dead last in the AL West.

King Felix's 13 victories were the fewest by a Cy Young–winning starting pitcher in a non-interrupted season. Carlton had more victories during his winning streak alone. As was the case with Zack Greinke, the rest of Carlton's numbers from 1972 dwarf the Seattle right-hander's statistics. Felix struck out 232 batters, made 34 starts, had six complete games and one shutout. His WHIP was 1.057. He did allow fewer earned runs (63) and walks (70) than Carlton. They both gave up 17 home runs.

The 2010 Mariners were very bad. But one could argue that the 1972 Phillies were worse. Not much, but worse. They played fewer games, but had they endured a full 162-game season, it's a safe bet that the '72 Phils would have lost 101 or more. At least the Mariners had Ichiro Suzuki, who had 214 hits and batted .315. There were no Ichiros on the '72 Phillies.

One thing more: In 2010, much like in the previous year, little or no mention was made of Carlton's accomplishment as the very first pitcher to win the Cy Young Award from a last-place team.

During the 20 years prior to 1972, baseball saw pitchers win 20 games 140 times. Of those 140, only 12 (nine percent) pitched for losing teams. All but one pitched for teams that were no more than 10 games below .500. Johnny Antonelli was the lone exception. He won 20 games for the '56 Giants, who had a record of 67-87. In the same 20-year span, there were fourteen 25-game winners. None were on losing teams. Seven pitched for first-place clubs, five finished in second place, one in third, and one in fourth. Of those 14, only four had won 27 games or more. Not only did Carlton go 27-10, but he did it for a team whose record was 38 games below the .500 mark. "When you go 27-10, even for a pennant winner, it's a remarkable season," says NBC's Bob Costas, "and he did it for a team that didn't win 60 games. Think about it, if you went 15-15 or 17-20 with a team that bad, you'd actually be pretty damn good. And this guy goes 27-10? That's ridiculous."

No National League pitcher has won as many as 27 games since. It would be another 18 years before any major league pitcher won 27 again. In 1990, Bob Welch won 27 games for the Oakland A's. Carlton and Welch are the only pitchers in Major League Baseball to win more than 25 games in the last 39 years.

The A's team that Welch pitched for in 1990 won 103 games and the American League title. Welch was the number-two starter on a staff in which four of the five starting pitchers won 13 or more. Welch went 27-6, but Dave Stewart went 22-11, and Scott Sanderson won 17. That's a far cry from the staff for which Carlton toiled.

While Carlton's record was 27-10, no other starter in the 1972 Phillies four-man rotation had more than four wins. The second winningest pitcher on the team was Darrell Brandon, whose record in 42 games (36 relief appearances) was 7-7. Remember that Ken Reynolds, the number-two starter based on number of starts, finished with a record of 2-15. Bill Champion won only four of his 22 starts. Woodie Fryman (4-10) made 17 starts. Wayne Twitchell made 15 starts that season and went 5-9. Dick Selma (2-9) started 10 games. And Jim Nash lost every one of his eight starts. So, the pitchers who made eight or more starts for the Phillies in 1972 had a combined record of 44-75. That's an astounding 31 games below .500. Meanwhile the guy at the top of the rotation was 17 games *above* the .500 mark. "I promise you," Tim Kurkjian of ESPN maintains, "that we will never see another season where one pitcher was so dominant on such a bad team, and was so much better than any other pitcher on his team."

Now consider that atrocious '72 Phillies offense. They finished with a team batting average of .236. They didn't have a single player hit higher than .284. No player hit 20 homers, or drove in as many as 70 runs. And yet for that team, Carlton went 27-10. In Carlton's 10 losses, his teammates put up 17 total runs. The Phillies scored three runs or fewer in nine of the 10. They were shut out twice, and on three occasions they scored only one run for their ace. At 59-97, the 1972 Phillies had a winning percentage of .378. At 27-10, Carlton's winning percentage was .730. The '72 Phillies were 29-12 in games that Carlton started.

"They played .707 baseball when Carlton started. That means he made them roughly as good as the 1927 Murderers Row Yankees," Tom Verducci points out. (The '27 Yankees had a winning percentage of .714.)

The Phillies were 29-12 with Carlton on the mound, and 30-85 the rest of the time. During Steve's 15-game winning streak, the team went

26-40. That's 15-0 for Carlton, and 11-40 for the rest of the club. "It seems impossible, when you look at that team, to do what he did," says Jayson Stark of ESPN. "But the idea that a guy could win 15 games in a row for a team like that boggles my mind more than any of it….30-85 means they were a tick better than the '62 Mets, the worst team of modern times. They lost six games a week; the only games they didn't lose were when he pitched, or something bizarre happened."

So where does Carlton's '72 season rank among the greatest single-season pitching performances of all time? It prompts the question: Is it the greatest single effort we've ever seen from a starting pitcher?

"There is no question that Carlton's '72 season ranks among the greatest ever, but the single greatest? That depends upon your definition," notes Ken Rosenthal of Fox Sports.

Who better to address the question than Bill James, the "Sultan of Stats"? James, Senior Advisor on Baseball Operations for the Red Sox and the father of sabremetrics, has made a career out of weighing players' values based on statistics. For years, he authored *The Bill James Baseball Abstract*, a series of books of statistical analysis, and he has come up with a number of statistical innovations that have found their way into many a baseball front office. "The first five things I look at are wins, losses, walks, strikeouts and ERA, and the sixth would be innings pitched," says James. "And then there are park factors you look at to an extent."

The next question is: Who are the other candidates? A diligent search of the pantheon of baseball history since 1900 yielded the following stats for consideration:

Cy Young, Boston Americans, 1901: 33-10, 1.62 ERA, 37 BB, 158 Ks, 371.1 IP

Christy Mathewson, NY Giants, 1905: 31-8, 1.27 ERA, 64 BB, 206 Ks, 338.2 IP

Walter Johnson, Washington Senators, 1913: 36-7, 1.14 ERA, 38 BB, 243 Ks, 346 IP

Dazzy Vance, Brooklyn Dodgers, 1924: 28-6, 2.16 ERA, 77 BB, 262 Ks, 308 IP

Lefty Grove, Philadelphia Athletics, 1931: 31-4, 2.06 ERA, 62 BB, 175 Ks, 288.2 IP

Hal Newhouser, Detroit Tigers, 1945: 25-9, 1.81 ERA, 110 BB, 212 Ks, 313 IP

Sandy Koufax, LA Dodgers, 1965: 26-8, 2.04 ERA, 71 BB, 382 Ks, 335.2 IP

Denny McLain, Detroit Tigers, 1968: 31-6, 1.96 ERA, 63 BB, 280 Ks, 336 IP

Bob Gibson, St. Louis Cardinals, 1968: 22-9, 1.12 ERA, 62 BB, 268 Ks, 304.2 IP

Ron Guidry, NY Yankees, 1978: 25-3, 1.74 ERA, 72 BB, 248 Ks, 273.2 IP

Dwight Gooden, NY Mets, 1985: 24-4, 1.53 ERA, 69 BB, 268 Ks, 276.2 IP

Roger Clemens, Boston Red Sox, 1986: 24-4, 2.48 ERA, 67 BB, 238 Ks, 254 IP

Greg Maddux, Atlanta Braves, 1995: 19-2, 1.63 ERA, 23 BB, 181 Ks, 209.2 IP

Pedro Martinez, Boston Red Sox, 1999: 23-4, 2.07 ERA, 37 BB, 313 Ks, 213.1 IP

Randy Johnson, Arizona Diamondbacks, 2002: 24-5, 2.32 ERA, 71 BB, 334 Ks, 260 IP

That's our list, with apologies for anyone who was overlooked. The next step is to whittle it down. Should consideration be given to the Dead Ball Era pitchers? In Jayson Stark's view, "before Babe Ruth showed up and started hitting balls in the street, it was a different game. When 12 home runs led the league, they were playing a different game than the one we're playing today." That is an excellent point. Therefore, we'll throw out Cy Young, Christy Mathewson, and Walter Johnson. Needless to say, their places in baseball history are secure.

That leaves us with 12 players remaining on our list. How do they compare to Carlton in '72? We'll start with Brooklyn's Dazzy Vance in 1924. He had more wins and fewer losses than Carlton. But Carlton had a lower ERA. Vance walked fewer batters in his super-season, but he also struck out fewer batters. Carlton pitched more innings. Vance's '24 Dodgers won 92 games and finished in second place in the National League. In the authors' opinion, advantage: Carlton.

Lefty Grove's '31 season earned him MVP honors. He won more games than Carlton. He had fewer losses and walks, but a higher ERA. Carlton had more strikeouts and pitched more innings. Let's throw complete games and shutouts into the mix, shall we? Carlton had more of both, and had a lower WHIP. By the way, the '31 A's won 107 games and the American League pennant. And what about this inconvenient truth: the game was segregated. In 1931, Grove didn't pitch against all of the very best baseball players the nation had to offer. Advantage: Carlton.

Hal Newhouser won the second of his back-to-back MVP awards in 1945. Fewer wins, one less defeat. Lower ERA, fewer innings pitched. Fewer strikeouts, more walks. Also, World War II was still under way—many of the games' star players were in military service, and this was before Jackie Robinson. Advantage: Carlton.

Now, what to say about Sandy Koufax? His 1965 (and his '66 for that matter) remains one of the truly dominant seasons baseball has ever seen. At the time, his strikeout total set a major league record. If there was anything that gave him an edge over hitters that Carlton did not enjoy, it was this: the mound was five inches higher back then. One cannot say objectively that this alone gives the advantage to Carlton. But how about this fact: In 1965, the Dodgers won 97 games and the World Series. Koufax pitched for a club that won as many games as Carlton's '72 Phillies lost. Do you see a pattern emerging?

Denny McLain is the last pitcher in history to win 30 games. He did it in 1968, which has been termed the "Year of the Pitcher." He had a better record than Carlton. They had comparable ERAs. McLain walked fewer, but struck out fewer, and pitched fewer innings. His WHIP was .905—better than Carlton's. But he had 28 complete games to Carlton's 30, and six shutouts to Carlton's eight. McLain pitched for a team that won the World Series that year; Carlton did not.

Bob Gibson's 1968 produced the sterling ERA of 1.12, a line of demarcation that all ERAs since have been judged against. Carlton's ERA was also under two. He had more wins, more strikeouts, and pitched more innings than Gibson. Carlton had two more complete games, but Gibson had five more shutouts. Also, Gibby's WHIP was .853—better than Lefty's .993. It was because of Gibson in '68 (as well as McLain, Marichal, and Drysdale, among others) that baseball decided to lower the mound from 15 inches to its current height of 10 inches. They wanted to "even the playing field" for the game's hitters. Hitting was so down that year that Boston's Carl Yastrzemski won the AL batting title with a .301 average. What separates Carlton from Gibson? We keep coming back to it—Carlton put up his superlative numbers with inferior talent around him. The '68 Cardinals won 97 games and lost to the Tigers in the World Series.

Ron Guidry, Dwight Gooden, and Roger Clemens all had historic winning percentages; 22 and 20 more wins, respectively, than losses. They each dominated their leagues in those seasons. But were they more dominant than Carlton? And each pitched for winning teams. Guidry's Yankees won 100 games and the World Series. Clemens' Red Sox in 1986 came one out short of winning it all in six games. And Gooden's Mets of 1985 won 98 and finished second in the NL East.

The seasons of Greg Maddux, Pedro Martinez, and Randy Johnson came smack-dab in the middle of the Steroid Age, which makes their cases a bit more interesting. Their ERAs were much better than their leagues' averages, in an era when scoring and home run hitting were at all-time highs. And yet, Carlton's line from '72 stacks up well against all three in most of the categories. What Maddux, Martinez, and Johnson cannot say is that they pitched for a last-place team. Maddux's Braves were World Champs, Pedro's '99 BoSox went to the ALCS, and the Big Unit's D-Backs won 98 games and the NL West.

Pedro's 2000 is a fascinating study. Pitching in arguably the best division in baseball, and facing a DH every night, Pedro's ERA was a stunning 1.74. The league average ERA was just over five. Pedro's was more than *three runs* lower than the league average!

The Red Sox righty struck out a league-best 284 batters while walking just 32 in 217 innings. He pitched seven complete games and averaged nearly 12 strikeouts per nine innings. His WHIP was an ungodly .737. But Pedro made only 29 starts in 2000.

Admittedly, we have given great weight to the team factor, which may slant the argument to Carlton. While this has been a rather unscientific and arbitrary examination, Bill James argues that it is also futile. He feels that it's impossible to determine which pitcher holds the distinction of having had the greatest single season in the game's history. "There comes a point in the comparison of pitchers that the kind of analysis I do becomes not very instructive," James granted. "The curves flatten out, and you can't really rely on what you see, if that makes any sense."

According to James, the greatest single seasons are so much greater than their league averages that it's impossible to differentiate the best because they are all so much better. "It destroys the normal frame of reference," he contended.

"What's interesting," says James, "is that it's easy to identify the candidates. There are about seven great seasons since 1969. Carlton's season is certainly among them. But when it comes to the point of saying which of those is better than the others, I honestly don't know how you'd say. I'm not saying that it isn't the best season ever, or since 1969, it may well be; I just don't know what's the right formula. He has two more wins than Guidry, but he has seven more losses. Guidry's ERA is lower, but Carlton pitched more innings. I don't know how to resolve it."

So, what say our panel of baseball media types? We asked Tim Kurkjian, Jayson Stark, Ken Rosenthal, and Tom Verducci for their opinions on the topic.

Here is Kurkjian on Pedro Martinez in 1999 and 2000: "In such an unbelievable hitting era that those two seasons were, for Pedro's ERA to be that far below the league average, doing it in a designated hitter league, the American League East, doing it back-to-back like that, I think I would have to put Pedro ahead of Steve Carlton's '72, but just barely because, again, the 27 of 59. You have to say that out loud to appreciate how astounding that is."

Here is Stark on Bob Gibson's 1968. "Just because the 1.12 ERA is such a magical number in the history of baseball and there's a certain romance to that season because of it. From there, it really depends on how you set up the criteria. If the defining criterion is how did this guy's season compare to everything that went on around him that year, in the context of how pathetic Carlton's team was that year, I don't know how Carlton's not number two, or number one with a bullet."

Rosenthal is also partial to Gibson's '68, and adds Greg Maddux in '94 or '95. "Using the statistic ERA+, Carlton's '72 doesn't appear off-the-charts special. A number of more recent pitchers, including Greg Maddux, Pedro Martinez, and even Kevin Brown (217 ERA+ in 1996 for the Florida Marlins, tied for 20th all-time), had better seasons by that measure. But, of course, none of them won 27 games for a 59-win team. Or threw 346 and a third innings. Or struck out 310 batters. Carlton might not have been Gibson in '68, or even Maddux in 1994 and '95, but his '72 season was a singular achievement."

Verducci is with Kurkjian when it comes to Pedro. "I don't know if it's above them all, but the 2000 season by Pedro Martinez is as good as it gets," he said. "If you go by ERA+, Martinez's is the best in the history of the sixty-foot, six-inch distance: .291," Verducci adds. "His WHIP is the best ever. Base runners were rarer against Pedro, in the middle of the Steroid Era and in the American League with the designated hitter, than against the very best of the deadball era," he said. "The one thing that holds Pedro back is that he made only 29 starts. But he was as good as there ever was in those 29 starts."

In 1972, Carlton made 41 starts. Pitching a four-man rotation factors into that equation. Martinez pitched every fifth day; Lefty every fourth. But that also means that Pedro benefited from an extra day's rest. Lefty made 31 starts on three days' rest; Pedro made no start on less than four.

The term "ERA+" has been mentioned. ERA+ refers to a pitcher's earned run average, adjusted to factor in his league and his home ballpark. It is a measurement devised and widely used by the website Baseball-Reference.com. "We compute ERA+ as the league average ERA, adjusted for ballpark, divided by the pitcher's ERA," says Sean Forman, president of Sports Reference LLC, the website's parent company.

Carlton's ERA in 1972 was 1.97. His ERA+ for 1972 was 182. An ERA+ of 182 basically means that he was 82 percent better than his league's average. But it ranks just 86th all-time. The top six ERA+ pitchers and seasons since 1900 are:

Pedro Martinez, 2000:   291
Dutch Leonard, 1914:   279
Greg Maddux, 1994:   271
Greg Maddux, 1995:   262
Walter Johnson, 1913:   259
Bob Gibson, 1968:   258

"Carlton's 1.97 ERA is obviously very good, but run scoring was pretty low in 1972, so he was starting from a much lower baseline than someone like Martinez in 2000, who was facing the DH as well," notes Baseball-Reference.com's Sean Forman. "This also increased the number of innings that Carlton was able to pitch, although his IP total was so much higher than Pedro's, he may have been more valuable," concedes Forman.

In Carlton's day, pitchers pitched more innings than they do today. Carlton, in '72, routinely lasted eight or nine innings. If he was used in the manner that starting pitchers are used today, and only expected to go six or seven innings, his ERA+ would certainly be higher. Also, the Vet was a pretty neutral park. It wasn't considered a hitter's park. It wasn't particularly pitcher-friendly, but it wasn't a hitter's haven, either. This could be a reason that Carlton's ERA+ for 1972 is not higher.

Baseball-Reference.com also has a feature called "neutralized pitching." It's a somewhat complex metric that allows one to "transport" a pitcher into another context, such as season, league, and ballpark. So we can put the Pedro Martinez of 1999 and 2000 in the 1972 National League, and with Veterans Stadium as his home park. For 1972, neutralized pitching converts the numbers to a 155-game schedule, and to an average team scoring 630 total runs. Here are Pedro's "neutralized" stats for '99 and 2000:

1999   19-4, 1.61 ERA, 207 IP, 32 BB, 304 K, .821 WHIP
2000   20-3, 1.33 ERA, 210 IP, 28 BB, 275 K, .662 WHIP

These numbers indicate fewer wins, fewer strikeouts, and also fewer innings pitched than Carlton, as well as a lower ERA, fewer walks, and a lower WHIP.

For Maddux:

1994   27-4, 1.34 ERA, 282 IP, 33 BB, 217 K, .681 WHIP
1995   22-3, 1.39 ERA, 227 IP, 22 BB, 196 K, .705 WHIP

The Maddux of '94, pitching in the '72 National League with the Vet as his home park, matches Carlton's win total, and has six fewer losses. The '95 Maddux has fewer wins and losses. He has a better ERA and WHIP in both seasons, fewer innings pitched, fewer bases-on-balls, and fewer strikeouts.

Bob Gibson, of course, did pitch in the National League in '72. As a 36-year-old starter, Gibson posted a 19-11 record for the Cardinals, with a 2.46 ERA in 278 innings. He walked 88 and struck out 208, and his WHIP was 1.129. His neutralized pitching numbers for 1972, with the Vet as his home ballpark, look like this:

19-10, 2.70 ERA, 267 IP, 88 BB, 200 K, 1.176 WHIP

Interestingly, it's the same number of wins, but one less loss. The ERA is higher, in less innings, and with fewer strikeouts.

While these statistical analyses can take into consideration such factors as league, scoring climate, and ballpark, what they don't account for is the level of talent surrounding each pitcher. The real question is this: What would the Gibson of '68, or the Maddux of '94 and '95, or the Martinez of '99 and 2000, or the Guidry of '78, or anyone else, have done with the '72 Phillies playing behind him?

It is difficult to discount the fact that Carlton was pitching with inferior talent around him, and yet was able to post such incredible numbers. In the words of ESPN's Kurkjian, "it just doesn't seem to add up."

All of the seasons that one would consider to be among the greatest single-season pitching performances of the modern era were achieved for winning teams, except for Carlton's. Of the 17 pitchers and seasons that we have compared and contrasted with Carlton's '72, none of those players pitched on teams that finished lower than in second place in their respective leagues or divisions. Most either won the World Series or appeared in the World Series. And in Carlton's case, the '72 Phillies weren't just a middle-of-the-division, below-average team, they were among the worst in baseball history—on the days, that is, that Carlton didn't pitch. Billy DeMars knows that as well as anyone. From 1969 to 1981, he was the Phillies' hitting coach. He watched every one of Carlton's starts in '72 from the Phillies' dugout. "It was the best pitching performance I ever saw in my 58 years of baseball," DeMars contends.

ESPN's Jayson Stark probably summed it up best when he stated, "If you're going to judge other seasons to be greater than Steve Carlton's, don't you have to say that it was more possible for another guy to do what he did? You look at the years that Maddux and Pedro had in the '90s, they were amazing seasons, but were they possible? They did what they did while pitching for great teams, winning teams. Carlton did what he did pitching for one of the worst teams of the last 50 years. It's impossible. He goes in a whole special category for me."

Special is what Larry Bowa has thought of Carlton since they became teammates in Steve's super-season of 1972. Ask him if it's the best performance ever by a pitcher, and he replies without hesitation. "By far, I don't think anyone else comes close. Even the year Gibson had with the ERA, he was on a good team. This was a bad team." This is a fact, as has often been pointed out, that is irrefutable.

"I've said to players, 'What do you think about a guy who won 27 for a team that won only 59 games?' They say, 'You've gotta be kidding me.' They don't even know about it," adds Bowa. "I'll say, 'Look up Carlton's numbers from 1972 on the Internet.' When they do, they can't believe it."

CHAPTER 19

Beyond '72

Spring training, a time of eternal hope, was about to kick off in 1973. For the 27th year in a row, the Phillies would train in Clearwater at the Carpenter Field Training Complex. As usual, pitchers and catchers were due to report first, followed by infielders and outfielders a week later.

Phillies traveling secretary Eddie Ferenz had the job of picking up Carlton from the Tampa airport. He asked his good friend, writer Hal Bodley, to come along for the ride. Bodley agreed and volunteered to drive. They arrived at the airport, loaded up Carlton's luggage, and headed back to Clearwater.

They motored along the causeway, across the crystal-clear bay waters. As the bright Florida sunshine washed down on the palm trees that lined the highway, Carlton lamented his hectic off-season schedule. "You wouldn't believe the winter I had," said Lefty from the back seat. "It was one thing after another. I could never get my training in. There were reporters covering everything I did." Carlton soon found out that the media blitz would continue during spring training, as writers from *Sports Illustrated* and all the major publications descended on Clearwater to inundate him with questions. To make matters worse, Carlton came down with a bout of bronchitis, which set him back in his preparation for the season.

Things became frenetic for Carlton not long after the '72 World Series ended. First came the awards and then came the banquets. In addition to winning the National League Cy Young Award, he was named left-handed pitcher on the Associated Press, the Newspaper Enterprise Association, and *The Sporting News* All-Star teams. He was presented with the Clark Griffith Memorial Award by the Washington (D.C.) Touchdown Club and the Sid Mercer Player of the Year Award at the New York Sportswriters Dinner.

To top it off, Carlton won the prestigious Hickok Belt, a trophy which since 1950 had been awarded to the year's top professional athlete. This encompassed all sports, not just baseball. The award was in honor of the founder of the Hickok Manufacturing Company, based in Rochester, New York, which made, you guessed it, belts. By winning the trophy in 1972, Carlton joined some very select company. Past winners included Willie Mays and Sandy Koufax; football's Jim Brown and Joe Namath; boxer Rocky Marciano; and golfers Ben Hogan and Arnold Palmer. Lefty accepted the trophy at a banquet in New York City.

Carlton was able to get his mind off baseball for a little while when he went on a hunting trip in December to Montana and British Columbia with several players, including Tim McCarver, Hank Aaron, and Jerry Koosman. His aim was as sharp in the hunting field as it was on the pitcher's mound—he shot an elk and a mule deer.

In January, Lefty returned to the Philadelphia area. His sudden super stardom had placed him in high demand as a speaker on the local banquet circuit. He made several appearances over the few weeks leading up to spring training. He worked out at Veterans Stadium—when he could fit the time in. Early in the winter, he also inked a one-year contract for $165,000, which made him baseball's highest-paid pitcher.

While Carlton was running from banquet to banquet in the off-season, Paul Owens was busy dismantling his team. He started by releasing 14-year Phillie Chris Short and then traded Don Money, Billy Champion, and reserve third baseman John Vukovich to the Brewers for four players, most notably Jim Lonborg, who had won the Cy Young Award for the Red Sox in 1967. Pitcher Ken Brett, George's older brother, was also acquired in the deal.

On November 1, 1972, Owens introduced 48-year-old Danny Ozark as the Phillies' new manager. Ozark had been in the Dodgers organization since 1942, the year he graduated from high school, as a minor league player and manager, and a third base coach for the Dodgers. Some regarded him as the heir apparent to Walter Alston as the Dodgers' manager, but instead of waiting for Alston to step down, Ozark took the job with the Phillies.

Owens wanted to supply Ozark with as much talent as possible to work with, so right after Thanksgiving, he made two more trades on successive days. First, he sent three players, including Ken Reynolds and Joe Lis, on their way to the Twins, and the following day, outfielders Oscar Gamble and Roger Freed were dealt to the Indians.

In January, Owens released John Bateman. He had been on the receiving end of 21 of Carlton's 27 wins. However, Bob Boone was ticketed as the Phillies' starting catcher, making Bateman expendable. Carlton and

Bateman were teammates for only three and a half months, but they developed a close bond, both on and off the field. Carlton would miss the sturdy, reliable, fun-loving Bateman. The manager of the team hotel in San Francisco would not. Bateman, 32 at the time, never played in the majors again. His career ended prematurely, and so did his life. He died in 1996 at the age of 56. The '72 Phillies were cursed in that regard, as several other members of the team did not live to be 60: Roger Freed (49), Deron Johnson (53), Chris Short (53), Dick Selma (57), and Joe Hoerner (59).

On the field in 1973, things went downhill rapidly for Steve Carlton. The constraints on his time and his inability to properly train in the off-season conspired against him. Lefty never got going. He finished with a 13-20 record and a 3.90 ERA. He'd gone from winning 27 to *losing* 20! Compared to his '72 season, Carlton had half as many wins, twice as many losses, and his ERA was twice as high. He led the league in losses and earned runs allowed. His control was shaky as he walked 3.46 batters per nine innings, a big jump from his 2.26 ratio in 1972. Carlton was really roughed up in a few starts. In a May game against the Dodgers, he gave up 13 hits and six runs. The Cardinals knocked him out in the fifth inning of a game in June to the tune of 10 hits and seven runs. He did not make it to the sixth inning in three consecutive starts in August.

So why the huge turnaround? Longtime Dodger Wes Parker asked Carlton the question at a card show in 2008. With a smirk, Steve responded, "The 'rubber chicken' [banquet] circuit got me." Invariably, attending numerous banquets in multiple cities in the off-season took its toll on Carlton and hindered his performance in '73.

There were other reasons, though. Bob Boone, who caught most of Carlton's games in that year, responded half-seriously when posed the question: "It was my fault." Boone explained, "He didn't have confidence in a rookie catcher catching his game. He changed signs. There was a lot of indecision. I couldn't get on the same page that Steve wanted me on. Steve struggled with me." Boone also observed that Carlton's curve wasn't an effective pitch in '73. "It would 'roll.' It didn't have the same snap; it didn't drop off the table."

Ray Rippelmeyer attributed the big drop-off in Carlton's performance largely to his reduced endurance. "When he joined the Phillies in 1972, he ran every step [with the other pitchers]. He won the Cy Young and thought he was invincible. [In 1973] Steve didn't think he needed to run and [consequently] didn't have the same stamina." Rippelmeyer, who did not have the authority to fine players, became so infuriated with Carlton's unwillingness to run that he complained to Paul Owens. "He won't do what I'm telling him." It fell on deaf ears. Carlton persisted in refusing to run, and neither Owens nor Ozark disciplined him.

To illustrate how Carlton's lack of stamina affected his pitching, Rippelmeyer recalled a game at the Vet in which Lefty started by throwing six strong innings. In the bottom of the sixth, Carlton hit a slow grounder to deep shortstop and legged it down the line, but he was thrown out for the third out. He went straight to the mound, huffing and puffing, and the first three batters in the top of the seventh hit bullets off him.

Carlton was frustrated with the way he was pitching, but he resisted suggestions. In the outfield before a game in Cincinnati, Rip approached Carlton. "Why don't we have a chat?"

"Sure," Lefty responded. "As long as it's not about baseball."

"Then we don't have anything to discuss." End of conversation.

It was during Carlton's trying 1973 season that his feud with the media was triggered. Up until then, he had enjoyed a good rapport with the writers. Lefty was a talkative, thoughtful, and quotable interviewee. "He was the most cooperative athlete I had been around up to that point," says Larry Shenk, who spent 44 years as the Phillies' public relations director. But Carlton became incensed when a Philadelphia sportswriter wrote an article intimating that Lefty's sub-par performance in 1973 was attributable to his zest for the night life. Carlton began to distance himself from the media, and over the next few years he became less and less accessible. It wasn't as much a single incident that turned him off to the media, but a series of things. "He would say, 'Why should I talk to the writers? I talk to them and then I pick up the paper the next day and they don't quote me accurately, they take things out of context,'" Shenk remembers. "'Why should I waste my time talking to them when they don't quote me accurately,' he would say. 'Let them be creative.'"

Finally, Lefty boycotted the media completely. "It was easy for me then," says Shenk. "The answer was always no."

"I stopped talking to them because they bothered me," Carlton told Hal Bodley in a 1989 interview. "They were affecting my skills on the field." Denny Doyle believes that Carlton was turned off by the writers' penchant for injecting criticism into their articles, not only about him, but about other players. "Controversy sells newspapers. Carlton didn't like people being put down in the paper. His attitude was, 'If you can't say anything good, don't say anything.'"

After Lefty stopped doing interviews, he was still cordial toward the writers. "He wasn't nasty like Dave Kingman," said Frank Bilovsky, the former *Bulletin* reporter. "If the guy in the locker stall next to him had a great game, and the crowd of media would spill over into his locker area, he would just quietly grab his clothes and dress in the trainer's room. He was not nasty at all. If visiting reporters would come up to him, he would just say very politely, 'I don't do interviews, it's nothing personal.' It wasn't like, 'Get the fuck out of here' [like Kingman might say] or anything like that."

Ironically, during the years when he was not doing interviews, Carlton would still talk to some of the writers whom he liked personally, including the AP's Ralph Bernstein and Bud Saidt from the *Trenton Times*—as long as the subject was not baseball. Carlton was a connoisseur of the grape and would sometimes discuss wine with the writers. But if a writer tried to sneak in a baseball question, even if he made it clear that the conversation would be "off the record," Steve would refuse to answer and issue his standard response: "Policy is policy." Bernstein would approach him every spring training, without pen and note pad in hand, to try and engage him in a baseball dialogue. "Ah, ah, ah, Ralph." Carlton would say. "Policy is policy."

In 1977, when Carlton was in the phasing-out stage with the media, a conditioning coach named Gus Hoefling gave his career a big shot in the arm. Steve had rebounded from his 1973 season with winning records during the next three years, including a 20-win season in 1976, yet he still had not regained the dominance that he had on the mound in 1972.

Much like Carlton's regular use of the slider in '72 elevated his game to another level, Gus Hoefling helped Carlton bring his game to an even higher place. Hoefling, who had been a conditioning coach with the Eagles until 1976, joined the Phillies staff in 1977, and Lefty became his star student. Under Hoefling's tutelage, Carlton began an intense conditioning program based on kung fu principles. The program was designed to strengthen him physically and mentally. One of Carlton's most rigorous exercises was filling a 30-gallon garbage can with rice and putting his arm all the way to the bottom. Jerry Koosman, who was a teammate of Carlton's for two years in the 1980s, described the benefits which Lefty derived from working with Gus. "He's the strongest guy that I have ever met in my life. I never saw somebody work that hard. He could do things nobody else could. His strength was a big reason for his success."

Hoefling also taught Carlton how to intensify his focus and positive outlook. Lefty would spend sessions in a behavior-modification room at Veterans Stadium with various stimuli which induced a state akin to self-hypnosis. Subliminal messages, stressing success and winning, were relayed to Carlton as he sat, eyes closed, in a trance.

Working closely with Hoefling paid immediate dividends, as Carlton won his second Cy Young in 1977, by winning 23 games and posting a 2.64 ERA, his best numbers since '72. He maintained his exceptional pitching over the next few years, winning the Cy Young again in 1980 and 1982. In '80, he won 24 games and struck out a league-leading 286 batters. He reached the pinnacle by winning the second game and the decisive sixth game of the World Series against the Kansas City Royals, helping the Phillies to their first World Series triumph. Characteristically, Lefty did not revel in the celebration with the rest of his teammates, choosing instead to sip champagne in the trainer's room. He was dazzling again when he won his fourth Cy Young in '82, as he led the National League in wins, complete games, shutouts, and strikeouts.

Carlton slowed down somewhat in 1983, posting a losing record, although he still led the National League in strikeouts. His downward slide started in 1985. By then, Steve was 40 years old and had thrown almost 4,800 innings. He spent time on the disabled list with a shoulder injury and finished with a 1-8 record. It got worse in 1986 when Carlton's ERA ballooned to 6.18 in June. Pitching coach Claude Osteen explained Carlton's fall from grace: "Hitters started to recognize his slider to lay off it. It was not the same slider. It may have broken as much, but the hitter saw what he previously did not see. He got behind hitters. I suggested that he use the slider as a slow pitch and get batters out with his curve. Steve was not receptive to my suggestion. His bread-and-butter pitch was his slider— he wanted to prove to everybody that he still had it. What makes a great pitcher is they never reach a point when they don't think they can get a guy out. They never quit. I can't fault Steve's determination, but sometimes you have to be realistic."

Phillies chairman Bill Giles implored Carlton to retire to spare him the embarrassment of being released. Carlton refused, insisting that he could pitch another 10 years. Giles felt that he had no choice but to let Lefty go. Determined to prove to his detractors that he could still win in the majors, Carlton spent the next two years bouncing from team to team. He pitched for the Giants, White Sox, Indians, and Twins. In between, the Phillies invited him to spring training in 1987 as a non-roster player. Carlton got hit hard in the exhibition games, and once again the Phillies were obliged to release him. The final blow came in April 1988 when the Twins cut Carlton loose. In 10 innings, Lefty's ERA was a monstrous 16.76.

After he retired from baseball, Carlton withdrew from society much like author J.D. Salinger did in the 1950s when he tired of the media intruding on his privacy. While the man who penned *The Catcher in the Rye* retreated to Cornish, New Hampshire, Lefty chose the remote mountain community of Durango, Colorado. Pat Jordan, a freelance writer based in Fort Lauderdale, Florida, interviewed Carlton at his Durango home in December 1993 and wrote an article that was published in the April 1994 issue of *Philadelphia* magazine. In the article, Jordan attributed several bizarre statements and beliefs to Carlton, among them that 12 Jewish bankers who meet in Switzerland rule the world; that the last eight U.S. Presidents have been guilty of treason; that the Russian and U.S. governments fill the air with low-frequency sound waves meant to control us; and that one of a number of conspiratorial groups will begin the new American Revolution. Carlton denied making some of the statements that Jordan attributed to him, and those that he admitted making were, he said, taken far out of context.

Steve Carlton is not the only member of the '72 Phillies who owns a home in Durango. Tommy Hutton and his wife have owned a second home in Durango since the mid-1990s. If Hutton knows he's going to be in town for a week, he will call Carlton and get together with him for dinner and maybe catch an afternoon of skiing, a post-baseball passion of Lefty's. "He's a maniac on the ski slopes," said Hutton with a laugh.

Carlton may not have endeared himself to the writers, but they could not deny his greatness. In 1994, they elected him to the Baseball Hall of Fame on the first ballot. He was well deserving of the honor. His 329 wins place him seventh on the all-time list of modern-day pitchers. He is fourth in career strikeouts, behind Nolan Ryan, Randy Johnson, and Roger Clemens. Carlton was the first pitcher in history to win four Cy Young Awards, which also puts him in an elite group; only Clemens (seven) and Johnson (five) have won the award more times; Greg Maddux also won four Cy Youngs.

Despite this impressive arsenal of accomplishments, some baseball experts feel that Carlton has not been given his fair due. "I think Carlton is given short shrift," says Bob Costas. "If you look at the quality of his career, almost 330 victories, his name doesn't come up as often as Koufax, or Gibson, or Nolan Ryan because of all the strikeouts and no-hitters. There are reasons why people hang their hats on other great performers, not that their performances weren't great, but it's a mystery to me why Carlton's name doesn't come up more often. If you look at the strikeouts and no-hitters, and the overwhelming speed, it's easy to see why Nolan Ryan was on the All-Century team; you can't make an objective case that Nolan Ryan was a better pitcher than Steve Carlton. It's impossible."

Veteran baseball writer Jayson Stark states that Carlton is the greatest left-handed starter that he has ever seen. "Steve Carlton had a quality that I have seen in very few starting pitchers. When he went to the mound in a big game, everyone in the ballpark thought 'W.' He was going to will his way to win any big game that needed to be won."

That is one of the reasons why, in his book *The Stark Truth*, Jayson lists Carlton as one of the game's most underrated players. "When the topic turns to the greatest left-handed starting pitchers in history, I'm shocked at how little you hear his name. I really think that for a 300-game winner who won four Cy Youngs, he's massively underrated. And I do think that has something to do with his relationship with the media."

While his career may have been underrated (as Hall of Fame careers go), there is no understating the unparalleled achievement that was Steve Carlton's 1972 season. Hitting him that year was indeed, as Willie Stargell said on that long-ago summer night, like trying to drink coffee with a fork.

Sources

Baseball-Almanac.com

Baseball-Reference.com

Collin, Lee. "20 Game Winners on Last-Place Clubs," *The Bleacher Creature* (May 2001).

Enders, Eric. *Ballparks Then and Now* (Thunder Bay Press, 2002).

The Evening Bulletin (Philadelphia)

Flood, Curt, and Richard D. Carter. *The Way It Is* (Trident Press, 1971).

Giles, Bill, and Doug Meyers. *Pouring Six Beers at a Time* (Triumph Books, 2007).

Hirsch, James S. *Willie Mays: The Life, the Legend* (Scribner's, 2010).

Jordan, Pat. "Thin Mountain Air," *Philadelphia* magazine (April 1994).

Leventhal, Josh. T*ake Me Out to the Ballpark* (Black Dog & Leventhal, 2003).

"The Midday Show," 610 WIP-AM, CBS Radio, Philadelphia, September 25, 2009.

MLB.com

Neft, David S., Richard M. Cohen, and Michael L. Neft. *The Sports Encyclopedia: Baseball* (St. Martin's Press/Griffin Books, 2005).

The New York Daily News

The New York Post

The New York Times

The Philadelphia Daily News

The Philadelphia Inquirer

Philadelphia Phillies Highlight Film (1972).

Shenk, Larry, ed. *Philadelphia Phillies 1972 Media Guide.*

Shenk, Larry, and Chris Wheeler, eds. *Direction '73: The 1973 Philadelphia Phillies Yearbook.*

The Sporting News

Sports Illustrated 2009 Almanac (Sports Illustrated Books, 2010).

The St. Louis Globe-Democrat

The St. Louis Post-Dispatch

USA Today

Videojug.com, "How to throw a slider in baseball."

Westcott, Rich. *Phillies Essential* (Triumph Books, 2006).

Westcott, Rich. *The Fightin' Phils: Oddities, Insights, and Untold Stories* (Camino Books, 2008).

Westcott, Rich, and Frank Bilovsky. *The Phillies Encyclopedia*, Third Edition (Temple University Press, 2004).

Wikipedia.com

Wulf, Steve. "Sports People: Steve Carlton," *Sports Illustrated* (January 24, 1994).

Zolecki, Todd. *The Good, the Bad, and the Ugly: Heart-Pounding, Jaw-Dropping, and Gut-Wrenching Moments from Philadelphia Phillies History* (Triumph Books, 2010).

Index

Aaron, Hank, 2, 64, 82-83, 112, 141, 144, 149, 181

Adams, Bobby, 52

Agee, Tommie, 63-65, 158

Alexander, Grover Cleveland ("Pete"), 111, 159

All-Century Team, 186

Allen, Mel, 46

Allen, Richie (Dick), 2, 76, 84, 130, 142

All-Stars/All-Star Game, 3-6, 21, 28-29, 48, 74, 78, 103-104, 109, 112-113, 123, 126, 135, 148, 165, 180

Alou, Felipe, 75

Alou, Jesus, 75

Alou, Matty, 26, 75, 151

Alston, Walter, 57, 181

American League, 21, 61, 68, 112, 126, 168-171, 173-174, 176

American League Championship Series, 21, 35, 85, 175

American League Eastern Division, 164, 176

American League Western Division, 84-85, 170

Anaheim Stadium, 85

Anderson, Mike, 28, 47, 50, 59, 66, 69, 76, 78, 167

Antonelli, Johnny, 170

Arizona Diamondbacks, 173, 175

Arlin, Steve, 55-57, 103-104, 107, 167

Arnold, Chris, 48, 50-51

Ashburn, Richie ("Whitey"), 41, 46-47, 59-60, 63, 71, 80, 101, 130, 132

Associated Press, 10, 24, 154, 180, 184

Astrodome, 79, 148

Atlanta Braves, 28, 77-79, 82, 112, 136, 139, 141, 143-145, 147, 149, 164, 166, 173, 175

Atlanta Falcons, 112

Atlanta-Fulton County Stadium, 112

Atlanta Hawks, 10

Autry, Gene, 85

Bailey, Bob, 80-81, 87-88, 90-91, 131

Baker, Dusty, 141-142, 144

Baltimore Orioles, 21, 27, 62, 66, 69, 155

Barber, Red, 46

Barnes, Lute, 158

Barton, Bob, 56

Baseball Hall of Fame, 7, 11, 15, 17-18, 26, 29, 31, 36, 41, 44-46, 52, 56-58, 65, 67, 81, 99, 109, 127, 139, 144, 155, 159, 186

Baseball-Reference.com, 176-177

Bateman, John, 78-82, 87-88, 90, 92, 101-102, 105-106, 111, 120, 135, 143, 145, 149, 154, 158-159, 165, 181-182

Bavasi, Buzzie, 55

Baylor, Don, 85

Beauchamp, Jim, 65, 153

Beckert, Glenn, 20, 31-32, 160

Bench, Johnny, 6, 31, 71, 73, 134-137, 148, 167

Bern's Steak House (Tampa), 135

Bernstein, Ralph, 154, 184

Berra, Yogi, 27, 63-65, 93, 158

"Big Red Machine, The," 71, 136

Billingham, Jack, 73

Bill James Baseball Abstract, The, 172

Bilovsky, Frank, 10, 30, 53, 69, 73, 110, 113, 120, 183-184, 189

Blass, Steve, 31, 125-27, 169

Blue, Vida, 21-22, 25

Boccabella, John, 88

Bodley, Hal, 8, 10, 14, 37, 41-42, 52-53, 150, 153, 180, 183

Bonds, Barry, 49

Bonds, Bobby, 48-50, 58, 99-100

Boone, Bob, 85, 153, 162, 181-182

Boston Americans, 61, 172

Boston Braves, 2

Boston Red Sox, 12-13, 27, 61, 68-69, 71, 85, 164, 172-176, 181

Bourke, Pat, 160

Bowa, Larry, 6-8, 18, 27-28, 30, 32, 36-38, 42-43, 47, 49, 51, 63, 66-68, 70-71, 75-76, 80-82, 90-91, 98, 104-105, 107, 110-111, 119, 136-137, 139, 140-141, 143, 146, 149, 152-153, 162, 165, 167, 169-170, 179

Bragan, Jimmy, 90-91

Brandon, Darrell ("Bucky"), 14-15, 68-69, 71-72, 76-77, 79, 83, 101, 119, 133, 171

Brett, George, 181

Brett, Ken, 181

Brewer, Jim, 60

Briles, Nelson, 67

Brock, Lou, 26, 38, 123, 151, 157

Brooklyn Dodgers, 172-173

Brown, Jim, 181

Brown, Kevin, 176

Brown, Ollie, 149

Brown, Oscar, 149

Browne, Byron, 5, 75-77, 165

Bryant, Ron, 58

Bull's BBQ, 160

Bunning, Jim, 7, 20, 29, 52, 84, 115, 151-152

Burkhart, Ken, 45-46, 48, 51

Burrell, Pat, 130

Busch, August, 3-5, 8, 21, 23, 41, 122

Busch Memorial Stadium, 23, 122, 157

California Angels, 27, 59, 84-85, 89, 148

California League, 73

Callison, Johnny, 84, 130, 142

Calloway, Ernie, 113

Campbell, Bill, 1

Candlestick Park, 43-44, 49, 51, 58

Carbo, Bernie, 12-13

Cardenal, José, 31-32, 62, 114, 160

Carew, Rod, 85, 112

Carey, Ron, 156

Carlton, Anne, 155

Carlton, Beverly, 116, 135, 138, 164

Carlton, Christina, 155

Carlton, Joanne, 155

Carlton, Joe, 155

Carlton, Steve, 2-4, 8-10, 12-16, 18-20, 25-26, 28-32, 35-52, 55-65, 69-83, 88-97, 99-141, 143-187

Carpenter, Bob, 2, 24, 72, 98

Carpenter Field Training Complex, 130, 180

Carpenter, Ruly, 24, 36, 102-103, 140

Carrithers, Don, 95

Carroll, Clay, 6, 71, 148

Carty, Rico, 144

Cash, Dave, 68-69

Cedeño, César, 75-76, 80, 112, 149, 167

Cepeda, Orlando, 27, 83

Chamberlain, Wilt, 77

Champion, Billy, 29, 58, 62, 70, 73, 77, 124, 133, 163-165, 171, 181

Chicago Cubs, 20-21, 25, 29-32, 40, 62, 75, 86, 113-114, 117, 160-161

Chicago White Sox, 77, 166, 185

Cincinnati Reds, 5-6, 45, 52, 56, 71, 73, 75, 77, 84, 104, 134-136, 139, 147-148, 164, 168, 183

Citizens Bank Park, 34, 130, 160

Clark Griffith Memorial Award, 180

Clearwater, Florida (spring training), 1, 9-11, 14, 22-23, 29, 130, 180

Clemens, Roger, 169, 173-174, 186

Clemente, Roberto, 19, 67-68, 126-127, 159

Clendenon, Donn, 122-123

Cleveland Indians, 13, 79, 89, 181, 185

Cleveland, Reggie, 36, 77, 122

Cline, Ty, 7

Clines, Gene, 67-68, 126-127

Cobb, Ty, 7, 26

Colbert, Nate, 105, 107

Comcast SportsNet, 136

Conlin, Bill, 10, 132

Concepción, Dave, 6, 136

Connie Mack Stadium, 5, 46, 86, 129-130, 135

Cooperstown, New York, 11-12, 44, 59. *See also* Baseball Hall of Fame.

Corrales, Pat, 99

Costas, Bob, 170-171, 186

Crawford, Shag, 152

Culver, George, 77

Cy Young Award, 13, 21, 26, 31, 57, 60, 63, 68, 125, 138, 169-170, 180-182, 184-186

Daly, Chuck, 10
Daulton, Darren, 130
Davis, Al, 22
Davis, Willie, 57-58
Day, Boots, 87
DeMars, Billy, 178
Detroit Pistons, 77
Detroit Tigers, 26, 35, 104, 172-174
Devine, Bing, 3, 8, 12
Diaz, Bo, 13
DiMaggio, Joe, 30
Dodger Stadium, 57, 166
Downs, Dave, 166
Downs, Kelly, 166
Doyle Baseball Academy, 7, 27
Doyle, Blake, 27
Doyle, Brian, 27
Doyle, Denny, 20, 27, 31, 38-39, 47, 49-50, 62, 67, 72, 78, 82, 87, 91, 104-107, 140, 145, 149, 157, 159, 162, 167, 183
Drew, J.D., 27
Drysdale, Don, 57, 174
Durocher, Leo, 32
Dyer, Duffy, 153

Eckersley, Dennis, 13
Elias Sports Bureau, 117
Ellis, Dock, 127-128
Ennis, Del, 142
ESPN/ESPN.com, 11-13, 106, 171-172, 178
Eugene (Oregon) Emeralds, 69, 76, 78-79, 89, 142
Evening Bulletin (Philadelphia), 10, 37, 41, 52, 99, 107, 110, 183

Fairly, Ron, 66
Fanzone, Carmen, 160
Feeney, Chub, 92
Fenway Park, 69, 85
Fenwick, Bobby, 76
Ferenz, Eddie, 9, 102-103, 180
Finley, Charlie, 22
Fisk, Carlton, 13

Flood, Curt, 4-5, 9, 21, 27-28, 30, 38, 76, 188
Florida Marlins, 106, 143, 176
Foli, Tim, 89, 91-92
Ford Frick Award, 46
Forman, Sean, 176
Foster, George, 134
Fox, Charlie, 47
Fox Sports, 172
Foxx, Jimmie, 61
Freed, Roger, 69-70, 75, 77, 82, 90, 108, 111, 119, 128, 157, 181-182
Fregosi, Jim, 120
Frisella, Danny, 65
Froemming, Bruce, 114
Fryman, Woodie, 25, 29, 35-36, 55, 58, 70-71, 163-165, 171
Fuentes, Tito, 48-50

Gaherin, John, 24
Gamble, Oscar, 5, 76-77, 81-82, 106, 108, 181
Garr, Ralph, 141, 143
Garvey, Steve, 57, 111
Gaston, Cito, 107-108
Gibson, Bob, 3, 26, 29-31, 36-42, 44-45, 49, 68, 81, 91, 121-122, 143, 173-174, 176-179
Gilbreath, Rod, 149
Giles, Bill, 34-35, 75, 129, 132-133, 169, 185, 188
Giles, Warren, 34
Giusti, Dave, 62, 67
Gold Glove Award, 4, 18, 57, 141, 154
Gomez, Preston, 55
Gooden, Dwight, 169, 173-174
Grapefruit League, 10, 22
Greinke, Zack, 169-170
Griffin, Tom, 80
Grimsley, Ross, 5, 71, 137
Gross, Greg, 40
Grote, Jerry, 63, 86
Grove, Lefty, 61, 172-173
Guidry, Ron, 173-175, 178

Hahn, Frank ("Noodles"), 168
Hall, Tom, 73
Halladay, Roy, 94
Hamels, Cole, 56

Hamilton, Steve, 32
Hands, Bill, 31, 62
Harmon, Terry, 7, 19-21, 24-25, 27, 59,
  75, 80-82, 91, 99-101, 119-120, 145,
  148-149, 161, 166
Harrleson, Bud, 63, 65
"Harvey's Wallbangers" (Milwaukee
  Brewers), 85
Hawaii Islanders, 144
Healy, Fran, 48, 50
Hebner, Richie, 67-68, 77, 127
Heintzleman, Ken, 111
Helms, Tommy, 6, 80, 149
Helms, Wes, 6
Henderson, Dave, 85
Henderson, Ken, 48-49, 58-59
Henderson, Rickey, 26
Hernandez, Enzo, 105-107
Hernandez, Felix, 170
Hernandez, Jackie, 127
Hershiser, Orel, 69
Hickman, Jim, 62
Hickok Belt, 181
Hiser, Gene, 160
Hochman, Stan, 8, 10-11, 108, 121
Hodges, Gil, 63
Hoefling, Gus, 184
Hoerner, Joe, 5, 25, 30, 32, 36, 67-69,
  77-79, 182
Hogan, Ben, 181
Hooton, Burt, 32, 62, 117, 167
Hot Pants Patrol (Veterans Stadium), 34
Houston Astros, 34, 46, 73, 75-80, 82,
  148-149, 165
Howard, Larry, 76, 80
Howard, Ryan, 130
Humphrey, Terry, 88, 90-91
Hundley, Randy, 160
Hunt, Ron, 88, 91
Hutton, Tommy, 23, 25, 27, 39, 44, 65,
  68, 71, 73, 77, 88, 98, 104-107, 114,
  118, 120, 122, 124-126, 142, 148,
  152, 157-159, 186

International League, 69

J.G. Taylor Spink Award, 52
Jack Murphy Stadium, 107
Jack Russell Stadium, 10, 14

Jack Tar Hotel (Florida), 9-10
Jackson, Grant, 69, 87
Jackson, Larry, 31
Jackson, Reggie, 85, 112
James, Bill, 172, 175
Jarry Park, 66, 88, 90
Javier, Julian, 71, 148
Jenkins, Fergie, 31, 36, 44, 81, 117, 143,
  167
Jobe, Dr. Frank, 110
John, Tommy, 31, 85, 109-111
Johnny Bench Show, The, 47
Johnson, Deron, 6, 27, 32, 39, 47, 49,
  51, 66, 73-76, 79, 89, 101, 104, 120,
  136, 142, 182
Johnson, Randy, 173, 175, 186
Johnson, Richard ("Kite Man"), 34-35
Johnson, Walter, 172-173, 177
Jones, Cleon, 63, 118-120, 153
Jordan, Pat, 185, 188
Jutze, Skip, 151

Kalas, Harry, 41, 46-47, 59, 63, 71, 101,
  114-115, 132, 144, 149
Kansas City Athletics, 46, 79
Kansas City Royals, 112, 118, 169, 185
Keidan, Bruce, 45, 100
Kelleher, Mick, 151
Kelly, Ray, 10, 52
Kendall, Fred, 106
Kendall, Jason, 106
Kessinger, Don, 160
Khayat, Ed, 113
Kiner, Ralph, 63, 65
Kingman, Dave, 49-51, 95, 183-184
Kirby, Clay, 104-108, 114
Kison, Bruce, 85
Knowles, Darold, 12
Koegel, Pete, 62-63, 77, 90
Konerko, Paul, 127
Koosman, Jerry, 31, 117, 120, 152, 181,
  184
Korbut, Olga, 147
Koufax, Sandy, 32, 45, 57, 60, 91, 110,
  172, 174, 181
Kranepool, Ed, 64
Kruk, John, 130
Kuehn, Harvey, 20, 85
Kuhn, Bowie, 5, 22

Kurkjian, Tim, 171, 175-176, 178
KYW-TV, 156

Lang, Jack, 29
Lasorda, Tommy, 57
Lee, Derrek, 27
Leonard, Dutch, 177
Lersch, Barry, 29, 66, 71, 79, 161
Lewis, Allen, 10
Lis, Joe, 88-92, 95, 105-106, 135, 149, 153, 181
Lonborg, Jim, 181
Lopes, Davey, 114
Los Angeles Dodgers, 23, 27, 40, 45, 55, 57-60, 97, 99, 106, 109-111, 114, 132, 166, 172, 181-182
Lowrey, Peanuts, 86-87
Lucchesi, Frank, 6, 29-30, 32, 41, 47, 58, 62, 66, 68-69, 71, 73, 75-80, 82, 91, 97-99
Lum, Mike, 144
Luzinski, Greg, 27-28, 30, 32, 37, 44, 47, 50, 62, 65, 76-77, 126, 130-131, 141-143, 149, 152, 156, 160-161, 165-167
Lynn, Fred, 85

Mack, Connie, 52, 61-62
Maddox, Garry, 48-50, 99-101
Maddux, Greg, 175-178, 186
Major League Baseball Players Association, 9, 20
Manager of the Year Award, 84
Mantle, Mickey, 27
Maravich, Pete, 10
Marciano, Rocky, 181
Marichal, Juan, 31, 44-45, 48-51, 58, 99, 174
Martin, Billy, 84, 164
Martinez, Pedro, 173, 175-178
Martinez, Ted, 158
Mashore, Clyde, 88, 90
Mathews, Eddie, 2, 144
Mathewson, Christy, 172-173
Matlack, Jon, 31, 69, 118, 127
Mauch, Gene, 61-62, 66, 84-90, 92-93, 131, 164
Maxvill, Dal, 12, 23

May, Lee, 75-76, 80
Mays, Willie, 32, 48, 51, 58, 63-65, 80, 82, 94, 119-120, 181
McAnally, Ernie, 88-92, 131
McCarver, Tim, 5, 14, 17-18, 27, 32, 37-39, 44, 47, 49, 51, 63, 65, 77-79, 88, 91, 181
McDowell, Sam, 64
McGinn, Dan, 63, 160
McGlothlin, Jim, 148
McGraw, Tug, 63, 77, 118, 158
McKay, Jim, 150
McLain, Denny, 173-174
McNally, Dave, 5
McRae, Hal, 73
Melendez, Luis, 151
Metzger, Roger, 76, 80
Miami Stadium, 56
Mike Douglas Show, The (Carlton appearance on), 156
Millan, Felix, 141
Miller, Marvin, 9, 20-22, 24
Milwaukee Braves, 2, 56
Milwaukee Brewers, 19, 28, 85, 163-165, 181
Minnesota Twins, 84, 89, 112, 181, 185
MLB.com, 10, 41
Monday, Rick, 31, 62, 160
Money, Don, 28, 30, 40, 47, 49-50, 66, 68, 75-76, 78, 81, 90, 99, 106, 114, 118, 120, 143, 148, 155, 160, 164, 181
Montañez, Willie, 7, 28, 32, 38-40, 50-51, 53-54, 63, 67, 73-74, 76-77, 82, 88, 92, 99-100, 105-106, 111, 115, 123, 126, 131, 141-142, 156, 167
Montreal Expos, 24, 35-36, 61, 66-67, 69, 78, 84-92, 128-129, 131, 133-135, 156-157, 160, 164
Montreuil, Al, 160
Moore, Balor, 157
Morales, Jerry, 107-108
Morgan, Joe, 71, 81, 112, 136, 148, 167
Morse, Bobby, 10
Morton, Carl, 66, 167
Most Valuable Player Award, 21, 23, 27-28, 59, 68-69, 73, 137, 173
Moyer, Jamie, 139

Murcer, Bobby, 112
"Murderers Row" (1927 Yankees), 171
Murphy, Bob, 63
Murtaugh, Danny, 66
Myatt, George, 30, 98

Namath, Joe, 181
Nash, Jim, 78-79, 90, 164-165, 171
National League, 11, 16, 27-29, 31, 34,
    40, 47, 56-58, 63, 76, 84, 92, 108,
    112, 118, 137, 159, 161, 163, 166,
    168-169, 171, 173, 177-178, 180, 185
National League Championship Series,
    23, 68
National League Eastern Division, 8, 30,
    66, 69, 113, 121, 126, 158, 160-161,
    174
National League Western Division, 52,
    134, 147, 175
Nau, Brad, 136, 138
Neibauer, Gary, 78-79, 82
Nelson, Lindsey, 63
Newcombe, Don, 57
Newhouser, Hal, 169, 172, 174
Newspaper Enterprise Association, 180
New York Daily News, 4
New York Giants, 63, 170, 172
New York Mets, 4, 29, 55-56, 58-59, 63-
    64, 69, 86, 89, 93-94, 106, 117-118,
    121, 126, 137, 152-153, 155, 163,
    172-173
New York Post, 44
New York Times, 29
New York Yankees, 23, 77, 86, 112, 171,
    173-174
Niekro, Joe, 139
Niekro, Phil, 31, 139-145, 147
Norman, Freddie, 56, 81
North, Bill, 160

Oakland A's, 21, 25, 35, 112, 166
Oh, Sadaharu, 17
Olean (New York) Oilers, 73
Oliver, Al, 18, 67-68, 126-128
Olsen, Andy, 40
Olympic Games (1972), 150, 153
Osteen, Claude, 59-60, 185
Owens, Marcelle, 1

Owens, Paul, 1-3, 9, 73, 78-79, 98-99,
    106-107, 119, 122, 131, 133, 143,
    145, 151, 153-154, 160, 164, 166,
    181-182
Ozark, Danny, 65, 181-182

Pacific Coast League, 49, 58, 142, 154
Palmer, Arnold, 181
Pappas, Milt, 21, 31, 113-115
Parker, Wes, 57-58, 99, 182
Payson, Joan, 63-64
Pepitone, Joe, 31
Perez, Marty, 143
Perez, Tony, 6-7, 71, 134, 148
Perry, Gaylord, 112
Philadelphia Athletics, 46, 52, 61, 130,
    172
Philadelphia Civic Center, 10, 155-156
Philadelphia Daily News, 8, 10-11, 103,
    132, 138
Philadelphia Eagles, 33, 113, 184
Philadelphia Flyers, 90
Philadelphia Inquirer, 10, 12, 22, 45, 98,
    100, 131, 144-145, 158
Philadelphia magazine, 185
Philadelphia Phillies, 1-12, 14-24, 26-42,
    44-52, 55-84, 86-97, 99-172, 174,
    178, 180-185
Philadelphia 76ers, 10
Philadelphia Spectrum, 10
Phillie Phanatic, 34
Phoenix Giants, 49
Piazza, Mike, 79
Pittsburgh Pirates, 22, 62, 66-69, 78, 89,
    106, 113, 125, 128, 150, 159, 161,
    166, 169
Plank, Eddie, 61
Plummer, Bill, 136
PONY League, 73
Powell, Lewis, 5

Quakers, Penn, 10
Qualcomm Stadium, 107
Quinn, Bob, 2
Quinn, John, 1-3, 8-10, 31, 72-73, 98

Rader, Doug, 76, 80
Randle, Lenny, 99

Reading Phillies, 87, 166
Reaves, John, 113
Reberger, Frank, 95
Reed, Ron, 77, 82
Reitz, Ken, 151
Reuss, Jerry, 31, 75-77, 82, 148, 167
Reynolds, Ken, 29, 69, 99-100, 117,
    124, 163-165, 171, 181
Richardson, Paul, 76
Ripken, Cal Jr., 62
Ripken, Cal Sr., 62
Rippelmeyer, Glenda, 164
Rippelmeyer, Ray, 16-17, 30, 39, 45, 53,
    66, 69, 91, 119, 163-165, 182-183
Riverfront Stadium, 5, 148
Roberts, Dave, 104
Roberts, Robin, 20, 52-53, 109, 111,
    113, 130, 159, 165
Robertson, Bob, 126-127, 159
Robinson, Bill, 106-107, 111, 118, 120,
    122, 135, 140, 143-145, 158, 160
Robinson, Frank, 57, 62, 111
Robinson, Jackie, 174
Rochester Red Wings, 69
Rojas, Cookie, 112
Rolen, Scott, 130
Rollins, Jimmy, 130
Rookie of the Year Award, 6, 28, 40,
    73, 118
Roque, Jorge, 151-152
Rose, Pete, 7, 71, 136-137
Rosello, Dave, 160
Rosenthal, Ken, 172, 175-176
Rossovich, Tim, 113
Rudolph, Ken, 160
Russell, Bill, 77
Ruth, Babe, 64, 173
Ruthven, Dick, 19
Ryan, Mike, 41, 71, 83, 91
Ryan, Nolan, 53, 186

Saam, Byrum, 46-47, 63
Sadecki, Ray, 118-119
Saidt, Bud, 10, 184
St. Louis Cardinals, 2-5, 9, 11-12, 17-
    19, 21, 23, 26, 28-29, 31-32, 35-36,
    42, 45, 56-57, 61, 67-68, 71, 74-75,
    78, 84, 91, 94, 100, 121-123, 125,

150, 152, 155, 157-158, 168, 173-
    174, 182
San Diego Padres (National League), 45,
    55-57, 85, 95-96, 103-105, 107, 111,
    114
San Diego Padres (Pacific Coast
    League), 16
San Diego Stadium, 107
San Francisco 49ers, 45
San Francisco Giants, 43-44, 47-53, 55,
    58, 63-64, 95, 99-101, 137, 140,
    166, 185
Sanderson, Scott, 171
Sanford, Jack, 140
Sanguillen, Manny, 19, 67
Santo, Ron, 31, 160
Santorini, Al, 151
Scarce, Mac, 100, 119, 148
Schilling, Curt, 130
Schmidt, Mike, 130, 142, 155, 157
Schneck, Dave, 119
Schoendienst, Red, 3, 40-41, 78, 122,
    151, 157, 168
Seattle Mariners, 89, 170
Seaver, Tom, 31, 57, 63, 65, 143, 158-
    159
Secretariat, 154
Selma, Dick, 25, 29-30, 58, 63, 66, 69,
    77, 82, 119, 163-164, 171, 182
Seminick, Andy, 11
Shea Stadium, 64, 69, 117, 119, 158
Sheffield, Gary, 27
Shenk, Larry, 9-10, 15, 72-73, 108-109,
    129, 183, 188
Shibe Park, 46, 52
Short, Chris, 29, 68, 71, 73, 84, 95, 131,
    165, 181-182
Sid Mercer Player of the Year Award,
    180
Simmons, Curt, 123, 128
Simmons, Ted, 19, 26, 36, 79, 122, 151
Singer, Bill, 57
Singleton, Ken, 88
Sizemore, Ted, 39-40, 123, 158
Skipper Lucchesi Show, The, 78
Souderton (Pennsylvania) Little League,
    136, 138
Spahn, Warren, 56

Spartanburg (South Carolina) Phillies, 166

Spectrum (Philadelphia), 10

Speier, Chris, 48, 50-52, 101

Spitz, Mark, 147, 150

Sporting News, The, 180

Sports Illustrated, 17, 169, 180

Sports Reference LLC, 176

Spring training, Phillies, 1, 9-11, 14, 22-23, 29, 130, 180

Stahl, Larry, 114

Stargell, Willie, 67, 127-128, 159, 187

Stark, Jayson, 12-13, 30, 162, 172-173, 175-176, 178, 186

Stark Truth, The: The Most Overrated and Underrated Players in Baseball History, 186

Staub, Rusty, 69

Stein, Bill, 151

Steinbrenner, George, 22

Stello, Dick, 40, 90-91

Stengel, Casey, 84, 163

Stennett, Rennie, 127-128, 159

Stewart, Dave, 171

Stewart, Jimmy, 7, 76

Stone, Ron, 32, 77, 80, 82, 165

Stoneham, Horace, 64

Strohmayer, John, 91

Sutton, Don, 31, 57, 99

Suzuki, Ichiro, 170

Swoboda, Ron, 4, 11

Texas Rangers, 69, 98

Thomas, Derrel, 105

Thornton, Andre, 78-79

Three Rivers Stadium, 66, 69, 124, 126

Tidewater (Virginia) Tides, 87

Tolan, Bobby, 71, 137, 148

Toronto Blue Jays, 108

Torre, Joe, 5, 8, 23, 26, 37, 45, 86, 122-123, 151, 157

Torres, Hector, 90

Torrez, Mike, 155-156

Trenton Times, 10, 184

Trillo, Manny, 40

Tulsa Oilers, 16

Turner, Ted, 22

Twitchell, Wayne, 53, 69, 104, 117-118, 125, 165, 171

Tyrone, Jim, 160

Tyson, Mike, 151

United Press International, 10

University of Pennsylvania Quakers, 10

Upshaw, Cecil, 83

USA Today, 41

Utley, Chase, 130

Valentine, Bobby, 59-60

Valenzuela, Fernando, 166

Vance, Dazzy, 172-173

Verducci, Tom, 169, 171, 175-176

Veterans Stadium, 8, 24-25, 33-36, 39-41, 59, 62, 66, 71, 75-76, 92, 95, 97, 104, 113-114, 116, 121, 128-129, 131, 133, 135-137, 140, 142, 151, 154-155, 158-159, 177-178, 181, 183-184

Virdon, Bill, 67

Vukovich, John, 7, 181

Wakefield, Tim, 27

Walker, Harry, 80

Wallenda, Karl ("The Great Wallenda"), 34, 128-129, 132

Washington Senators, 16, 172

Washington Touchdown Club, 180

Watson, Bob, 75-76, 80-81

WCAU-AM, 47

Weiss, Walt, 27

Welch, Bob, 171

Westcott, Rich, 11-12, 109, 189

Wheeler, Chris, 9-11, 20, 30, 70, 89, 101, 108-109, 117, 129, 133-134, 141, 144-145, 188

"Wheeze Kids" (1983 Phillies), 106

"Whiz Kids" (1950 Phillies), 11

Williams, Billy, 31, 62, 114, 160, 166

Williams, Charlie, 51

Williams, Dick, 84

Williams, Earl, 28, 144

Williams, Ted, 11

Wilmington *News Journal*, 8, 10, 52, 150

Wilson, Billy, 117, 119, 121

Wilson, Don, 79-80

Wilson, Willie, 118

Wine, Bobby, 87

Wise, Rick, 2-3, 5-13, 30, 39, 53, 72,
    74, 76, 130, 157-158
Woods, Ron, 88, 90
Woods, Tiger, 156
World Series, 3, 10, 13, 26-27, 30, 56,
    59, 66, 68-69, 84-85, 99, 104, 106,
    108, 118, 130, 136, 154, 163, 174,
    178, 180, 187
WPHL-TV, 40, 47

Wrigley Field, 25-26, 31, 160-161
Wynn, Jimmy, 79-82, 149

Yastrzemski, Carl, 174
Young, Cy, 61, 172-173

Zeiser, Anne, 130
Zeiser, Betty, 11, 116-117, 129-130
Zimmer, Don, 55, 57, 85-87, 103-104,
    107